FORESTRY AND THE NEW INSTITUTIONAL ECONOMICS

Forestry and the New Institutional Economics

An application of contract theory to forest
silvicultural investment

SEN WANG
Canadian Forest Service
Victoria, Canada

G. CORNELIS VAN KOOTEN
University of Nevada, Reno, USA
University of British Columbia, Vancouver, Canada
Wageningen University, The Netherlands

Routledge
Taylor & Francis Group

LONDON AND NEW YORK

First published 2001 by Ashgate Publishing

Reissued 2018 by Routledge
2 Park Square, Milton Park, Abingdon, Oxon OX14 4RN
711 Third Avenue, New York, NY 10017, USA

Routledge is an imprint of the Taylor & Francis Group, an informa business

Publisher's Note
The publisher has gone to great lengths to ensure the quality of this reprint but points out that some imperfections in the original copies may be apparent.

Disclaimer
The publisher has made every effort to trace copyright holders and welcomes correspondence from those they have been unable to contact.

ISBN 13: 978-1-138-73387-9 (hbk)
ISBN 13: 978-1-138-73384-8 (pbk)
ISBN 13: 978-1-315-18752-5 (ebk)

Contents

List of Tables

List of Figures

Foreword

Dr. Wang and Professor van Kooten, and their colleagues at the Forest Economics and Policy Analysis (FEPA) Research Unit at the University of British Columbia, have introduced foresters, forest researchers and forest policy analysts to the important effects that institutions have on business practice, forest management and, indeed, the condition of the forest itself. Economists, like everyone else, recognize the immense importance of legal institutions and administrative structures in determining business conditions and performance. Yet economists have largely integrated institutional distinctions into their analyses only in the last 35 years. Despite the fact that governments control well over half of the world's forests, forest economists and policy analysts have only begun to examine institutional behavior in the last twelve years. The UBC group has led this effort.

Nowhere do institutions have a greater influence on forestry than in British Columbia, where 96 percent of the forest belongs to the Crown. Nowhere is forestry more important to the economy than in British Columbia, where it provides the foundation for three of the four largest sectors of the economy – forestry itself, forest products and tourism. Therefore, it seems only appropriate that Sen Wang and Cornelis van Kooten have used the perspective of British Columbia to introduce institutions to the economics and policy of forestry. The British Columbia experience has lots to teach all of us everywhere – about market performance, about contracts for forest management, and about the contrasting performance of government and private agents.

The analysis of this book is careful and thorough in its investigation of these issues. It is also illustrative and inviting. It illustrates how we can, and should, be asking similar questions about the comparable institutions of forestry in other economic and political environments around the world. It is inviting because it tempts any thoughtful reader to inquire about the other critical forestry institutions that are more important outside of British Columbia.

Contractual arrangements for private harvests of public lands, increasing public regulation of private forestlands (the "taking" issue), and the different performance of central and local government or mixed central-local management of public forests are among the least examined, but most contentious issues of forest policy today. Yet our understanding of the relative performance of these institutions is weak at best. Sen Wang and Cornelis van Kooten have provided the leadership with their analyses in this book. They, and the rest of us, have a responsibility to continue the good work.

William F. Hyde
Visiting Professor, Environmental Economics Unit, Goteborg University
Senior Associate, Centre for International Forestry Research

Preface

This book is an outgrowth of Sen Wang's doctoral research conducted at the University of British Columbia. When Peter Nielsen, Editor of Ashgate Publishing, first approached us in February 1999 with an interest in converting Dr. Wang's dissertation into a book, we accepted the offer gladly. However, after just a short while, we realized that this would be a good opportunity of going beyond Sen's dissertation to blend the latest achievements of the new institutional economics with some interesting applications in the field of forestry, particularly silviculture.

As the title suggests, the book is principally concerned with forestry and its institutional environment. It addresses the economics of institutions, institutional change and transaction costs in the context of forestry. Forestry serves as an excellent area for applying the theory of the new institutional economics because, in addition to producing commercial timber products, forests provide non-timber forest products and non-market amenities that often conflict with commercial logging activities. The response to this conflict has been the evolution of new regulations. As conflict is greatest in regions that rely most heavily on harvests from primary forests, British Columbia's forestry sector provides a fruitful arena for studying the evolution of public policy and new institutional arrangements.

Our book extends the theory of the new institutional economics by setting out the ramifications of market failures in the context of British Columbia's forestry sector, with a clear focus on silvicultural investment at the contractual level. Using the results of in-depth surveys, we analyze the evolution of forestry institutions and public policy with an emphasis on silvicultural investment as a means of addressing environmental concerns. We investigate the organizational decisions of forest companies to contract out silvicultural activities or to perform them in-house and to choose appropriate payment schemes such as piece wages and time rates. Our approach to economic analysis of forestry investment problems emphasizes an understanding of the linkages between the biological and institutional attributes of forestry activities. We believe that our book makes a significant contribution to the study of institutional change in forestry and will be useful to academic, government and industry analysts.

As always, our debts are many. Deep gratitude is due Professor Ilan Vertinsky, Director of the Forest Economics and Policy Analysis Research Unit, University of British Columbia for his full support. We would like to acknowledge with appreciation the contribution by Dr. Bill Wilson to Chapters 6, 8 and 9 and his moral support for our efforts. The institutional support of the Canadian Forest Service is sincerely acknowledged. We are also very grateful to Professor William F. Hyde for his kindness in writing a foreword for us.

In completing this book, it has been our good fortune to work with Berry Carroll, Carolyn Court, Rosalind Ebdon, Adam Hickford, Jan Lloyd and others of the Ashgate editorial staff. Their unfailing assistance is graciously acknowledged. Finally, we are grateful to our families whose unseen support is both real and decisive in helping turn this book into a reality.

Sen Wang
G. Cornelis van Kooten

1 Introduction

Forests are one of the most important natural resources on the planet, covering some 4.3 billion hectares (ha) or one-third of the world's land area. Yet, this is less than the area capable of growing trees, which amounts to some 40% of the earth's landmass. Forests are important as a source of income and employment because of the wood products industry, but they also contribute ecosystem services such as a carbon sink and weather regulation functions, absorb pollutants, provide recreational and scenic amenities, contribute wildlife habitat, and protect watersheds. Therefore, management of forestlands for both commercial timber production and other amenities is vital to the overall well being of society.

Of the globe's forested area, 2,900 million ha or 68% is considered productive forestland, defined as land capable of growing merchantable stands of timber within a reasonable period of time (see Table 1.1). It is estimated that the standing volume of timber on productive forestlands is some 320 billion cubic meters (m^3). Canada's forests account for about 10% of the world's forested land and 8% of its productive forestland; the United States accounts for about 7% of the world's total forested land and the same proportion of productive forestland. As a country, only Russia has greater forest resources (Table 1.1).

The USA is the largest producer of softwood lumber and wood products in the world, followed by Canada and Russia (Tables 1.2). Some 70% of total roundwood and 90% of all the paper products produced globally come from forests in northern latitudes (Table 1.2). The majority of wood products are produced from coniferous forests in the Northern Hemisphere.

Production of pulp from hardwood species has become increasingly important as a result of technical advances in pulp making and the existence of substantial indigenous (boreal) stands of mixed hard and softwood species, and the use of hardwood species in plantation forests. Principal producers of pulp and softwood lumber are the USA, Canada, Sweden, Finland, Russia and Japan. Among tropical countries, only Brazil produces globally significant amounts of pulp, although the amount is relatively small

1

(less than 5% of world production). Countries such as Chile, New Zealand and Australia are also expected to become important, at least in export markets.

Table 1.1: World Forest Resources

Country/Region	Total forestland (10^6 ha)	Productive forestland (10^6 ha)	Timber volume (10^9 m^3)
Canada	418	245	25.0
United States	298	217	29.0
South and Central America	988	739	97.0
Africa	744	236	25.0
Europe (excl. former USSR)	195	141	15.2
Former USSR	957	770	86.7
Asia and Oceania	767	585	44.0
WORLD	4,367	2,933	321.9

Source: United Nations (2000); Natural Resources Canada (1997).

Table 1.2: World Forest Products Output (1997)

Country/Region	Industrial roundwood (10^6 m^3)	Sawn-wood (10^6 m^3)	Wood-based panels (10^6 m^3)	Paper products (10^6 tonnes)
Canada	185.9	64.8	11.3	19.0
United States	416.1	111.4	38.5	86.3
South & Central America	141.7	35.2	7.2	13.8
Africa	67.1	9.0	1.9	3.2
Europe (excl. USSR)	290.5	89.3	43.6	83.5
Former USSR	103.0	25.7	4.7	3.8
Asia & Oceania	318.5	103.5	48.4	88.5
WORLD	1,522.8	438.9	155.6	298.1

Source: FAO (1999).

Tropical forests do not contribute large amounts to global industrial wood output. Even for countries such as Brazil that are significant in terms of pulp production, fiber comes from plantation forests. Less than one-third of the world's industrial wood harvest originates with old-growth forests, or forests that have not previously been commercially exploited (Table 1.3). Commercial timber production from old growth occurs principally in Canada, Russia, Indonesia and Malaysia (Sedjo 1997). Industrial plantations account for more than one-third of industrial wood harvest, with the remainder accounted for by second-growth forests. The continuing trend toward intensively managed plantation forests occurs for both financial reasons and concerns related to security of supply, with increasing investment in the technology of growing trees stimulated by declining global reliance on old growth – the dwindling of the "old growth overhang" (Sedjo 1997). Increasingly trees are considered an agricultural crop, with rapidly growing trees competitive with annual crops as a land use (as is the case with loblolly pine (*Pinus taeda*) plantations in the US South and hybrid cottonwood plantations on irrigated agricultural lands in the US Pacific Northwest).

Table 1.3: Global Timber Harvests by Management Type

Management Type	Proportion of industrial wood production
Old growth	30%
Second growth, minimal management	14%
Indigenous second growth, managed	22%
Industrial plantation, indigenous species	24%
Industrial plantation, exotic species	10%

Source: Sedjo (1997, p.11).

Canada is the world's foremost exporter of wood products followed by the USA and the countries in Nordic Europe. Compared to other timber producing regions in the world, Canada and Russia are likely at a disadvantage in timber production because of climate (particularly in the interior regions of these countries); to a lesser degree, the same might be true of the Scandinavian countries.

Timber shortfalls have been forecast for the US Pacific Northwest and South and Canada, particularly British Columbia (BC). In BC, a "fall down" in timber production is predicted because of the time lag between the availability of virgin forests and second growth. This is caused by past delays in plantings and silvicultural investments and the mere fact that old-growth forests contain greater timber volume and are increasingly being set aside as protected areas. Globally these shortfalls will likely be covered by production of radiata pine (*Pinus radiata*) from Chile and New Zealand. Unless adequate investments are made in planting and silviculture, countries such as Canada will decline in importance in terms of world timber production. Unfortunately, reforestation and silvicultural investments on many sites are often uneconomic and it may well be that forests in these regions provide non-timber benefits to society that exceed their commercial timber value.

This book is about silvicultural investment and forest institutions, with particular focus on British Columbia. BC is chosen because it is currently the largest forest products exporting region in the world and its economy is likely more dependent on forestry than any other economy in the world (Wilson et al. 1998). Thus, the rapid technological and social (e.g., increasing demand for environmental services of forests) changes that are occurring in the sector are going to have a profound impact on the Province's economy and institutions. Although this book focuses somewhat narrowly on British Columbia and silviculture, the lessons that it provides have implications, nonetheless, well beyond the Province and the world's forestry sector. Even so, it is enough to consider only forestry and silvicultural investments in temperate forests because forests harbor much of the globe's biodiversity, serve as a symbol of the planet's health and are profoundly affected by silvicultural decisions in one location because the forest products sector is a globally-interdependent whole.

1.1 Background on British Columbia's Forestry Sector

Within Canada, the Province of British Columbia, which is the country's westernmost province, accounts for about half of all wood products output. BC has a population of 3.7 million and covers 96 million ha, of which forestland accounts for about 64%. Productive forest amounts to 51.1 million ha. A major factor in the exploitation of forest resources and the development of forest policy is that more than 95% of the forestland is publicly owned, almost entirely (excepting National Parks) by the Province (Natural Resources Canada 1999). This level of public ownership is the highest of any political jurisdiction (Table 1.4), and a reason why much public policy focuses on forest tenure issues. It has also caused forest companies to devote greater attention to the Provincial political scene, as opposed to ensuring their competitiveness in the global economy. In the short term, more may be gained (or lost) by influencing Provincial policy makers than competing in the international marketplace.

Table 1.4: Working Forest Area, Public Ownership, Annual Growth and Harvest, Selected Jurisdictions (Data for Early- to Mid-1990s)

Country/ Region	Working forest (10^6 ha)	% public	Average annual growth (10^6 m^3)	Annual harvest (10^6 m^3)
Finland	20	29	77	63.6
Sweden	23	13	98	68.0
New Zealand	2	4	22[a]	17.0
Chile	2	neg.	22[b]	20.0
Russia	446	90	617	300+[c]
United States	198	45	612	469.0
- PNW	16	56	82	73.0
- South	37	11	128	117.0
Canada	227	94	233	183.0
- BC	51	96	72	71.0
- Alberta	25	96	22	20.3

Source: Wilson et al. (1998, p.13).
[a] New Zealand's annual growth is expected to rise to some 25 million m^3 by 2005.
[b] Chile's annual growth is expected to reach 47 million m^3 in 2018.
[c] Russian harvests have fallen to some 232 million m^3, but have exceeded 300 million m^3 previously.

For one and a half centuries, the forest resource has served as the cornerstone of the BC economy. However, the patterns of forest utilization have undergone changes over time. For the longest time, forests have essentially been "mined" (Pearse 1976). Concern for forest conservation did not emerge until the beginning of the twentieth century. Since then, changes in forest structure and species composition occurred, in part, due to enhanced utilization standards that became the norm as a consequence of demand and technological changes that were spurred by public policy. Aside from the sustained-timber-yield policy adopted as a result of a public inquiry in the early 1940s (Sloan 1945), relative scarcity of forest resources, concerns for production costs and heightened awareness of environmental issues contributed to the emergence of a distinct silviculture sector.

To understand the nuances of public policy related to forestry in BC, it is first necessary to grasp the essentials of the current tenure system. While the Province owns the majority of productive forestland, timber is harvested under basically two forms of tenure arrangement. The first grants forest companies long-term rights to harvest timber from a designated area, known as a Tree Farm License (TFL). Companies are permitted to harvest an amount of timber determined in conjunction with the BC Ministry of Forests (MoF), also known as the BC Forest Service (BCFS). Harvest levels are based on growth to ensure sustainability of the resource. For a license holder, the basis for timber operations is the five-year plan that the Licensee prepares and the Ministry approves. In managing a TFL, a company is encouraged to include its privately-held forestland in the overall plan. The Licensee is responsible for certain environmental aspects of forest management, most notably regeneration. TFLs are area based and guarantee holders access to timber for a period of 25 years, although the holder can renew the license for an additional 25 years after 15 years have expired. In return, the Licensees have built sawmills and pulp mills that ensure a level of jobs – perhaps the principal focus of government.

The second form of tenure is a volume-based license that permits a forest company (or individual) to cut a certain volume of timber from a particular area, known as a Timber Supply Area (TSA). The government manages TSAs. Again, jobs are a prime concern in the awarding of licenses to harvest timber. In the awarding of contracts to harvest trees on a TSA under the Small Business Forest Enterprise Program (SBFEP), for example, a low bid is only one criterion; others include a provision favoring "small business" and local job creation. TSAs dominate in the Interior of the Province, while TFLs are the predominate form of tenure on BC Coast.

Given the tenure arrangements, the relatively short history of silviculture in the Province bears out the necessity of integrating private initiatives into the undertaking of production and management activities on public land. The choice to retain public (referred to as *Crown*) ownership of forestlands, while allocating timber harvest rights to individuals and private companies via the sorts of leasing and licensing arrangements indicated above, seems to have worked effectively only in removing timber (Pearse 1988). The difficulty of having logged-off sites rapidly and appropriately regenerated had been a central concern to policy makers up to the late 1970s, and institutional restructuring to promote silviculture has been a key element in the overall reform of BC's forest policy sector since the 1980s.

There have been four major trends in the evolution of BC's silviculture. First, beginning with seedling production, silvicultural activities proceeded from planting merely for the purpose of reforestation of harvested sites toward forest renewal with greater emphasis on the enhancement of multiple forest values. After several decades of slow progress, this process has accelerated over the last 20 years.

Second, the institutional structure has evolved from a Provincial Forest Service focus and responsibility to one that placed greater responsibility for silviculture on forest tenure holders. For instance, in the 1950s, forest regeneration on the part of TFL holders was encouraged by government, although they under-performed this task as they lacked the necessary economic or mandatory incentives. Some replanting did occur on private land, however. During the 1960s, holders of harvest licenses were encouraged to perform reforestation in the TSAs, then known as Public Sustained Yield Units. The 1970s saw the implementation of the "credit against stumpage" system, whereby forest companies were effectively paid for forest regeneration activities. By the late 1980s, full responsibility for basic silviculture, at least the physical component, had been transferred from the Forest Service to the major licensees, except for operations under the SBFEP.[1]

Third, in parallel, financial obligations for basic silviculture have gradually shifted from the Forest Service to the major licensees. It began with the government supply of seedlings for reforestation, free of charge, to private forestland owners in the 1950s; it progressed to a "stumpage offset" system (based on approved costs) that was initially adopted in 1964 and became "credit against stumpage" in the form of "Section 88" of the 1979 Forest Act; and culminated in 1987 with mandatory financial obligation for basic silviculture residing with the major licensees.

Lastly, quality standards have risen steadily in an increasingly regulated environment. For example, companies had to commit to replanting to free-to-grow status[2] (initially introduced in 1979) and the development of a pre-harvest silvicultural prescription (formally introduced in 1987) that was subsequently replaced by a five-year silvicultural plan (officially introduced in 1995). Indeed, the Forest Practices Code introduced fairly onerous harvest and renewal obligations that were phased in from 1995 onwards.

The first trend is concerned with the growth patterns, in terms of both scope and scale, of silvicultural programs. The second trend is reflective of the evolution of institutional structures for physical operations. The third trend is concerned with the financial arrangements necessary for carrying out silvicultural activities, while the final one is concerned with regulatory aspects of silvicultural operations. Specifically, silvicultural prescription is,

---

[1] Basic silviculture refers to activities required to regenerate desired forest species at specified densities and stocking levels. Major licensees are those that hold major licenses such as Tree Farm License, Forest License, Timber License and so forth.

[2] A free-to-grow condition refers to a state where trees are of sufficient height that they are not choked out by shrubs and other vegetation.

conceptually, a good idea because it ensures the important position of silviculture in that cutting cannot proceed until a silvicultural plan is in place. Literally, silvicultural prescription becomes a key task that can have system-wide effects, the delay of which may hinder or jeopardize progress on cutting operations.

A chronology of the trends and other major events that shape BC's silviculture sector is provided in Chapter 6. It is the evolution of historical driving forces behind institutional changes that provides the context in this book for analyzing silvicultural activities. Importantly, given these changes and the shifting of the financial burden of silviculture onto the forest companies, it is little wonder that the companies have focused much of their efforts on influencing the political process in the Province. One consequence has been that companies have neglected, at least to some extent, other aspects of the global wood products business.

1.2 Silvicultural Investment and Institutions

Williamson (1996) points out that changes in the institutional environment trigger shifts in production and organizational parameters that, in turn, lead to the redesign of governance structures.[3] In this book we focus on institutional arrangements as they pertain to silvicultural investment (tree planting, pruning, thinning, fertilizing, etc.) in British Columbia. Typically, the choice of governance structures for silvicultural operations in BC has been dichotomous in the post-1987 period. Some silvicultural activities are performed in-house by forest companies (through internal hierarchical structures), while others are contracted out to specialized silvicultural contractors. While the latter represents market-oriented contractual arrangements, the former falls into the category of vertical integration. Of course, a variety of hybrid or intermediate forms exist between these polar opposites.

Reforms in the institutional structures governing *basic* silviculture (i.e., primarily tree planting as opposed to other activities, such as pruning and thinning, that constitute *incremental* silviculture) constitute the focus of the research reported here. Since 1987, a series of reforms have unfolded and these reforms have significant implications for governance choices by which silvicultural work is organized, resulting in changes in the cost

---

[3] The term "governance" refers to the institutional framework in which contracts are initiated, negotiated, monitored, adapted, enforced, and terminated (Palay 1984, p.265), and was first used in this context by Williamson (1979).

structures and incentive schemes of individual operations. Based on the institutional evolution of responsibility over (basic) silviculture and the characterization of BC's silviculture sector, several questions are addressed.

1. Why has decentralization of silvicultural activities occurred under an increasingly onerous regulatory environment?
2. Given the changes in the institutional environment, why do governance structures differ in the sense that firms choose vertical integration (in-house performance) for some silvicultural activities, while electing to relegate responsibilities to independent contractors (contracting out) for other activities? What firm and silvicultural activity characteristics cause some forest companies to perform a certain activity in-house, while another company contracts it out?
3. What is the rationale behind the private sector taking certain actions in order to meet basic silvicultural obligations, and to what extent do these actions successfully match the attributes of the chosen governance structures?

In order to answer these narrow questions, we also consider the larger question concerning the role of government in setting forest policy, and guiding industry in a particular direction. More broadly, we might ask whether the Provincial government's environmental and tenure policy in forestry has been a hindrance to the success and efficient performance of silvicultural operations, and what effect this has had on the evolution of the forestry sector in general. In addressing this issue, we not only wish to take into account the non-commercial aspects of forest ecosystems, but also the role of institutions and economic incentives in influencing the forestry sector. We begin this task in the next chapter by examining the theory of institutions and, more specifically, property rights and transaction costs as these are applied to forestry.

1.3 Outline of the Book

The first part of the book, comprising Chapters 2 through 5, provides a theoretical background to property rights, transaction costs and the new institutional economics (NIE) more generally, particularly as these relate to forestry and forest economics. In Chapter 2, we discuss market failure within the framework of the NIE, thereby also providing an overview of the NIE. The particular focus is on transaction costs and mechanisms for coordinating economic activity to address market failure.

Market failure and forestry are the focus of Chapter 3. We begin by considering how market failure can be addressed within the framework of the literature on rotation ages. However, we end up concluding that, because forestland owners (or tenure holders) do not take into account public goods and spillover benefits, regulations are used to manipulate cutting cycles to correct market failure. Regulations are discussed from the perspective of British Columbia where the Province is the major forestland owner. These themes are taken up again in Chapters 4 and 5.

In Chapter 4, we focus on contract theory because, in the case of a public landowner, tenure arrangements and contracts are important means of correcting market failures in practice. This chapter also provides the background theory for our subsequent studies of silvicultural contracting. Then, in Chapter 5, we discuss the role of organizations, public regulation and culture in examining market failure in the forestry sector. Particular policy instruments are considered in the light of organizational theory, regulation and culture, with application to the BC situation. Finally, in the last section of Chapter 5, sustainable forestry is examined within the framework of the NIE.

The second part of the book focuses on silvicultural activities as, in addition to land set asides, silviculture is the principal means used to deal with market failure in forestry. Although applicable to other forestry regions, the discussion here focuses on British Columbia because of data availability. A history and overview of silvicultural activities in BC is provided in Chapter 6, followed by two chapters that rely on survey results to make conclusions about the efficiency of silvicultural activities in BC. In Chapter 7, we examine why some major forest companies conduct silvicultural activities in house, while others contract them out. In Chapter 8, we study means for paying silvicultural workers. One finding is that basic silviculture (planting trees on logged-off sites) can be done efficiently, but that incremental or enhanced silviculture (e.g., pruning, thinning) do not deliver adequate benefits, either private or public – it is too expensive to undertake.

Finally, in Chapter 9, we consider silvicultural investment more broadly in light of our theoretical and empirical information. We conclude that, from the point of view of the NIE and the empirical results, it will be necessary to make some major structural adjustments to forestry institutions in British Columbia if market failure is to be adequately addressed. On economic efficiency grounds, there is certainly a need to restructure institutions.

2 Property Rights, Institutions and Market Failure

Economics is concerned with the study of human choices and the efficient allocation of scarce resources. Economics also has to do with "the institution of the market, the price mechanism as a market-regulating process, and marginal analysis as a means of calculation" (Simon 1962, pp.1-2). In recent decades, economists have given increasing attention to the interrelations between institutional structures and economic behavior.

There is no standardized definition of the term "institutions". Institutions are commonly understood to refer to formal or informal social devices that constrain human behavior. Generally speaking, institutions fall into three basic categories: constitutional order, institutional arrangements, and normative behavioral codes (Feder and Feeny 1991). Constitutional order refers to the fundamental rules about how society is organized – it is the rule for making rules, or a nation's Constitution. In modern society, institutional arrangements emerge organically and spontaneously from among the forces underlying the social fabric, or are artificially created within the rules of the Constitution (usually via legislation or as a result of a court decision).[1] These arrangements include laws, regulations, property rights, contracts, and so forth. At the fundamental level, cultural values influence and shape all institutional arrangements and play a role in constraining human behavior (Fukuyama 1999).

In this chapter, we examine the role of institutions in economics, and particularly that of property rights. In this regard, it is important to consider the New Institutional Economics, or the NIE, which has its origins both in traditional institutionalism and neoclassical or mainstream economics. However, we begin by defining what property rights mean.

---

[1] Constitutional choice refers to the study of how society chooses the rules for making the rules under which the social system operates, procedures for making selections among alternative constraints. Buchanan and Tullock (1962) are representatives of the public choice literature.

2.1 The Notion of Property Rights

Property rights are important to institutional arrangements, but there is much confusion about what property rights entail and their role. Property rights are an important class of institutional arrangements. The development of the theory of property rights is attributable to generations of philosophers and scholars. The section of David Hume's *A Treatise of Human Nature* (1739) entitled "Of property and riches" is often cited as the fountainhead of studies of property (Bracewell-Milnes 1982). What has come to be known as the property rights (PR) approach was first developed by Alchian (1965a, 1965b), Demsetz (1966, 1967), and Alchian and Demsetz (1973). The PR approach is concerned with three basic and interrelated questions (Alchian and Demsetz 1973, p.17):

- What is the structure of property rights in a society at any point of time?
- What consequences for social interaction arise from a particular structure of property rights?
- How has this property right structure come into being?

2.1.1 Characterizing property rights

According to Carmichael (1975), property is "a constellation of highly complex adjustments of entitlements and expectations" (p.749). Property is considered to be a bundle of recognized relations (rights, obligations, claims, powers, privileges or immunities) between people in regard to some good, service or "thing" that has economic value (Pryor 1972, p.407). Property rights define relations among human beings and specify the norm of behavior with respect to scarce resources (Pejovich 1990). Most importantly, property rights define the relationship between individuals with respect to the right to a resource. It is not the resource itself that is owned, but, rather, a property right constitutes a bundle, or a portion, of rights to use a resource that is owned. In other words, to own something is really to own the rights to use resources. In essence, property rights are defined not as relations between people and things, but, rather, as the behavioral relations among people that arise from the existence of things and pertain to their use. Structured property rights ensure that people observe the prevailing behavioral norms respecting property and that they are penalized for non-compliance (Pejovich 1990).

In addition to being perceived as a bundle of quantitative or numerical claims and obligations, property rights are also described as a bundle of more abstract characteristics or attributes. In order to facilitate free exchange of assets for all transactions and contingencies, a well-defined system of property rights must have the following four characteristics (Randall 1975; Bromley 1989; Feder and Feeny 1991).

1. *Comprehensive.* Ownership to all assets must be assigned to a specified economic agent (individual, firm, state, other legal entity) with all entitlements to use or dispose of property known in advance. Comprehensiveness implies that the property right is secure from involuntary seizure or encroachment by other economic agents, including the state. Of course, this is subject to some risk, but this risk must be known a priori, as must the course to restitution or compensation in the event that property rights are taken, either through the taking of title or through a regulation that affects what one can do with property (see van Kooten and Bulte 2000).
2. *Exclusive.* All benefits and costs pertaining to the use and/or disposal of property accrue to the owner. Exclusiveness tightens the relationship between the welfare of the owner and the consequences of her actions, creating incentives for putting resources to the highest-valued uses. Of course, property rights can hardly be expected to convey totally exclusive and unrestricted use – there will always exist various social constraints to the use of property.
3. *Transferable.* The rights to property must be transferable to another agent in a voluntary exchange.
4. *Enforceable.* No property rights, regardless of their degree of comprehensiveness, transferability and exclusiveness, can be held without some assurance that there is proper enforcement of those rights by the state. That is, in a complex society, property rights only exist because the state permits them to exist. Without adequate enforcement, *de jure* private property rights become *de facto* open access, a scramble for the benefits from property that is open to all.

Property rights can be said to be complete if they are comprehensive, exclusive and transferable. When property rights are complete this diminishes uncertainty, and thereby provides adequate information for guiding behavior. Complete property rights are established in law. That is, *de jure* rights exist if property rights are given lawful approbation by formal, legal institutions – they are protected by law that is upheld by the state. Such *de jure* rights form the predominant system governing land use in developed nations. In many developing nations, *de jure* rights either do not exist or are not upheld by the state. Thus, there is greater reliance on *de facto* rights, on what is not opposed and thus possible, although not necessarily legal or explicitly recognized by government. An example is where loggers harvest trees without rights, or peasants grow and harvest crops on land as squatters rather than rightful owners. In these cases, land is often needlessly degraded because the user does not take into account the future value of the resource, or its user cost.

The ability to transfer property or rights over property encourages resources to gravitate from less productive owners to more productive ones. Land transactions generally increase efficiency in resource allocation, as agents with high potential marginal productivity of land are induced to acquire land from agents with low marginal productivity (Feder and Feeny 1991).

2.1.2 Types of property rights

There are four forms that property rights take: private property, state ownership, communal ownership and open access. These are summarized in Table 2.1, along with their main characteristics. Exclusivity is generally considered the most important characteristic of property rights (Alchian and Demsetz 1973), and private ownership grants the highest degree of exclusivity. Private property is likely the most understood form of property right, granting almost exclusive say over use and disposal to the owner. Yet, rights only exist because they are bestowed and protected by the state, *de jure* and *de facto*, with the state specifying the conditions under which use (exploitation) can occur.

With state ownership, it is the state that either directly manages the property or resource, or grants usufructuary rights to economic agents (e.g., individuals, firms, community groups, cooperatives, and so on) to use the resource for a specified period of time. Failure by government to exercise proper control over the resource, via management and enforcement, can and often does lead to open access exploitation, and its attendant problems.

Communal property represents private property at the group, community or cooperative level. In some respects, it is another form of state ownership, except that the "commune" or community can exclude others who may or may not be citizens of the state. It is the fact that the community of owners is readily identifiable while some can be excluded that is the main distinguishing feature of this type of ownership. Certain rights and duties respecting use and maintenance of the common property resource bind the individual members of the ownership group. Such rights and duties may be *de jure* or *de facto*, although the latter are more prevalent. For example, custom often dictates how many animal units a member of a group can graze in the common pasture, and/or how much time or expense the member must devote to (invest in) improving the commons. However, as a result of Hardin's (1968) paper on "The Tragedy of the Commons", common property is often confused with open access.

Table 2.1: Classification and Characteristics of Property Rights

Type	Characteristics	Implications for economic incentives
Private property	Exclusive rights assigned to individuals	Strong incentives for conservation of resources and for investment as well
State ownership	Rights held in collectivity with control exercised by authority or designated agency	Creating opportunities for attenuation of rights; managers have incentives for personal gains
Communal ownership	Exclusive rights assigned to all members of a community; approaching private property	Creating free-riders problem and low incentives for conservation
Open access	Rights unassigned; lack of exclusivity	Lack of incentives to conserve; often resulting in resource degradation

Open access is a situation where neither *de jure* nor *de facto* rights exist for a specified resource. In essence, property rights are absent. As a result, users fail to take into account the user cost of exploiting the resource; they neglect the benefits from leaving some units of the resource unexploited today because they yield a higher benefit in the future. This is the true "tragedy of the commons". The problem of open access is that "everybody's property is nobody's property" (Ciriacy-Wantrup and Bishop 1975, p.713; Pejovich 1972). When a resource is physically and legally accessible to anyone, what one user gets comes at the expense of another, with no one having the incentive to conserve the resource for possible future use. In the case of a nonrenewable resource, such as an oil reserve, this might imply pumping at too rapid a rate to permit extraction of all of the resource. For renewable resources, irreversibility is a likely outcome (e.g., a forest is converted to agriculture, thereby depleting all nutrients and preventing future re-establishment of tree cover), often implying extinction (say, of a species or fishery).[2]

Apart from the adverse effect of accelerated exploitation of the resource stock, open access results in a lack of incentives for conservation (as already noted) and investment. The reason is twofold. First, the investor is uncertain that she will be able to capture the expected future benefit of her investment decision. This would shorten her time horizon, raise the discount rate and, consequently, investment activity will stop short of what it would otherwise be. Indeed, open access exploitation is similar to private or communal exploitation if the discount rate is infinite (van Kooten and Bulte 2000). Short-lived property rights offer less flexibility of resource use than more permanent ones, so short-lived property rights are correspondingly less valuable.

Second, the absence of property rights in a resource is also likely to affect the form of investment activity. Only if property rights are completely specified is it possible for the resource user, for example, to defer resource use to a future date, thereby choosing in favor of conservation. Conservation is a form of investment.

In conclusion, from the social point of view, the establishment of property rights is a powerful and necessary condition for more efficient allocation and use of resources. From the individual's point of view, the complete specification of property rights, and their enforcement, is associated with an ability to employ property in a way that best enhances well being or utility (Pejovich 1972). The same is true for other economic agents that have entitlement to property rights.

2.2 The New Institutional Economics

Institutional economics goes back to Thorstein B. Veblen (1857-1929) who is widely regarded as the founder of American institutionalism. Representing an extreme in the institutionalist thinking, Veblen viewed institutions as "habits of thought which prevail in a given period" (Hutchison 1984). Institutionalism signifies "a concern with economic institutions, or organizations, such as industrial, labor, or monetary institutions, or with the property framework and legal institutions, together, in some cases, with an emphasis on collectivism, and group institutions, or

---

[2] The problem of open access in the fishery has been extensively examined, beginning with Gordon (1954) and Scott (1955).

organizations, rather than individuals, as the main economic agents or actors" (p.20).

The publication of John R. Commons' *Institutional Economics* in 1934 marked the formation of institutional economics as a distinct school of thought. However, institutional economics did not make significant headway until after the 1940s, thanks to the contributions of Clarence E. Ayers, who ushered in the era of neo-institutional economics (Gruchy 1972). In contrast to neoclassical economics, which emphasizes the profit motive, the desire for monetary gains, and maximization of individual and social utility (utilitarianism), institutional economics pays greater attention to the role of technology.[3] Institutional economists believe that the basic dynamic force in economics is technology, or the accumulation of technical knowledge (Gordon 1980). Historical and comparative analytical approaches are employed to investigate institutional dynamics. It is historical in its attempt to explore the role of history in institutional emergence, perpetuation and change, and it is comparative in its attempt to gain insights through comparative studies over time and space (Greif 1998).

Stressing the importance of habits and customs, the earlier institutional approach is sharply critical of neoclassical theorizing and its fundamental assumptions about rationality and knowledge. Persistently critical of the excessive abstractions of classical and neoclassical theorizing, institutionalists focus on "descriptive realism" (Dugger 1979, p.902). However, in spite of some fundamental differences in ideologies and philosophies between the old institutional economics approach and neoclassical economics, the positions of institutionalists have softened recently.[4] Dugger (1977) admits that institutional economics is not really a substitute for neoclassical economics. Instead, it is an effective complement because the domains and explanations of the two schools are complementary. "Where one leaves off, the other begins" (Dugger 1977, p.449). More recently, the objection of the old institutionalist approach to theorizing is found to have weakened the power of this approach for analytical purposes (Coase 1998).

---

[3] Neoclassical economics refers to the rejuvenation of the classical economics of Smith and Ricardo by marginalists, such as Jevon, Menger and Walras, and to the theoretical framework developed in Alfred Marshall's *Principles* and Paul Samuelson's *Foundations* (Dugger 1977). However, some economists feel uncomfortable with the term 'neoclassical' (Dahlman 1980, p.219).

[4] Hamilton (1970) suggests that the institutional economics is based on a Darwinian conception of the world, while neoclassical economics is based on a Newtonian conception.

The "New Institutional Economics", a term coined by Oliver Williamson to distinguish it from "old" institutional economics (Coase 1998, p.72), descends from both the earlier institutional economics and neoclassical economics. In the remainder of this section, we provide a brief background to the NIE.

Institutions are defined as "humanly devised constraints that structure human interaction. They are either formal or informal: formal institutions consist of formal constraints, e.g., policy rules, regulations, laws, constitutions, contracts, property rights, bargaining agreements, [while] informal institutions concern informal constraints, e.g., norms of behavior, conventions, self-imposed codes of conduct" (CPB 1997, p.42; also North 1990, 1994). Included in the definition of institutions are "a set of moral, ethical behavioral norms which define the contours that constrain the way in which the rules and regulations are specified and enforcement is carried out" (North 1984, p.8). The new institutional economics evolved in response to the fundamental need to include explicitly institutions into economic analysis. However, while descending out of the institutional economics associated with Veblen and Commons, the NIE was as much a response by neoclassical economists to perceived weaknesses in the assumptions underlying mainstream economics (Eggertsson 1990; Acheson 1994; Pejovich 1995; Furubotn and Richter 1997). While the NIE is "a science of institutions," its practitioners emphasize that economics is still a "science of choices."

Mainstream or neoclassical economics assumes that decision-makers are rational economizers who have perfect knowledge; markets are perfectly competitive, homogeneous goods are traded and prices contain all of the important information; transaction costs are ignored as is market failure more generally. The NIE differs from neoclassical economics in some fundamental ways (Acheson 1994).

1. The NIE takes the position that economic agents are rationally bounded, while information is costly to obtain. As Williamson (1985) points out, agents do not have perfect information but are often opportunistic, acting in their own self interest with guile. That is, people are only weakly rational and weakly moral, often withholding information when it is in their interests to do so (Acheson 1994, p.8). Bounded rationality and opportunism *cause* transaction costs (CPB 1997, p.46). Transactions take place even though information is incomplete or distorted. Further, people do not always have exclusive rights to what is traded. This then leads to a great deal of uncertainty and incomplete contracting.

2. There are costs to using markets because of market imperfections and outright market failure.
3. It is the case in many transactions (including ones that deal with provision of nature) that price is not the sole consideration. There exists a range of social and legal ties among people; and non-market (or beyond market) transactions also occur, especially within the same organization.
4. Finally, a key assumption of the NIE is that institutions have a strong impact on the economic system and that institutions are often the result of political processes.

In essence, the NIE is concerned with the evolution of institutions or history (North 1990, 1991, 1994), property rights (Alchian 1961, 1965a, 1965b; Demsetz 1967; Alchian and Demsetz 1973), transaction costs (Williamson 1979, 1985, 1996), and uncertainty (a form of market failure). As Coase (1937, 1960) has pointed out, without transaction costs the firm and law have no role to play.

2.2.1 Coordination mechanisms: Public versus private provision

Economists have applied insights from the NIE to question whether public or private provision of goods and services is preferred. Shleifer (1998) and Hart et al. (1997) make the case for private provision of health care, schools and other services that are usually associated with government provision. The reasons for private provision are that it leads to incentives for innovation and cost minimization, but possibly at the expense of quality. Where cost of provision is important and quality is less important, the case for private provision is strongest. However, even where quality is important, the ability of government to use contracts to get what it wants could mitigate the need for public provision. While private firms providing a service have an incentive to innovate in order to reduce costs, contracts can be written in ways that prevent deterioration of quality related to cost minimizing efforts or encourage innovation to improve quality (e.g., via performance incentives). Public ownership or provision may be preferred when the adverse effect of cost reductions on quality is large, quality improvements are unimportant, or government employees have weaker incentives to improve quality than private owners (Hart et al. 1997).

In addition to the quality-cost of provision trade-off, corruption and patronage are important in deciding whether public or private provision is preferred. Corruption and patronage are opposite sides of the same coin.

Corruption occurs when private firms are effectively able to lobby or "bribe" government officials to extend them favors (e.g., providing contracts for provision of services with weak or vague performance clauses). Patronage occurs when government (elected) officials favor particular constituents in return for their support (e.g., public service union workers are provided large pay raises, environmental groups are given freedom to protest even if they break the law). Where corruption is a severe problem, the case for in-house (public) provision is enhanced; where patronage is a problem, the case favors privatization.

2.2.2 Market failure and coordination mechanisms

Other factors enter into the supply decision in addition to the raw choice between private and public provision of a good or service. These depend on the source of market failure, of which four sources can be identified.

1. Market power can result from economies of scale and scope, or collusion by firms in oligopolist industries.
2. Interdependencies outside the price system occur because of so-called spillovers. When economic agents fail to take into account the costs (benefits) their actions have on other agents, they produce (consume) at a level where marginal social cost exceeds marginal social benefits. This is the classic case of externality. Another form of market failure occurs when there is no incentive to provide a good or service, or amenity, because the provider cannot capture enough of the social benefit of provision. This is the case of public goods; there is no incentive for a single economic agent to invest in the protection of biodiversity (provision of nature), because benefits accrue widely and cannot be captured privately.
3. Investment in relation-specific assets, or specificity, leads to what is known as the hold-up problem. By investing in specific assets, the supplier of a good or service (or nature) is subject to hold-up because what was agreed to *ex ante* is not what the demander (say government) pays *ex post*. *Ex post* could be well over 10 years in the case of nature (forest ecosystem) provision.
4. Finally, risk sharing deals with fundamental uncertainty. However, risk sharing leads to problems of moral hazard (agents take fewer precautions to avoid risk once they are part of risk sharing scheme) and adverse selection (only those with the highest need to share risk participate in the scheme).

Four economic coordination mechanisms are available for dealing with market failure:

1. competition,
2. control (or government regulation/ownership),
3. cooperative exchange (contracts), and
4. common values and norms.

Cooperative exchange, and common values and norms, are intermediary between the extremes of competition and control. Competition may be more appropriate in a heterogeneous society, while common values and norms develop more easily in a homogeneous society (CPB 1997, pp.42-44).

The ability to implement a coordination mechanism (if at all) depends crucially on the existing institutional arrangements, or governance structure, within the jurisdiction. It is not possible, for example, to implement a system of transferable development rights if private property rights are not enforceable and upheld by the courts. Where such institutions do no exist, it is not possible to have transferable rights to timber or logs on public land. If forestland ownership and forest exploitation have been in public hands, organizations within government will oppose their privatization. Indeed, such organizations might be supported by others (e.g., environmental groups) who feel that privatization of forestland (and maybe even of its exploitation) will result in a decline in the quality of forests (or nature). This may make it difficult to change tenure systems, regulations and other forest governance structures. The underlying governance structure may prevent implementation of some of the coordination mechanisms for dealing with market failure. The extent to which this is the case will vary from one jurisdiction and situation to another.

The potential strengths and weaknesses of the four coordination methods are summarized in Table 2.2. Competition is aided by such instruments as transferable development rights (e.g., to harvest trees on public lands), *ex ante* payments or subsidies, and/or insurance markets that guarantee firms protection against political whims and the possibility of default on payments. Making markets more competitive by removing such impediments as onerous government regulations can lead to a reduction in market power, as can more vigorous enforcement of anti-trust laws.

Economies of size and scope may limit competition – scope because it may be more efficient to provide two amenities, say commercial timber benefits and extra-market amenities, together rather than separately.

Uncertainty and lack of commitment may also characterize competition, although one advantage of reliance on competition to provide certain products and services is that society gets greater diversity in the types (qualities) provided.

Table 2.2: Strengths and Weaknesses of Coordination Mechanisms for Providing Nature

Coordination Mechanism	Implementation	Potential Weaknesses	Potential Strengths
Competition	Transferable development rights, *ex ante* payments, reallocate revenues, insurance markets	Economies of scale & scope, certainty, commitment, solidarity	Diversity/variety, experimentation, external flexibility, incentives
Control	Regulation, public provision, nationalization, ownership, uniform conditions	Diversity, experimentation, flexibility, incentives	Economies of scale & scope, certainty, enforcement, solidarity
Cooperative Exchange or Contracts	Intermediary, covenants, encompass interest groups, co-determination, monitoring, restrict freedom to act, delegation	Enforcement, certainty, flexibility	Commitment, accountability, internal flexibility
Common Values & Norms	Information, reputation, private-group charity	Enforcement, privacy	Commitment, in-group solidarity

Source: Adapted from CPB (1997, pp.61-74).

Control is exercised through public ownership or regulation, with regulations usually uniform across agents even though costs and benefits vary. The advantage of control is that society is more certain that the desired good or service is supplied. State ownership is usually required to ensure provision of wilderness areas, for example, because it is a public good, although wilderness itself is a vague concept, with society unsure as to what it wants in this regard. Direct regulation or public ownership also can be used to avoid problems related to economies of size and scope, and enforcement is usually direct as it relates to regulations. Problems here are similar to those identified above. The means for implementing cooperative exchange, and common values and norms, is also provided in Table 2.2. For both, enforcement is a problem, while commitment is a strength.

In some jurisdictions forestland and even agricultural land is publicly owned. In some cases, logging may even be performed by state-owned enterprises. In others, private companies may have harvesting or other property rights that, in a civil society, require compensation if commercial activities are no longer permitted on the land – the government cannot simply decree that the land will be protected (converted from the commercial activity to supply nature). Even where logging occurs by state-run enterprises, it is not a simple matter to induce such enterprises to focus less on logging and more on silviculture, for example.

Where land is privately held, some form of inducement is also needed to get owners to provide (more) nature (by investing in silviculture) in lieu of the current activity. The government could simply use regulations to force companies to perform silvicultural activities (create more nature), but, as noted in Table 2.2, this has its disadvantages and will generally not be permitted unless compensation is forthcoming. The state could purchase silvicultural services, or it can perform these by forming a state run agency to perform such services. Both have their own budgetary implications, with the former possibly cheaper (e.g., if private silvicultural contracts are less prone to becoming unionized compared to state-owned agencies). Clearly, government will prefer to regulate forest companies via a legislated forest practices code, for example, so that the private companies provide the desired silvicultural services at no cost to the public treasury.

Private provision of many forms of nature (especially where exclusion is not possible and private benefits are few) only occurs if the state uses broad-based incentives or contracts to obtain desired levels (supplies) of nature from private landowners. Contracts will vary by the quality of nature desired (viz., wilderness areas where little human activity is permitted versus bird nesting cover on private farmland), local institutions and the costs of providing nature, and the ability to reallocate funds from demanders of nature to suppliers. To provide wilderness it may be necessary to prohibit all commercial activities (e.g., stop logging of mature forest), while it may only be necessary to restrict the size of clearcuts and require replanting to provide desired environmental benefits on private forestland.

In some areas or jurisdictions it may simply be difficult or even impossible to provide some types of nature (such as primary wilderness). For example, it is impossible to prohibit human use of forests in Sweden (where tradition allows all citizens access for recreation purposes) or harvesting of trees in Austria (where, for example, in the Montafon Valley historic user rights guarantee residents can harvest timber).[5] While the private supplier of nature will seek to minimize costs, contracts are often vague about quality. Contracts are incomplete and generally complex because all contingencies cannot be accounted for and the "thing" to be supplied (nature or the silvicultural "outcome") is necessarily ill-defined, and sometimes even difficult to measure.

Contracts refer to the "arrangements" between the "principal" who demands the nature and the "agent" who supplies it. The principal is usually the government (acting on behalf of citizens who demand more nature), an environmental non-governmental organization (ENGO) that represents a particular constituency (e.g., The Nature Conservancy, Ducks Unlimited), or even a private company desiring to purchase silvicultural services. It does not matter, however, whether nature is publicly or privately provided. In the case of public provision, the agent responsible for carrying out the activity of supplying nature (planting or tending trees, monitoring compliance, managing wildlife populations, constructing trails and campsites for recreationists, etc.) is a government employee or someone specifically contracted to perform one or more specific activities. In the case of private provision, the agent responsible for supplying nature is the landowner. Assuming that the government is the principal, there is a significant difference between the case where the agent is an employee or a private landowner.

Provision of nature – the creation or protection of natural forest or silvicultural investment to provide forest ecosystem amenities – is not costless, but it could be made costlier by inappropriate choice of a coordination mechanism.

2.3 Market Failure and Property Rights: Further Thoughts

At a broad level, institutions are said to evolve organically and incrementally (North 1994). Property rights (PR) scholars contend that

---

[5] In the Austrian case, the common property forest is managed by *Stand Montafon*, a company owned by the local municipalities. Historic user rights guarantee the citizens of the region rights to use wood for heating and construction. In recent times, to prevent exploitation, residents have been allocated a share of the allowable harvest each year for heating, while wood cannot be used for new construction but only for repair of existing structures (Linda ten Klooster, pers. com., March 3, 1999). See Glüeck et al. (1999) for additional examples.

institutions evolve in response to emerging social conflicts because humans constantly compete for limited resources and, therefore, the desire for greater incomes and wealth provides a rationale for the emergence and creation of property rights (Pejovich 1972, 1990).

Demsetz (1967) is one of the first PR scholars to have examined the origins of property rights. He analyzed the development of private property rights in land among American native Indians. Specifically, the advent of the fur trade resulted in a sharp increase in the value of furs to the Indians and, consequently, increased the scale of hunting. Traditional open access gave way to increasingly private ownership in the form of territorial hunting and trapping by individual families, eventually to the appropriation of land and exclusive hunting and trapping domains.

> "New techniques, new ways of doing the same things, and doing new things – all invoke harmful and beneficial effects to which society has not been accustomed...It is my thesis...that property rights takes place in response to the desires of the interacting persons for adjustment to new benefit-cost possibilities. Property rights develop to internalize externalities when the gain from internalization becomes larger than the cost of internalization. Increased internalization, in the main, results from changes in economic values, changes that stem from the development of new technology and the opening of new markets, changes to which old property rights are poorly attuned" (Demsetz 1967, p.350).

Echoing Demsetz, North (1972, p.86) traces the development of property rights in Medieval Europe to changes in cost-benefit calculations. Pejovich (1972) and Dahlman (1980) summarize the various findings in two points. First, property rights emerge to reflect changes in social relations with respect to the allocation of scarce resources. Second, the creation and specification of property rights over scarce resources takes place in response to human desire for greater income and wealth.

The driving force for the creation of a specific property rights arrangement lies in the role played by incentives. Humans respond to economic incentives. Whenever the benefits of undertaking a certain activity exceed the costs, the economic agent desires to pursue the activity. In the case of externality, if the benefits of internalizing the externality exceed the costs of doing so, new structures or institutions emerge to bring this about (Demsetz 1967). Changes in benefits and costs occur as a result of:

1. New technologies and the opening up of new markets (e.g., introduction of computers and the Internet) affects benefits and costs, among other things.
2. Changes in relative factor scarcities and factor prices affect economic allocations of resources. North (1972) illustrates this using the example of Western Europe's change in population relative to land availability in the 13th century.
3. The actions of the State (laws, regulations, economic incentives) affect the allocation of resources (Demsetz 1967; Pejovich 1972).

Thus, the creation and specification of property rights occurs in response to human desires, and modification of extant property rights is prompted by changes in opportunities (benefits and costs).

If property rights are completely specified, problems associated with spillovers (externalities) are easier to resolve, in many cases without government intervention (Coase 1960). This result has been codified in the so-called Coase Theorem, which states, in effect, that it is proper specification of property rights that matters, and not their assignment – assignment of property rights only affects the final distribution of income, but not the economically efficient outcome. This may well be true in the neoclassical world of zero transaction costs, but it is not true in a world where transaction costs do affect the outcome, possibly preventing attainment of a social optimum. Coase (1960, 1998) was well aware of this, but believed that many externalities could be mitigated through litigation. In this sense, he anticipated the NIE by suggesting that, while complete specification of property rights is important, other factors also need to be taken into account, including transaction costs and bounded rationality (as evident in the litigation process).

In summary, therefore, property rights are an important institution within society because they establish exclusive rights over resources so that individuals have a clear understanding as to who must pay whom in the event of disputes over the use of scarce resources. However, along with proper specification of property rights and their enforcement, norms of behavior (among other things) are important in governing interactions among individuals and the potential for efficient outcomes (Furubotn and Pejovich 1972; Fukuyama 1995, 1999; Berns et al. 1999). Thus, a major function of property rights is allocative in that they determine the distribution of gains and losses, and resolve conflicts in the course of resource use (Alchian and Demsetz 1973; Seitz and Headley 1975). Further, well-defined property rights help reduce uncertainty and promote efficiency in market transactions (Alchian and Demsetz 1973; Demsetz 1967). However, it is crucial to note that proper specification of property rights is only a necessary and not sufficient condition for bringing this about.

3 Market Failure and Forestry

Managing forests solely for their commercial timber values leads to market failure because too much forestland is harvested relative to what society desires, or it is harvested in ways that are considered detrimental to other forest values. Market failure occurs because markets do not adequately capture the benefits associated with the environmental amenities that forests provide, so that the level of provision of those amenities is below what is economically optimal – these associated environmental amenities are a public good. As the forestland owner, the government of British Columbia must balance commercial or financial aspects of the forest against the environmental amenities of forests, particularly forest ecosystem functions such as carbon sink and uptake (to mitigate global warming), watershed protection, and wildlife habitat and biodiversity protection. Also important to the people of the Province are the outdoor recreational opportunities provided by forests, their role in attracting tourism income and scenic amenities. Again, these amenities are not traded in markets and are sub-optimally provided if focus is only on commercial timber values.

Much effort has gone into measuring non-market or spillover benefits and using them to recommend appropriate forest policy (e.g., van Kooten 1999). However, while measurement of such benefits is a difficult task in and of itself, employing such measures to guide forest policy and management is also complicated. In this regard, it is important to recognize the following:

1. Because forests provide environmental benefits in addition to their commercial (primarily timber) gain, the government must provide economic incentives to forestland owners or tenure holders on public lands to take into account such non-market values in their management decisions.
2. Alternatively, the government can use a regulatory approach to address market failure, although this has the drawback that it often leads to *policy failure*. Policy failure results from the inability of the authority to provide appropriate (socially optimal) levels of commercial and/or

environmental amenities because of political interference and/or bureaucratic bungling, often analyzed via the principal-agent approach.[1]

3. Institutions play an important role in determining the outcome between the commercial and environmental, private and social, interests in the public forest.

4. While the total value of environmental amenities from forest ecosystems might be large and, indeed, might even outweigh the benefits of harvesting trees, decisions are made at the margin. Society does not decide to clearcut all of the forestland in one fell swoop, but makes decisions about whether to harvest the next stand or hectare of forest and how (e.g., clearcut versus selective harvesting). At the margin, the environmental spillover effects are likely very small (van Kooten and Bulte 1999).

In this Chapter, we address the issue of non-market values, or spillovers. We do this by first examining how one might adjust rotation ages to take account of non-timber and non-market values. How do spillovers or externalities affect decisions about when to harvest trees? For example, if amenity values are related to the age of a stand, it may make sense to prolong harvest ages to take such values into account, although it does not necessarily imply that harvest ages are extended indefinitely. This is the market-based or incentive route to addressing market failure – the route of increasing competition. We then consider more fully the role that regulation plays in addressing market failure or externality. It is this approach that has been followed in most forest jurisdictions, particularly British Columbia (see Wilson et al. 1998).

3.1 Economic Incentives and Forest Management via Rotation Age

Harvesting timber provides benefits to society that are given by the stumpage value of standing trees. The decision of when to harvest trees depends on prices, including importantly the interest rate (or opportunity cost of cash). On the other hand, by harvesting trees too soon or too late, environmental benefits could be foregone. The authority needs to provide economic incentives that cause forestland owners or concessionaires to

---

[1] For a discussion of policy failure see Hart et al. (1997), Shleifer (1998), Shleifer and Vishny (1998), and La Porta et al. (1999).

harvest trees at a time that is optimal from society's point of view rather than solely from a private, commercial point of view. To determine what these incentives might be, we examine various criteria that are used to determine the age of harvest.

3.1.1 Maximizing sustainable yield

Maximum sustainable yield (MSY) is used by biologists to determine optimal harvest ages for timber. As implied by its name, the objective is to find the forest rotation age that leads to the maximum possible annual output that can be maintained in perpetuity. The allowable annual cut (AAC) is based on the MSY concept. The AAC is the amount of timber that can be harvested each and every year without diminishing the amount that can be harvested in the future. It is simply the net increase in timber volume in a region or district that results from tree growth – the *mean annual increment* (MAI).

Denote the growth of a stand of timber over time by $v(t)$. In the parlance of production economics, this is the total product function, where time or age, t, replaces the usual inputs labor or capital. Then average product is simply MAI, which is given by $v(t)/t$. Current annual increment is analogous to marginal product, and is given by $v'(t)$. It is well known that the marginal product curve intersects the average product function (from above) at the point where average product attains its maximum. Thus, the MSY rotation age, t_M, is simply the culmination of mean annual increment, and is found by setting the MAI equal to current annual increment:

$$(3.1) \quad \frac{v(t)}{t} = v'(t).$$

Rearranging (3.1) gives the usual relation for finding the MSY rotation age:

$$(3.2) \quad \frac{v'(t_M)}{v(t_M)} = \frac{1}{t_M},$$

where the LHS of this expression is the rate of growth of the timber stand.

As an illustration, consider two functions that can be used to describe the growth in the yield of commercial timber for a stand of trees (Table 3.1). One function describes the growth of native spruce (*Picea spp.*) trees, while the other describes that of fast-growing, hybrid poplar. The maximum sustainable yield rotation ages for slow-growing spruce and hybrid poplar are 50 years and 13 years, respectively.

Table 3.1: Comparison of Various Rotation Ages for Different Functional Forms for Stand Growth

| Rotation | Functional Form[a] | |
	Spruce[b] $v(t) = k\,t^a\,e^{-bt}$ $k = 0.25$, $a=2.00$, $b=0.02$	Hybrid poplar[c] $v(t) = \gamma(1-e^{-\varepsilon t})^{\phi}$ $\gamma=300.00$, $\varepsilon=0.15$, $\phi=3.00$
MSY (t_M)	50 years	13 years
Fisher (t_S)	33 years	17 years
Faustmann (t_F)	23 years	11 years

[a] Timber volume v is measured in m^3.
[b] This function is easy to estimate and $v'(t)/v(t) = (a - bt)/t$.
[c] This is referred to as the Chapman-Richards growth function. Binkley (1987) demonstrates that, for fast-growing species, the financial rotation age can exceed the MSY age.

For plantation forests and under an MSY rotation, the AAC is set equal to the MSY. For uneven-aged forests consisting of mature, over-mature, and young stands of trees, the AAC and MSY are subject to vagaries of harvesting and planting. If one's desire is to maximize society's well being, the MSY rotation may not be appropriate, however.

The problem with maximum sustainable yield is that it is a knife-edge rule, with harvests exceeding the sustainable level if growth does not, for whatever reason, achieve its expected level. The reason for this is uncertainty related to weather, fire, wind and disease. While this is not a major problem in forestry, since any mismatch between sustainable and actual yield can easily be corrected in the future, it is a problem for resources where the stock is unknown and even unknowable, as in the fishery. However, even for forestry, the stock may be unknown if society does not make investments in measurement and stock assessment.

3.1.2 Maximizing benefits from a single cut: Fisher rotation age

Suppose the objective of forest operations is to maximize the net benefit from a one-time harvest of the forest so future harvests are not considered. The objective is then to

(3.3)   Maximize$_t$ $(p - c)\,v(\text{t})\,e^{-rt}$,

where p is the price of logs at the mill and c is the associated cost of felling, bucking, yarding, loading and hauling the logs to the mill. For simplicity, it is assumed that the cost of harvest is a constant marginal cost that can be subtracted from price to obtain a net price or stumpage value.

The first-order conditions for a maximum give:

(3.4) $\quad \dfrac{v'(t_S)}{v(t_S)} = r,$

where r is the (instantaneous) rate of discount (interest rate). The rotation age found from (3.5) is known as the Fisher rotation age, t_S (where S denotes single harvest). This condition states that trees should be left standing as long as their value (rate of growth) increases at a rate greater than the rate of return on alternative investments, as represented by the discount rate r. When the rate of tree growth is falling, the trees should be harvested the moment the rate of growth in value equals the discount rate. The forest (woodlot) owner simply keeps her investment tied up in trees until more can be earned by liquidating the investment (cutting the timber) and investing the funds from their sale at the alternative rate of return, or discount rate. Assuming a discount rate of 4%, the single rotation age is found to be about 33 years for spruce and 17 years for hybrid poplar (Table 3.1).

Note that the decision to harvest is independent of price as can be seen by multiplying both the numerator and denominator in conditions (3.2) and (3.4) by net price. (Alternatively, and without loss of generality, we can scale the output units so net revenue per unit is 1.0.) However, price is important in the decision for one reason: if price is too low, so that the net revenue from harvesting a stand of trees is negative, then the trees will not be harvested regardless of their rate of growth. If the cost of harvesting (c) cannot be expressed on a per unit basis, then the cost of harvesting trees can be incorporated in the decision by modifying equation (3.4) as follows:

(3.5) $\quad \dfrac{pv'(t)}{pv(t)-c} = r.$

3.1.3 Faustmann or financial rotation age

Assume that forestland is to be used only for the purpose of growing and harvesting trees, that it has no potential for non-timber sources of revenue, and that speculative factors are ignored. (The impact of each of these upon land value will be discussed below.) Then, the value of land depends on whether the land is managed, whether trees are currently growing on the site and whether the land is part of a larger management unit.

Begin with a situation where there are no trees growing on the site (bare land). Let V denote the discounted value of returns from all future harvests, or the value of bare land, which is also referred to as the *soil expectation*. The soil expectation is given by:

$$(3.6) \quad V = \lim_{n \to \infty} \sum_{k=1}^{n} (p-c)\, v(t)\, e^{-rkt} = \frac{(p-c)v(t)\, e^{-rt}}{1 - e^{-rt}},$$

where $v(t)$ is the volume of timber growing on the site at time t, p and c are as above, and r may include a risk premium. Maximizing (3.6) by setting the first derivative with respect to t equal to zero gives:

$$(3.7) \quad \frac{v'(t_F)}{v(t_F)} = \frac{r}{1 - e^{-rt_F}}$$

where the t_F denotes the optimal Faustmann rotation age. Compared to the cutting rule in equation (3.4), the fact that the denominator on the RHS of (3.7) is less than one but greater than zero has the same effect as that of increasing the discount rate in (3.4). An increase in the discount rate would cause one to harvest sooner (see Table 3.1).

What is not taken into account in the Fisher (single-harvest) case is the possibility that, once timber is harvested, a new stand of trees can be generated on the land. The second growth can be harvested at a later date. By taking into account the potential of the land to grow another stand of trees, the harvest period is actually shortened. The reason is that, by cutting trees sooner, it also makes available a second and third harvest sooner than would otherwise be the case.

Regeneration can be hastened through reforestation and silviculture. In the one-period case, initial planting costs do not affect the optimum unless net returns are less than zero, in which case there is no solution (Samuelson 1976, p.472). The same is true in the multiple-period case. Rotation ages for other situations, such as when the forest is of uneven age (the manager does not begin with bare land), are discussed by Montgomery and Adams (1995).

For spruce, the Faustmann or financial rotation age is just over 20 years of age, while it is about 11 years for hybrid poplar (Table 3.1). The financial rotation age is below that which maximizes sustainable yield.

Where institutions permit (e.g., public ownership), biological considerations have led governments to legislate harvest ages that exceed the Faustmann age. While this has resulted in lower timber benefits, it is not clear that it has also resulted in lower overall benefits to society.

3.1.4 Hartman rotation age: Non-timber benefits

Where growing forests provide non-timber benefits, an economic argument can be made for extending rotations beyond the financial age. Standing trees have value to society in addition to commercial timber value; these values are derived from scenic amenities, watershed functions, waste receptor and carbon uptake services, non-timber products such as mushrooms, wildlife habitat functions, and so on. If non-market values are related to timber volume, then, if society is to maximize its welfare from managing the forest, the Faustmann rotation age needs to be modified to take into account these values. External benefits need to be correlated with timber (forest) growth before it is possible to determine directly the optimal harvest age that would take external values into account. The difference between commercial timber and non-timber benefits in determining optimal rotation age is that commercial timber benefits accrue only at the end of the rotation, when the trees are harvested. Non-timber benefits, on the other hand, accrue continuously (or annually in the discrete case).

The Hartman (1976) rotation age is based on the maximization of external or amenity values. Suppose that amenity values, denoted $\gamma(t)$, are an increasing function of the age of a forest stand, with $\gamma'(t) > 0$ and $\gamma''(t) < 0$.

The amenity benefits over a rotation are then given by $A(t) = \int_0^t \gamma(s)e^{-rs}ds$.

The objective is to choose the rotation age that maximizes the discounted stream of such benefits, recognizing that benefits fall to zero each time the stand is cut. Substituting $A(t)$ for $(p - c)\, v(t)$ in expression (3.6) gives the following problem:

$$(3.8) \quad \max_t \left[\frac{A(t)e^{-rt}}{1 - e^{-rt}} \right] = \max_t \left[\frac{\left(\int_0^t \gamma(s)e^{-rs}ds \right)e^{-rt}}{1 - e^{-rt}} \right].$$

Maximizing expression (3.8) yields

$$(3.9) \quad \frac{\gamma'(t_H)}{\gamma(t_H)} = \frac{r\,e^{-rt_H}}{1-e^{-rt_H}}$$

If one solves (3.9) for the Hartman rotation age, t_H, one finds that it is longer than the Faustmann age, but only if amenity values increase with stand age; if they decline with age, the Hartman rotation is shorter. This is explored further below.

For now, suppose amenity values for a stand of spruce increase with age according to the following function:

$$(3.10) \quad \gamma(t) = 0.125\, t^2\, e^{-0.0132t},$$

where $\gamma(t)$ is measured in dollars per ha. In this case, the Hartman rotation age is some 150 years, exceeding even the MSY rotation age (Table 3.1).

3.1.5 Hartman-Faustmann rotation age

Consider the case where the manager seeks to maximize the combined commercial timber and non-timber amenities over an infinite planning horizon. In the usual formulation, the manager begins with bare land, plants trees and maximizes the present value of total forest benefits (Swallow et al. 1990; Swallow and Wear 1993):

$$(3.11) \quad \underset{t}{\text{Max}} \left[\frac{((p-c)v(t) + A(t) - C)e^{-rt}}{1-e^{-rt}} \right],$$

where $(p-c)v(t)$ is the commercial timber benefit, $A(t)$ amenity benefits over rotation t, and C regeneration costs. The necessary conditions for an optimum give:

$$(3.12) \quad [(p-c)v'(t_{HF}) + \gamma(t_{HF})]\left(\frac{1-e^{-rt_{HF}}}{r} \right) = (p-c)v(t_{HF}) + e^{-rt_{HF}} A(t_{HF}) - C.$$

The Hartman-Faustmann rotation age (denoted t_{HF}) should be chosen so that the marginal present value of delaying harvest, or marginal benefit of delay (MBD), equals the marginal opportunity cost of delay (MOC). The latter is given on the RHS of (3.12) as the immediate timber benefits minus regeneration costs if the stand is harvested today, plus the amenity benefits received over the next growing period.

The forest manager who is interested in commercial timber production only would need to be subsidized to take into account non-timber amenity values. The policy would provide a subsidy of $\gamma(t)$ to those who hold timber of age t, or pay $[r/(1 - e^{-rt})]$ e^{-rt} $A(t)$ to managers who harvest at age t.

The problem is that there are many non-timber values (e.g., wilderness preservation, provision of forage for wild ungulates, wildlife habitat) that vary in different ways with forest age (see, e.g., Calish et al. 1978; Bowes and Krutilla 1989). Indeed, some amenities are unrelated to forest age. Examples of the relationship between a forest stand's age and non-timber amenities are provided in Figure 3.1. For example, amenity flows might represent the value of wildlife species (e.g., herbivores) adapted to young forests with plentiful forage (I), wildlife values that are independent of forest age (II), and the value of species reliant on more mature forests, such as trout and spotted owls. Benefit stream IV could be the sum of several amenity flows (Swallow et al. 1990). When such non-timber values are combined with commercial timber benefits to form the objective function in (3.11), the second-order conditions associated with a solution for the optimal cutting (Hartman-Faustmann rotation) age are likely to be violated, which implies existence of a *nonconvexity*.[2]

A relevant nonconvexity prevents a tax/subsidy policy from achieving the socially desirable rotation age. The reason can be illustrated with the aid of Figure 3.2. From (3.12), the first-order conditions for a socially optimal solution occur where the marginal opportunity cost of delaying harvest equals the discounted marginal benefit of delay, or MBD = MOC.

Suppose that the Faustmann rotation age is given by rotation age t_F. Points x and y, with accompanying rotation ages t_x and t_y, represent cases where (3.12) is satisfied. The second-order conditions are violated at x but not at y. Providing the forest manager with a myopic subsidy equal to the value of the non-timber benefits will result in a rotation age, t_x, that is shorter than the financial rotation age t_F, but this is not the socially optimal solution. However, a policy that rewards the forest owner or manager with a subsidy of $\gamma(t)$, with $t_x < t \leq t_F$, will achieve the desired solution at y.

---

[2] A sufficient and necessary condition for maximizing a single objective function is that the function be concave. In general, for constrained maximization, the objective function should be concave and the constraints convex; otherwise the second-order conditions for a maximum may not hold. Other conditions hold for minimization. But the term "nonconvexity" has come to mean any violation of the second-order conditions.

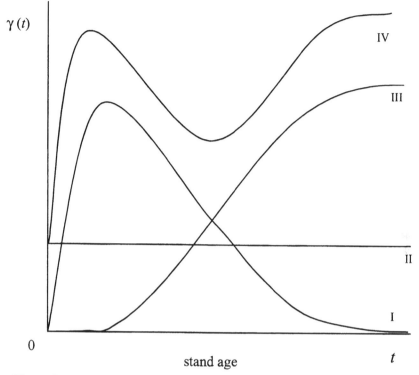

Figure 3.1 Relationship between Stand Age and Amenity Value, Various Amenities

Although the discussion in this sub-section used bare land as a starting point, for some existing forests the external or amenity benefits (which would include preservation value) might be so great that it would not be economically feasible to harvest the forest. In this case, it may be preferable to delay harvest or never harvest. In the context of Figure 3.2, this would be the case if equilibrium points existed at ages beyond those indicated in the diagram (e.g., MOC and MBD may intersection again, with MOC upward and MBD downward sloping). If this is the case and society inherits "ancient" forests, it may be worthwhile delaying harvests, perhaps indefinitely.

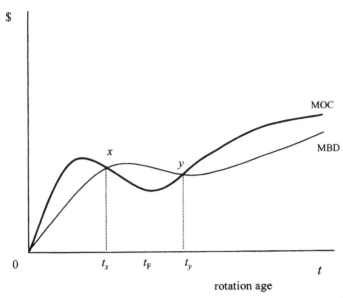

Figure 3.2 Nonconvexities and Optimal Hartman-Faustmann Rotation Age

Finally, Swallow and Wear (1993) and Swallow et al. (1997) extend the notion of convexities and external benefits to multiple use across forest stands. First consider two sites, one publicly owned and the other private. Suppose that harvest of the private forest stand affects the flow of amenity benefits from the public stand, thus shifting both the MOC and MBD functions at the public site. While it may be optimal to harvest the public stand, the public manager may wish to delay harvest in anticipation of felling of the private site, thus extending the public rotation age beyond that which would be socially optimal in the single-stand case (Swallow and Wear 1993). When both sites are managed together for their joint commercial timber and amenity values, Swallow et al. (1997) demonstrate that the sequence of harvest schedules can take rather odd forms. For example, even though two forest stands may be nearly similar in all respects, it might be socially optimal to permit one site to mature to beyond 100 years before harvesting it, while the other site is harvested several times during this period. Vincent and Binkley (1993) reach a similar conclusion about specialization, recommending zoning rather than subsidies as a public policy for increasing social well being.

Summary

A summary of the MSY, financial and combined financial-Hartman criteria for determining rotation ages is provided in Table 3.2. The variables are defined as above. In Table 3.3, the first-order conditions for these three criteria are given for the general growth function for spruce found in Table 3.1.

Table 3.2: Alternative Criteria for Determining Rotation Age

Item	Mathematical Statement Maximize:	First-Order Conditions
Average Annual Output (MSY)	$\dfrac{v(t)}{t}$	$\dfrac{v'(t)}{v(t)} = \dfrac{1}{t}$
Net present value of timber (Faustmann)	$\dfrac{[(p-c)v(t) - C]\,e^{-rt}}{1 - e^{-rt}}$	$\dfrac{(p-c)v'(t)}{(p-c)v(t) - C} = \dfrac{r}{1 - e^{-rt}}$
Present value of timber plus non-timber benefits[a] (Hartman-Faustmann)	$\dfrac{[(p-c)v(t) - C]\,e^{-rt} + A(t)}{1 - e^{-rt}}$	$(p-c)v'(t) + \gamma(t) = r(p-c)v(t) + r\left(\dfrac{[(p-c)v(t) - C]\,e^{-rt} + A(t)}{1 - e^{-rt}}\right)$

[a] $\gamma(t)$ refers to non-timber benefits as a function of growth, with $A(t) = \displaystyle\int_0^t \gamma(s)e^{-rs}ds$.

3.2 Control: Regulation in Forestry

In the past several decades, one response to market failure has been to increase emphasis on multiple use management, and even more recently on forest ecosystem management. While managing for multiple use is commonly understood and accepted by foresters (e.g., see Bowes and Krutilla 1989), the same cannot be said about ecosystem management (Sedjo 1996). The problem is that it is not at all clear what the objectives of ecosystem management might be – they are vague and ill defined – and there is no way of knowing when objectives are achieved. This makes scientific management difficult if not impossible.

Table 3.3: Criteria for Determining Rotation Age (for $v(t) = k\, t^a e^{-bt}$)

Average Annual Output (MSY)	$t = \dfrac{a-1}{b}$
Net present value of timber (Faustmann)	$\dfrac{(p-c)\left(\dfrac{a}{t}-b\right)v(t)}{(p-c)v(t)-C} = \dfrac{r}{1-e^{-rt}}$
Present value of timber plus non-timber benefits[a] (Hartman-Faustmann)	$(p-c)\left(\dfrac{a}{t}-b\right)+q = \dfrac{r\left((p-c)-\dfrac{C}{v(t)}\right)e^{-rt}}{1-e^{-rt}}$
	$+\dfrac{\dfrac{rq}{v(t)}\displaystyle\int_0^t v(s)\,e^{-rs}\,ds}{1-e^{-rt}}+r(p-c)$

[a] Assumes $\gamma(t) = q\, v(t)$, where q is the proportionality constant.

In the previous section, we reviewed a market-based approach to address multiple use management. Non-timber, non-market values can be taken into account by choosing the appropriate rotation age of various stands. As noted, work is ongoing to determine optimal rotation ages when harvest decisions on one stand affect non-market values on other stands, but this is a technical issue that has been solved in practice by a variety of mathematical programming methods (see Hof 1993; Buonginoro and Gilless 1987). The point is that, in order to get firms to harvest forest stands at times that confer the greatest benefits to society, it is possible to harness the power of the market (or competition, as we referred to it in section 2.2) via taxes and subsidies, for example. In practice, however, governments have eschewed this approach, preferring instead to rely on control, either direct ownership or regulation, or a combination of these.

In the past decade, many countries have implemented new forest acts that have included forestry regulations of one form or other (see Wilson et al. 1998). Both Finland and Sweden have new forest acts meant to protect nature. However, the most onerous and detailed regulations have been implemented in British Columbia in the form of a detailed Forest Practices Code. (Surprisingly, as we show in sub-section 3.2.2 below, BC also appears to have the highest public ownership of forestland of any jurisdiction.) Countries have also put in place harvest restrictions, particularly by setting aside environmentally important ecosystems. This has been most evident in the US Pacific North West and BC, where large tracts of old growth have been removed from the working forest and protected in perpetuity.[3] Rather than considering interactions among various forest stands, or even interactions across a much larger landscape, this approach is best described as zoning. The problems with zoning are well known (see van Kooten 1993), particularly that it leads to variances that, in the case of forestry, have led to slow erosion of protected areas (Sinclair 2000). Nonetheless, zoning has been promoted for California (Vaux 1973) and British Columbia as appropriate means for conserving non-timber amenities (Sahajananthan et al. 1998), for addressing market failure.

There are several problems with state intervention via regulation. First, as already alluded to in the previous paragraphs, it is likely to be expensive and ineffective in the longer run. Regulations lead to bureaucratic red tape that increases costs above what they need be. This has been the case in BC where the Forest Practices Code is estimated to add more than $1 billion annually to the costs of harvesting trees on public lands, namely, increasing harvest costs by $10/m^3 on the Coast and by $8/m^3 in the Interior (Haley 1996). In comparison, social benefits appear small (van Kooten 1999). A regulatory environment also creates opportunities and incentives for corruption: those enforcing regulations can be bribed in various ways (not always monetary) to overlook certain contraventions of the law (perhaps because regulations can be interpreted in more than one way), while politicians might grant variances in order to gain support ("bribes") from industry or to please voters (e.g., local communities, forest-sector workers).

Second, politics enter into decisions that should be made on scientific grounds. Thus, Sinclair (2000) complains that governments have been quick to identify protected ecosystems, but have not made available adequate funds to protect them from encroachment. Pressey (2000) demonstrates that governments have been unwilling to purchase important ecologically-sensitive lands from private owners, a complaint echoed by Sinclair (2000), while putting into reserves only public lands, often lands that are marginal for protection of biodiversity. Governments want to be seen as promoting biodiversity, as providing nature, but are unwilling to incur the budgetary costs that are required. They are also unwilling to rely

---

[3] In response, there have been a good many studies that have attempted to determine the optimal level of protection of old-growth forests. Most addressed concerns about irreversibility (quasi-option value) (e.g., Clarke and Reed 1989; Reed 1993; Reed and Ye 1994; Conrad and Ludwig 1994; Conrad 1997), while others included all amenity values in a deterministic framework (e.g., van Kooten and Bulte 1999).

on markets on ideological grounds, even when there are benefits to so doing (for a discussion of this point, see Sowell 1999; see also Pearse 1998).

Third, a regulatory environment often leads to a classic principal-agent problem. This is truer for regulations involving harvesting methods and silvicultural investments that are aimed at protecting nature than for the case of zoning or wilderness set-asides. With regulations that involve silvicutlural prescriptions to provide more nature, there remains the problem that the product, nature, is ill-defined or vague in that it is not precisely clear when the outcome has been achieved. Even when outcomes are defined in terms of specific silvicultural tasks, such as reforesting a site to the point where trees are "free to grow," there remains a certain amount of ambiguity. For instance, what is the state of trees at the time they are "free to grow"? What proportion are likely to survive? How many stems were planted? Are they appropriate species for the site? Are they native or exotic species, or genetically engineered to grow quickly for a short period in order to satisfy other requirements (e.g., green-up and adjacency)? Are non-timber values promoted?

Finally, there has been increasing demand by buyers of wood products for guarantees that such products come from forests that are sustainably managed, or managed in an environmentally preferred way. In response, a variety of certification schemes have been proposed, included ones that are sponsored by the state (e.g., BC's Forest Practices Code, but also efforts through the Canadian Standards Association and ISO 14001), industry (Canadian Pulp and Paper Association's Environmental Profile Data Sheet) and ENGOs (Forest Stewardship Council Certification). To a large extent, private sector (including ENGO) efforts have mitigated the need for regulations such as those embodied in BC's Forest Practices Code. While such regulations remain in place, they do serve as an impediment to certification through some of the other avenues. Further, in the case of BC, its forest practices have reduced its flexibility in addressing costs, as any attempt to ease restrictions will be regarded by the United States as a subsidy to the wood products industry.

British Columbia relies primarily on control to address market failure in forestry. As the focus in this book is on silvicultural investment in British Columbia, the next several sub-sections provide a more detailed background on BC's forestry institutions.

3.2.1 Emergence and evolution of forestland ownership

While many have studied land ownership and tenure (e.g., Powelson 1987, 1988), research specifically focused on forestland is limited. The UN Food and Agriculture Organization (FAO) accorded considerable attention to land tenure and property rights in forestry during the 1980s,[4] but its emphasis was mainly on management of forest resources and the policy framework, with particular focus on Europe.

The history of the advancement of human civilization is sometimes described as a history of deforestation – the conversion of forestland to agriculture (Bechmann 1990; Perlin 1989). As cultivation expanded and became more permanent, because of growth in population and advancement in technology, society forged a "more durable relationship of the cultivator to the soil" (Lewinsky 1913, p.16). This led to a more permanent life pattern, with the cultivated land as its center.

The evolution of forestland tenures tended to follow a sequence from open-access exploitation to communal ownership, then state property, and finally private (individual and corporate) ownership, primarily as a consequence of the intensification of human activities (Bechmann 1990). Transitions from open access to other ownership forms tended to be gradual, organic processes. In Africa and Asia, communal (tribal) ownership was an ownership characteristic that was skipped in other regions, particularly North America (Jeppe 1980; Dahlman 1980). Bechmann (1990, p.232) cites the "Law of Beaumont" as resulting in communal ownership in Europe as kings granted woodlands to hundreds of communities in the Middle Ages. It was perpetual usage rights that were granted and not freehold title, with such rights revocable by the feudal rulers. State ownership of the forest in Europe in the Middle Ages was the rule rather than exception.

In North America, forests are extensively owned by the federal or state government, although some of it tends to be marginal. The reason is that high-quality and easy to access forestland was privatized first, but that, as a result of the conservation movement, governments stopped granting forestland to private holders beginning in the latter part of the 1800s. In the US, this began with the creation of the Yellowstone National Park in 1872, but was followed shortly thereafter by the creation of the National Forest system. However, National Parks were designed as set asides, while the National Forests were originally created as a timber reserve, when timber

---

[4] FAO publications include de Saussay (1987), FAO (1988) and Hummel (1989).

from private land ran short. Of course, lands that were marginal in the late 1800s and early 1900s are no longer marginal today.

In other regions, culture and political systems had an impact on forestland ownership. In particular, communism led to state ownership in Russia, China, the Ukraine, and many other countries.

So how did private ownership of forest develop? Three reasons come to mind (Bechmann 1990). First, in Europe in the Middle Ages, the king and the nobles granted freehold rights to individuals for the services that they rendered, especially during wartime. Second, farmers could become owners of smaller pieces of forestlands by clearing and developing larger areas for the original owner under a labor-for-partial-title deal. Finally, merchants, artisans and lawyers could purchase forestlands with cash payments, but this process was essentially limited to the period before the 1200s.

The extent of private forest ownership is a function of culture, economic and political institutions, personalities (viz., Gifford Pinchot establishing the US Forest Service), historical precedence, the size of the forest resource, the relation of forests to other resources, and a host of other factors.[5] For instance, private ownership of forestland is more common where land was at some time in the past used extensively for agriculture. If the forest has traditionally been a major source of fuel and timber, private ownership is not inevitable; instead, forest tenure involves usufructuary rights for fuelwood and construction timber rather than fee simple title. Corporate holdings of forestland appeared between the 1600s and 1800s, primarily in Sweden and, to a lesser extent, Finland, in Sweden because it developed early on an iron industry that required charcoal (see Wilson et al. 1998). Today, corporate ownership of forestland remains a tenure characteristic in Nordic Europe. In the United States, all lands west of the Appalachians began as federal lands gained as a result of war and/or land purchases from other countries, but most were transferred to private ownership as a result of the Homesteader Act (Steen 1992; van Kooten 1993). Remaining (marginal) lands were transferred into State hands or kept as BLM and Forest Service lands. Forest companies acquired their forest holdings through decades of purchase from the government as well as from small, private forest owners.

---

[5] For a discussion of the role of culture, institutions, climate, education, and other factors in the creation of national wealth, see Landes (1999). See also Vickers and Yarrow (1991).

The extent of private, state and communal ownership of forestland is provided in Table 3.4 (see also Table 1.4). Different forms of ownership can and do co-exist within jurisdictions, but private property appears to be the most important and perhaps dominant form of forestland ownership in many parts of the world. However, it is difficult, a priori, to say that one form of ownership is preferred over another. Indeed, it is argued that public ownership of forest resources enables the public to protect and enhance the values of forestlands that are economically unattractive to private owners, and provides the state with powerful means of shaping the pattern and pace of economic development in a jurisdiction (Pearse 1976). Nonetheless, theoretical and empirical evidence presented by Hart et al. (1997), Shleifer and Vishny (1998), and La Porta et al. (1999) suggests that the state may not be an efficient manager of public lands for reasons noted in the previous section. Perhaps this helps explain why the governments of Sweden and New Zealand have recently reduced their holdings of productive forestlands in an effort to promote not only efficient timber production but also better environmental performance (see Wilson et al. 1998).[6]

Where there is widespread public ownership, exclusive use rights are generally given to private loggers; these are referred to as concessions in developing countries and contractual or tenure arrangements in developed countries. The usefulness of these arrangements depends on the degree of certainty that the concession or tenure provides, particularly with respect to duration, renewability and replaceability. If the property or usufructuary rights are transferable with few limitations, and contracts are of sufficient duration (e.g., exceeding normal rotation age), then there is very little difference between private property rights and concessionaire rights with public ownership of forestland. However, if a concession or tenure is of short duration (say, shorter than a rotation length), loggers' efforts are oriented only on timber harvesting, and not on preservation of soil fertility and timber growing. There are no incentives for the licensee in this case to maintain and develop the forest resource. Lack of clarity concerning property rights leads to incentive failure (Vickers and Yarrow 1991; also Pearse 1998).

---

[6] For Mexico, Heath (1992) fails to find significant differences between farmers operating on private farms and those on lands that belong to the state. The reason, however, is that there is only a *de jure* but not *de facto* difference in small farmers' control over resources between the tenure types. Farmers simply find a way around any restrictions on state lands.

Table 3.4: Forestland Ownership in Selected Jurisdictions

Country/ Region	Forest (10^6 ha)	Forest cover (%)	Managed forest by ownership (%)[a]				
			Public		Private		
			State	Other[b]	Individual	Industry	Other[c]
North America							
Canada	244.6	26.5	84.3	0.2	11.9	3.6	-
USA[d]	217.3	23.7	34.9	9.9	25.8	23.8	3.5
East Asia							
Japan	24.1	66.0	30.0	11.0	42.7	6.3	10.0
Korea (South)	6.5	65.3	22.0	7.0	71.0	-	-
P.R. China	133.0	14.3	45.0	55.0	-	-	-
Taiwan	1.9	52.1	83.0	7.0	10.0	-	-
Europe							
Austria	3.8	46.5	13.7	2.7	69.1	-	14.5
Belgium	0.6	21.3	10.8	32.4	55.1	0.2	1.6
Denmark	0.4	10.5	26.8	5.0	45.5	-	22.7
Finland	21.9	71.9	29.6	-	55.6	9.2	5.5
France	15.2	28.0	10.1	16.0	62.1	-	11.7
Germany	10.7	31.0	33.4	19.9	46.7	-	-
Greece	3.4	25.7	74.8	8.8	10.7	-	5.7
Ireland	0.6	8.6	69.3	-	30.7	-	-
Italy	9.9	33.5	5.1	94.3	0.6	-	-
Netherlands	0.3	10.0	36.6	14.3	20.7	-	28.3
Norway	8.7	28.4	10.8	3.1	75.4	4.5	6.3
Portugal	3.4	37.2	5.8	40.9	6.5	46.7	-
Spain	13.5	27.0	0.4	20.1	79.5	-	-
Sweden	27.3	66.8	1.9	7.1	51.4	39.6	-
Switzerland	1.2	30.0	1.0	64.9	30.5	-	3.6
UK	2.5	10.2	42.0	3.8	38.0	1.2	15.1
Oceania							
Australia	156.9	20.6	57.3	-	42.7	-	-
New Zealand	7.9	29.3	21.8	2.7	6.3	32.6	36.6

Source: United Nations (2000); Wang (1999).
[a] "Managed forest" refers to the forest that is available for wood supply; the total may not add up to 100% due to rounding.
[b] "Other public ownership" refers to that owned by municipal government and local authorities, collectives, church and so on.
[c] "Other private ownership" refers to that owned by private institutions.
[d] Approximately 2% of the managed forest in the United States is owned by indigenous or tribal peoples.

Recent evidence from Sweden, New Zealand and other jurisdictions indicates that forestland ownership forms do change (Wilson et al. 1998). These are related to, among other factors, changes in (1) the relative scarcity of forest resources, (2) relative prices of forest products, (3) technology that results in new investment opportunities, (4) societal values, or perception of the extent of market failure, and (5) the economic circumstances of the state owner. Although large areas of forest plantations were successfully privatized in some countries, privatization may not be a panacea for addressing policy failure, just as control (regulation, state ownership) may not be appropriate in solving instances of market failure. It is useful to note, however, that privatization itself is a public choice, with attendant, even large, distributional and political consequences. The process of asset transfer may open new opportunities for the pursuit of private agendas by political decision-makers. The effects of privatization in any particular context will, therefore, be highly dependent upon the wider institutional framework, and socio-cultural milieu, in which it is implemented (Vickers and Yarrow 1991).

In some cases, rapid privatization might leave inadequate time for the creation of durable incentive structures for efficiency. For example, without market liberalization, many of state-owned enterprises might simply be transformed into private monopolies. As events in a number of Eastern European countries suggest, other institutional changes may be required to permit proper functioning of private markets. Primary among these is a court system that protects property rights and contracts. Such things as honesty, trust and other social capital may also be required (Fukuyama 1995, 1999; Berns et al. 1999; Landes 1999).

3.2.2 Institutions and BC's forestry sector

Forestland covers 60.6 million ha, or 64% of BC, with a standing inventory of some 8,000 million cubic metres of mature timber. Productive forestland comprises some 26 million ha. About 93% of the forest is coniferous, giving BC nearly half of Canada's softwood inventory. The Province's forestland is, by and large, publicly owned, except for about 4% that is owned by private individuals and companies. This is the highest degree of public ownership of forestland of any jurisdiction in the industrialized world, with the exception of Russia and China (see Tables 1.4 and 3.4).

The forest tenure system is, without question, the driver of BC's forest policy and institutions. The central position that the forest tenure system has occupied in the Province's forestry development has been examined by, among others, Pearse et al. (1974), Pearse (1976), Haley and Luckert (1986, 1990), and Drushka (1999).

Historical Background

The British Crown colonies of Vancouver Island and mainland British Columbia were established with the signing of the Oregon Boundary Treaty in 1846, while BC joined Canada as a province in 1871. From 1846 until 1896, logging companies were granted freehold or fee simple title (exclusive possession and use in perpetuity) to land that was bestowed as a grant from the Crown to the initial private owner. The Crown grant included exclusive right to all timber resources as well as surface ownership of land; such grants constituted a frontier policy that aimed to promote settlement and economic growth. Primarily as a result of these grants, present private forestlands amount to 2.55 million ha, or less than 5% of the Province's forest area. Of course, the land is still subject to taxation, common law and statutory land use restrictions (Pearse et al. 1974).

After the granting of fee simple title stopped, only rights to timber harvest were provided, so the Province's title to the forestland was not severed. Five temporary tenures were designed to promote the economic development of the Province – timber leases, pulp leases, timber licenses, pulp licenses, and timber berths. A license typically expired when the timber inventory was liquidated. By 1907, temporary tenures covered some 4.4 million ha (for further details, see Drushka 1999).

The issuing of the temporary tenures abruptly ended in 1907 because of fear that it might lead to future timber shortages. The Fulton Commission of 1910 estimated that two-thirds of the Province's merchantable forestland had already been alienated, so further alienation would be undesirable. The Commission recommended the use of "Timber Sales", or Timber Sale Licenses, to prevent timber falling into the hands of speculators or a combine of operators who could restrict market competition (Pearse et al. 1974; Drushka 1999).

Sustained yield forest management became the centerpiece of BC's forest policy as a result of the Sloan Commission of 1945. Consequently, the Forest Management Licenses, which were later renamed Tree Farm Licenses (TFL), were introduced as a new form of forest tenure. It enabled owners of Crown-granted lands and old temporary tenures to combine their holdings with additional unencumbered public land in a management unit capable of yielding, theoretically at least, a continuous harvest of timber in perpetuity. All other tenures held or acquired by the licensee within the boundaries of a TFL were to be included in the license unit. In terms of composition, Crown grants and old temporary tenures were called "Schedule A" land, while the remaining area, consisting of otherwise unencumbered Crown land, was referred to as "Schedule B" land. Once timber was removed from an old temporary tenure, the land was automatically transferred to "Schedule B". The TFL system committed the licensee to manage the entire area according to sustained yield principles under the general supervision of the Forest Service. In return, the licensee was given an exclusive right to harvest public timber within the license area. The new tenure system was a timber-supply-in-exchange-for-sustained-yield-forest-management deal.

Besides, Farm Woodlot Licenses were also created in 1947, but they were quite limited in both acreage and influence. A number of other forms of tenures were created in response to changing circumstances. In the 1960s, volume-based Timber Sale Harvesting Licenses were introduced, committing the Crown to make available to the licensee a specified volume of timber each year from a designated Public Sustained Yield Unit (PSYU), typically for a period of 10 years. This system was designed to encourage the development of PSYUs, enabling operators to consolidate operations previously scattered among several short-term sales.

In 1978, following the Pearse Royal Commission, Woodlot License, Pulpwood Agreement and Forest License were introduced as new tenures replacing equivalent older tenures with new conditions. An "evergreen" clause was adopted to allow regular renewal of licenses, and Timber Supply Areas (TSAs) were introduced to replace the PSYUs. The most recent substantial change in the tenure system took place in 1987. Responsibility for basic silviculture was shifted from the government to major licensees (TFLs and Forest Licenses, or FLs). Meanwhile, 5% of AAC on each TFL and FL was retrieved over a two-year period, and allocated to the Small Business Forest Enterprise Program. Two years later, a moratorium was announced by the government on processing of new TFLs or additions to existing ones, and this policy marked the end of the consolidation of forest tenures as recommended in the Pearse Royal Commission report that was released in 1976.

The foregoing overview reveals the most conspicuous features of BC's forest tenure system. As forest tenures have historically formed the heart of the Province's forest policy, efforts aimed at understanding the patterns of the Province's forest development have naturally centered on tenure arrangements. However, due to the fact that adequate knowledge about the forest tenure system can hardly be deduced from the statutes or contracts alone, attention frequently has to be assigned to administrative procedures, practices and regulations, and changing industrial circumstances (Pearse et al. 1974). Due to the predominance of public ownership, BC's forestry institutional structure is characterized by schemes designed to motivate private initiatives for productive activities on public properties. Hence, the principal government policy has traditionally been the use of various forest tenure arrangements that grant timber cutting rights to the private sector without relinquishing the Crown's title to the land (Drushka 1999). Table 3.5 summarizes the status quo of BC's forest tenures.

Table 3.5: British Columbia's Forest Tenures

Tenure category	Number	Main features
Forest License	190	volume based, 15 years replaceable
Tree Farm License (TFL)	34	area based, 25 years replaceable
Timber License outside of TFL	270	area based, reverted to Crown after cut
Timber License within TFL	400	area based, reverted to Crown after cut
Timber Sale License (non-SBFEP)	8	small volume, variable durations
Timber Sale License (SBFEP)	1,773	small volume, some replaceable
Pulpwood Agreement	24	area based, 25 years, some replaceable
Woodlot License	516	area based, 15 years replaceable
Road permit	1,500	itemized permit
License to cut	1,381	short-term licenses
Christmas tree permit	125	itemized permit

Source: BC Ministry of Forests (Annual Report 1996/97, 1995); Vance (1990).

The Property Rights Approach to Forest Tenure Analysis

In the 1980s, research on forest tenures in BC began to be enlightened by the property rights theory advanced by scholars such as Alchian, Demsetz, and so on. According to Haley and Luckert (1986), the property rights theory fit the BC forest tenure system very well in that the system's chief characteristics of separation of control from ownership could find explanation in the usufructuary rights arguments. This understanding enabled them to find a suitable starting point in their handling of the dual relationship of predominant public ownership of forestlands and heavy reliance on private initiatives in managing the forest resource base.

The new approach was particularly appealing in the analysis of TFLs because, for a typical TFL that entails many characteristics and relationships, the PR approach reveals its advantage over the historical approach with its capability of analyzing multiple dimensions. Specifically, Haley and Luckert (1986) focused their attention on the following characteristics in their investigations: comprehensiveness, duration, transferability, right of licensee to economic benefits, exclusivity, use restrictions, and so on. They used the PR approach to provide a comprehensive description of the major tenure types across the country. In essence, the approach enabled them to treat the various characteristics of tenures as a bundle of rights and, once the composition of characteristics were identified, analysis could proceed by various combinations according to availability of information and purposes.

The question of forest tenures in BC boils down to the issue of institutions for silviculture. Luckert and Haley (1993) examined Canadian forest tenures and the silvicultural investment behavior of rational firms. Starting from the proposition advanced by Reed (1985) that forest companies in Canada rarely used conventional financial analysis for allocating funds to silviculture, they argued that the discrepancies between the theoretical and actual behavior of firms in the Canadian forestry sector resulted from the failure of analysts to account for the institutional context. They claimed that forest firms were consistently rational, and the problem of any seemingly irrational behavior arose from public policy constraints. Specifically, they pointed out that no silvicultural program in BC could pass the conventional economic analysis using discounted cash flows due to the fact that the conventional method failed to reflect the entire cost and benefits. They found that in many companies silviculture was treated as costs against harvests rather than as investments. The implication of this finding is that returns to silvicultural expenditures get disbursed in upstream operations like wood processing. So, silviculture is often done as a condition in exchange for securing AAC, hence, a benefit arising from the "allowable cut effect" (see section 5.4). From the practice that firms may be rewarded for undertaking silvicultural activities beyond contractual requirements by increases in AAC, they concluded that firms' returns from harvesting stocks of mature timber are attributable to their silvicultural activities. So, they came to the belief that many analysts failed to find net benefits for silvicultural expenses because they used the conventional economic analysis that was designed to maximize "land rent" only. They pointed out that, actually, some of the benefits of silviculture may be found in "stock rent". In other words, by land rent maximization criterion, there is no incentive for silviculture, but by stock rent maximization rule, there may exist an incentive for undertaking silviculture.

In terms of specific empirical findings, they concluded that neither FLs nor TFLs provided the necessary incentives for adequate management. But, comparatively, TFLs were superior to FLs in that the former, despite its lack of security in terms of replacement and renewability, still facilitates contracting between licensees and the Crown to include management clauses. But, it would be much harder to incorporate management requirements beyond planting whereas in the case of TFLs licensees can be expected to manage up to the free growing stage.

More recently, the implications of tenure for forestland value and management in BC have been examined based, essentially, on Zhang's doctoral work (Zhang 1994; Zhang and Binkley 1995; Zhang and Pearse

1996, 1997). This body of research was based on the employment of multiple regression techniques to quantitatively test several hypotheses: (i) How do the characteristics of forest property rights affect the value of the property? (ii) What is the role of tenures in determining silvicultural investment? And (iii) how do tenures affect outputs and silviculture performance? Based on the proposition that TFLs are superior to FLs in terms of the major property rights characteristics such as comprehensiveness, security, duration, exclusiveness, flexibility, and so on, Zhang attempted to empirically determine how much more a TFL holder invested than a FL holder in silviculture. To a lesser degree, timber licenses and private lands within TFLs were also included in the analysis. It was found that the amount of silvicultural investment was correlated with the security of the forest tenures. For the study period of 1987 to 1994, for every dollar spent under the FL category, $1.24 was spent on Crown lands within TFLs, and $1.73 on private lands within TFLs.

In essence, the objective of Zhang's research was to test how forest tenures affect inputs and outputs. This approach was highly appropriate from a PR perspective. Traditionally, institutions were assumed to be invariant and researchers tended to focus on the relationship between inputs and outputs. In contrast, Zhang purposefully sought to test the relationship between tenures and a number of economic indicators so that the effects of various forms of forest tenures could be inferred. Fundamentally, Zhang's approach was similar to Luckert's insofar as the employment of the PR approach was concerned. But, the employment of econometric methods as Zhang did was more demanding in terms of data collection and the quality of the empirical results hinges upon the acceptability of underlying assumptions and the quality of data.

Because of the historical evolutions that BC has undergone, it is not surprising that analyses of forestry institutions in the Province are necessarily focused on forest tenures. The PR approach operates at the level of forest tenures and is largely concerned with the incentive implications of various property rights structures. Consider the following question: "What are the changes in economic incentives and how do they influence the behavior of the economic agents involved?" In the context of this question, the PR approach is certainly a fruitful avenue of enquiry. However, because the PR approach depends on analyzing the several dimensions that include exclusiveness, duration, transferability and so forth (Haley and Luckert 1986), and since BC's forest tenure structures have not changed nearly as much as the contractual relationships among the players, investigation into the effects of forest tenures on silvicultural investment and performance may be difficult.

In spite of the usefulness of the approaches such as the historical approach and the PR approach, a third approach with a view to the role of transaction costs is likely to hold considerable promise for improved understanding of the increasingly complex institutional structure of BC's forestry sector. It is a hypothesis awaiting empirical testing that the creation of TFL in the early times and the switch of responsibilities for basic silviculture from the Crown to the private sector represented, on both occasions, attempts at reducing transaction costs. It is even possible to use the transaction cost approach to explain the government's policy framework regarding various silvicultural arrangements. It appears that the transaction cost approach is a logical step to follow the PR approach in the analysis of BC's forestry institutions, particularly in regard to the economic rationale of contractual arrangements. In BC's context, it seems appropriate to adopt a two-level or two-step approach. The first step is to analyze the contractual relations between the Crown and the major licensees, which is the main relationship characterized by public ownership of forestlands and private initiatives in production. The second step is to investigate the contractual arrangements between the major licensees and contractors, and at this level, microeconomic models such as the principal-agent one may be suitably used with an emphasis on the issue of resolving information deficits and asymmetries between the agents involved. The purpose is to show that institutionally efficient arrangements have advantages in diminishing transaction costs.

To conclude this chapter, economics may be viewed as the study of property rights over resources, and the allocation of scarce resources in a society is the assignment of rights to uses of resources. Property rights structures vary from one to another, and these variations affect the allocation of resources, composition of output, income distribution and so forth. Essentially, the question of economics should be posed in terms of how property rights are defined and traded, and on what terms.

As an extension of the traditional theory of microeconomics, the PR approach has become an analytical instrument capable of addressing economic problems with emphasis on differences in the incentive structures among various institutions. The PR approach provides a useful model for analyzing economic problems. The recognition of the role played by transaction costs lends help to broadening the scope of the PR approach in explaining many economic problems under various socio-economic systems. Transaction cost economics is the subject matter in the next chapter.

4 Contracts, Information and Transaction Costs

Contracts are important because any exchange of products and services must be coordinated by some form of contract, be it explicit or implicit (Hart 1989). There are a variety of approaches to the analysis of contracts. The most common is principal-agent theory, also known as the incentive contract paradigm. Ross (1973) was one of the first to model formally principal-agent relationships. Among others, Grossman and Hart (1983), Holmström (1979, 1982), Harris and Raviv (1979), Calvo and Wellisz (1978), Mirrlees (1976), and Becker and Stigler (1974) also studied the principal-agent question. In this pursuit, the typical model takes the following form: the principal maximizes some objective function subject to the agent's utility constraint (Hart and Holmström 1987; Sappington 1991).

In agriculture, to produce a certain crop, a landowner has several options:

1. produce it alone,
2. pay cash to hire another to produce it, and/or
3. produce it under a sharecropping agreement.

The first option is one in which the landowner encounters no incentive problem but also bears all of the risks. In 2 and 3, contracts are involved explicitly; by hiring another farmer, the landowner may suffer from possible shirking on the part of that farmer, but the landowner no longer bears the full risk of the undertaking. Clearly, in order to maximize the payoff, the landowner must adopt appropriate contractual forms with built-in incentive schemes that induce optimal levels of effort. Therefore, a typical principal-agent model generates a trade-off between risk avoidance and incentive implications. Most principal-agent models assume risk neutrality for the principal and risk aversion for the agent. Braverman and Stiglitz (1986) examined input cost sharing using such a model. The relationship between risk preferences and optimal crop mix was examined by Apland et al.

(1984), who explored the incentive conditions and the implications of various share-leases and risk aversion on optimum farming under mixed tenancy. Farm leasing studies commonly focus on the impact of contract terms on farm operators' incentives under tenancy (Heady 1947; Johnson 1950; Reid 1975). One difficulty with these types of models is that the modeler has to be specific about the risk preferences of the economic agents concerned. Assuming risk neutrality for both the principal and the agent, Allen and Lueck (1993) adopt an approach that permits joint wealth maximization. This is identical to maximizing the expected net value of the contract, given the characteristics of both the farmer and the landowner, the desired crop to be produced, and the attributes of the land. In this way, the need to define who is the principal and who is the agent is relaxed.

Unlike the risk-incentive approach, contracts can also be examined using a transaction cost approach. This approach still uses the principal-agent framework, but focus has shifted to things like job attributes and agent characteristics. The objective of the principal is to choose contractual forms ranging from direct hiring and contracting out, and, once a contractual form is picked, efforts are made to synchronize the vectors of job attributes with agent characteristics. The purpose is to economize on transaction costs. In this chapter, we examine the theory of contracts from the perspective of transaction costs. First, we develop a theory of contracts. Then we discuss the problem of information given the crucial role that information plays in economic decisions. Various issues concerning transaction costs are explicated. Finally, we discuss the application of contract theory to the issue of forest renewal.

4.1 Theory of Contracts

Beginning with the production function, it is customarily posited that production in the primary sectors entails the use of essential inputs including land, labor and capital:

(4.1) $Q = f(K, L, H)$.

Q is output, f is a production function that is linearly homogeneous, and increasing and concave in its arguments, K refers to capital inputs (e.g., machinery, tools, seeds, or forest seedlings in the case of tree growing), L is labor, and H is land.

Following routine specifications (see Lazear 1989; Allen and Lueck 1993; Eswaran and Kotwal 1985; Braverman and Stiglitz 1986), the theory of contracts may be derived from the standard production function (4.1). First, the economic world is assumed to be characterized by a competitive environment in which two individuals form a contractual relationship. These two individuals are known as the principal and the agent. The contractual relationship arises because the principal chooses to hire the agent to do the work in producing commodity Q. As a result of negotiation, an incentive contract is reached between the two parties, whereby they agree to share the outcome of the contract. As the principal does not do the work personally, she has a utility function, V, which is a function of her share of the product only. It is assumed that V is monotone increasing, and concave (implying that she is either risk neutral or risk averse).

The agent is assumed to have a utility function, U, which is strictly concave (implying that he is risk averse, in other words, $U' > 0$; $U'' < 0$). Clearly, the agent's utility function depends on his share of the product, which is, in turn, a function of his effort. It is further assumed that the agent prefers leisure to work, other things equal.

Logically, the output of the contract is affected by both the agent's effort and by some exogenous random variable that may be interpreted as the outcome of any exogenous uncertain event, such as weather. Hence, the relationship among the value of the agent's output, his effort, and the realization of the random variable may be expressed as the following simplified production function:

(4.2) $\quad Q = Q(E, \theta)$,

where E is the level of effort, or action the agent chooses, and θ is the state of nature.

It is reasonable to assume that greater effort by the agent will result in greater output for any value of E and θ, i.e., $Q_i > 0$ for all E, θ. For simplicity, assume away the influence of the state of nature. Then the objective function of the principal is simply:

(4.3) $\quad \text{Max}_Q \, F(Q, E) - C(E)$,

where $F(Q, E)$ represents the compensation schedule that the principal provides the agent, and $C(E)$ is the agent's cost of effort function, or the monetary cost associated with supplying effort level. The principal does not decide on the level of effort and must take it as given in problem (4.3).

Essentially (4.3) boils down to an incentive problem because, facing a given compensation scheme, $F(Q, E)$, the agent must choose a level of effort or action, E, to maximize the total payoff, or the expected value of the product resulting from his effort. Hence, the objective function of the agent is:

(4.4) $\text{Max}_E\ F(Q, E) - C(E)$.

The agent's effort supply function may be derived by solving the first-order condition associated with (4.4). Since Q is a function of E and, using the chain rule, we have:

(4.5) $C'(E) = (\partial F/\partial Q)\ dQ/dE + \partial F/\partial E$,

which indicates that the agent sets the marginal cost of his effort equal to its marginal return to him. The transformation of effort into output, i.e., dQ/dE, depends on the production function. It turns out that an incentive contract arises when $F(Q, E)$ is selected subject to the agent behaving according to (4.5).

There are two basic types of incentive contracts, namely, input-based contracts and output-based contracts. The former amounts to a wage payment according to input, while the latter is a payment according to output. Both schemes require measurement. In the case of an input-pricing scheme, the magnitudes of the inputs contributed by a participant need to be accurately measurable. In the output-based scheme, it is the resulting output that is measured rather than the input contribution. Needless to say, there are costs in measuring and dividing both output and inputs between the two parties (Allen and Lueck 1993). Very often, inputs are more costly to measure than output (Kleindorfer and Sertel 1979). In agriculture, cropshare contracts are ones that involve the sharing of both output and input. Allen and Lueck (1993) developed a theoretical model that determines the optimal sharing rule for both the crop output and the variable input costs. We consider output-based contracts, then input-pricing contracts.

4.1.1 Payment according to output

Sharecropping

Based on output, sharecropping is one of the most common incentive contracts in agriculture. In sharecropping, the principal usually owns the land and the agent farms the land. Inputs required in the production may be shared with, for instance, the farmer paying share q $(0 \le q \le 1)$ and the landowner providing $(1 - q)$. Whenever, q is less than 1, the farmer has an incentive to overuse the shared inputs because he bears less than their full marginal cost (Allen and Lueck 1993).

Aside from agreements on the sharing of inputs, the two parties agree to split the output of the contract. What is shared is the crop, not profits. At harvest, the crop is divided between the landowner and the farmer, with the farmer collecting γQ and the landowner receiving $(1 - \gamma) Q$, where $0 < \gamma < 1$. The set of possible values for γ excludes 0 and 1 because, if $\gamma = 1$, the contract becomes a cash rent; if $\gamma = 0$, the contract becomes a hired farm labor contract. Since γ indicates a fixed proportion that is agreed upon beforehand, a utility maximizing agent should be motivated to produce more but, in the meantime, he may put forth an insufficient level of effort simply on account of the fact that $\gamma < 1$. This is because, under a cropshare contract, the farmer will always receive less than the full marginal product of his own inputs, hence, he is apt to supply less of his effort than he would if he owned the entire crop. Cheung (1969) concludes that people's attitudes toward risks and the presence of transaction costs tend jointly to foster share contracts in agriculture for crops with greater variance in output. Considered in their totality, both from the principal's perspective and from the perspective of total output, there is always room for efficiency improvement in sharecropping. Nevertheless, the prevalence of sharecropping as a preferred contractual form to other alternatives, such as cash rent leasing of farmland, may be due to the spreading of risks across the two parties (Eswaran and Kotwal 1985).

Rent

Recognizing that sharecropping may be economically inefficient, the principal can choose to rent the land to the agent and permit the agent to keep all of the output. Under a form of rental, which is payable by either a pre-determined quantity of crop or cash, the agent's compensation becomes $(Q - \text{Rent})$. Renting may solve the problem of insufficient effort on the part of the agent. However, there may be other problems associated with renting. Allen and Dueck (1993) argue that cash rent may be inferior to a sharecrop contract, especially when the potential for soil exploitation is high and the measurement costs of dividing the crop are small. Lazear (1989) also points to the agent's lack of incentive to maintain properly the land by preserving the fertility level of the soil, and suggests that the ultimate solution may be to sell the land to the agent, on the proposition that he will then have full incentive to take good care of the land. But the sale may not come about if the agent has a capital constraint, lacks entrepreneurial spirit, has an aversion to risk, *et cetera*.

Piecework

In output-based contracts, piece-rate compensation may also be used. That is, the principal pays the agent in cash or in kind according to some function of output, say, a linear piece rate in the form of s dollars per unit of Q, or sQ. In other words, the agent faces compensation in the form of sQ instead of $F(Q, E)$. In such schemes, the agent's compensation depends on the number of units produced and, indirectly, on the level of effort that he exerts. A major advantage of piece rates is that they encourage the agent to choose higher levels of effort in order to earn more. Lazear (1989) discusses some variation of the standard piece rate approach by introducing the concept of capital in the contract. In that case, the principal charges the agent for the cost of using the capital involved.

The labor market tournament approach is also used on occasion. When a principal hires more than one agent, in order to encourage hardwork, she may choose to pay the more productive agent a higher wage at the expense of the less productive agent. Clearly, in spite of its incentive for one agent over another, tournament-type contracts typically discourage cooperation (Lazear 1989).

4.1.2 Payment according to input

Input refers primarily to the effort of the agent. If a time wage is used as compensation that depends only on the agent's input, then $F(Q, E)$ takes the form $S(E)$. In the case of an hourly wage, irrespective of the amount that is produced during the hour, the agent receives a fixed amount that depends only on E, or the number of hours worked. It is commonly thought that an hourly wage does not provide workers with the appropriate incentives, but whether or not this is true depends on the connection between the measurement of time and measurement of effort (Lazear 1989). The allegation that payment on the basis of effort does not provide adequate incentives has much to do with the discrepancy between hours and effort. If hours were a perfect proxy for effort, then payment of an hourly wage would be an optimal incentive contract. However, because workers vary in productivity and diligence on an hourly basis, the connection breaks down. Payment by the hour provides appropriate incentives for choice of the number of hours, but does not deal with what is done within the hour (Lazear 1989).

A salary recognizes the difficulty of linking effort, performance and hours worked. Hence, a salary permits some leeway in effort per hour under the often unwritten understanding that overall effort will achieve a certain minimum, which is often left unspecified and is difficult to measure. The agent is free to vary effort level across hours, and even work beyond the usual stated time period, so that overall effort or performance targets, which may be soft, are met.

There is a link between payment schemes and product quality. Unlike piece rates that induce the worker to rush the job, time based payment schemes, such as salaries and hourly wages, provide lower pressure to go for speed and, therefore, product quality may be high. But there are shirking problems and other transaction cost issues associated with either payment schemes and an in-depth examination of this topic is provided in Chapter 8. Table 4.1 summarizes the basic contract categories and payment schemes.

Table 4.1: Contract Category and Payment Scheme

Contract type	Principal's payoff[a]	Agent's payoff[a, b]
Cash rent	R	Q
Sharecropping	γQ	$(1 - \gamma) Q$
Hired Labor	Q	W: Piecework: $s\,Q$
		Time wage: hourly wage or monthly salary

[a] R is cash rent paid by the agent to the principal, Q is output, and γ is the proportion of the output shared between the two parties.
[b] W is payment to the agent by the principal and s is the piece rate.

4.2 The Problem of Information

In the principal-agent problem, the principal is always assumed to want to induce her agent to behave in a way that is beneficial to the principal. However, the principal's effort is fraught with difficulty due to lack of information – she either has difficulty observing what the agent does or has difficulty interpreting the agent's actions.

Actors in the marketplace do need information other than prices and quantity for making transaction decisions. But, often, knowledge about other actors with whom one has to deal is either little or non-existent, or may be acquired only with considerable cost. In this regard, Knight (1921) argued that, given imperfect knowledge and ignorance (uncertainty), the economic problem of choice should shift from "doing it" to "deciding what to do and how to do it" (p.268). What is significant about this shift is that the acquisition and communication of knowledge and information become central questions of concern to economists. In this perspective, contracts may be viewed as information-conveying mechanisms.

Economic activities are associated with various types of information. Frequently, the availability of information may be part of a convention. As economic decisions are shaped by customs, habits or institutions (Hutchison 1984, p.25), changes in knowledge result in changes in production functions, market values and aspirations (Demsetz 1967). However, the availability of information is more often than not limited, incomplete or irrelevant.

Strictly speaking, there are two aspects to the information problem, information deficiency and information asymmetry (Ross 1973; Stiglitz 1974). Although both impair the process of concluding a contract, they differ in their nature and effects. Information deficiency represents a natural barrier that arises from the incompleteness of information and the difficulty of making information available. The causes are twofold. The first one has much to do with the nature of unforeseen future events because, in a world of uncertainty, knowledge is never complete. The second one is the formidable cost associated with collecting, verifying, processing, transmitting and updating scattered information from various sources. Obtaining information of relevance to economic decisions is not effortless. Information has positive costs, with the efficiency of production and exchange processes subject to the level and the cost of the information utilized (Furubotn and Richter 1984). The process of generating information to diminish uncertainty requires real resources, including time. Therefore, obtaining additional information represents an additional cost, and the possibility of reducing such a cost is equivalent to the expansion of exchange opportunities.

Information asymmetry represents a human barrier that arises from human behavioral problems. Again, using the principal-agent setting, the agent has an incentive to hide from the principal some crucial information in order to exploit opportunities for seeking (optimizing) self-interest. This is also known as "moral hazard", which may be defined as the "propensity of human agents to behave opportunistically (Williamson 1985, p.51). Because the principal has difficulty in effectively monitoring her agent's conduct without incurring considerable costs, the problem of moral hazard or shirking arises. Some economists call it a problem of "hidden action" (Klein 1983; Arrow 1985). Hidden action on the part of the agent is possible, because he not only has an incentive but also the opportunity to promote his own interest over that of the principal. Sometimes the agent is said to have hidden information that is not available to the principal. Arrow (1985) argues that, in the event of hidden information problems, the agent has made some observation that the principal has not made, and the agent could use this observation in making decisions to his own advantage, often to the detriment of the principal.

It may be difficult to say which of the two aspects of the information problem is more serious – information deficiency or asymmetry. Both impair the bargaining process and hinder the parties in reaching fully contingent contracts (Kostrisky 1993). Neither of the two can be eliminated although there seem to be ways of reducing some effects. While technological change is capable of reducing the cost of handling the information deficiency problem, appropriate economic instruments may reduce the size of the problem of asymmetric information. For instance, to mitigate shirking, three private strategies have been identified. First, a principal may attempt to minimize shirking by screening a potential agent before entering in a contract – trying to discern *ex ante* whether the agent's preferences are likely to conflict with the principal's. Screening describes *ex ante* efforts by one party to identify the individual characteristics of the other, in order to "eliminate the quacks and the lemons" (Leland 1979), thereby minimizing costly efforts *ex post*. Nevertheless, screening devices can be very costly. Second, the two parties may employ bonding strategies, under which the agent agrees to special limitations on his delegated power (Kreps 1988). With bonding, the agent might experience a loss if he does not perform in accordance with the principal's objectives. Third, *ex ante* incentive alignment schemes may be designed to make the agent's compensation depend on a measure of his level of effort via, preferably, an output-based scheme (Lazear 1989).

A major distinction between the NIE and conventional economic approaches lies in the treatment of knowledge and information. Specifically, conventional models of production describe a firm as having a given technology characterized by feasible transformations of inputs into outputs. In such models, information is not a decision variable and is treated as perfect and complete. Sadly, the constant changes that characterize production technology and the relationships among economic agents are ignored (Wilson 1975). Similarly, the standard model of consumer behavior asserts that individuals have unlimited information-processing capacity, which allows them to solve their choice problems in a strictly optimal manner, irrespective of the difficulty of the problems (de Palma et al. 1994).

In contrast to the standard assumptions of homogeneous products given stable consumer preferences and perfect knowledge, the NIE treats information as variable, imperfect and incomplete. Achievements have been made in understanding, first, that individuals have only limited information-processing capacity. Individuals acquire information from various sources, and they perceive, interpret and evaluate this information by drawing upon past experience and the context in which the information is obtained. When deciding among alternative courses of action, individuals use simple, local and myopic choice procedures, which adapt choice behavior to their capacity limitations. The quality of a choice rule reflects the ability to choose (de Palma et al. 1994).

Second, information pertinent to individual decisions "never exists in concentrated or integrated form, but solely as the dispersed bits of incomplete and frequently contradictory knowledge which all the separate individuals possess" (Hayek 1945, p.519). Information about economic alternatives is dispersed among the individual members of a society, so the societal decision maker (e.g., a legislative assembly) utilizes information in the decision calculus that is not known to any one individual or legislative body in its entirety (Lohmann 1994).

Third, in addition to the important flows of information between buyers and sellers regarding price bids and offers, economic agents are in constant need of nonprice information that can be acquired, stored and processed only at a cost (Dohan 1976). For instance, a buyer must incur search costs in seeking low prices, and this process of seeking out and processing additional information continues until the expected marginal benefit is equal to its expected marginal cost (Stigler 1961).

Fourth, economic organizations are viewed as centers that achieve informational efficiency. Other social institutions, along with culture and/or customs, affect information costs. As a result, trust, honesty, reputation, brand names, licensing, product certification and labeling standards have become forms of social capital (Dohan 1976; Fukuyama 1999; Landes 1999).

Fifth, contracts are comprised of certain promises with regard to the product, its price and payments. Contracts can be viewed as a social institution with two important roles: (1) facilitating the specialization of information between buyer and seller, and (2) improving the quality of information offered in the market. In a contract, each party specifies what (product or service) is promised, along with explicit or implicit penalties if either fails to fulfill the terms of the contract (Dohan 1976).

The NIE logic insists that every economic decision require information about the available alternatives. The social institutions and physical mechanisms for producing, acquiring, transmitting, storing and processing such information are described by the term *information structure* (Dohan 1976, p.431). Certain types of production and purchase decisions are characterized by high cost information structures, and these high information costs often cause a breakdown of incentive structures, resulting in problems, such as cost-indifferent behavior and, ultimately, economic inefficiencies. As the cost of obtaining decision-relevant information independently of the seller rises, buyers are led to rely increasingly on information contained in messages supplied by a single or a few alternative sellers. As a result, both the efficiency of resource use declines and unavoidable transfer payments from buyer to seller occur. Buyers tend to depend on a seller's information, and this dependence is a frequent cause of the failure of the incentive structure to generate cost minimizing behavior. High information costs are frequently encountered in economic decision-making. This is especially the case in modern society where decisions require technical information that is highly specialized, complex, and difficult to acquire and use. Dohan (1976) found that, the higher the cost of information from a source, the less information would be acquired from that source by the buyer, ceteris paribus. Surprisingly, evidence indicates that high information costs can even induce cost maximizing behavior.

Internal information may be privately held (Kwon et al. 1979), and information holdout impedes agreement (Wiggins and Libecap 1985). Problems can arise in situations where information asymmetry prevails, with the market for used cars being the classic example (Akerlof 1970). Markets with asymmetric information tend to degenerate to the lowest-quality level (Leland 1979). To solve the problem, producers of the highest-quality product or services could "signal" their superiority by using product guarantees, self certification and so on (Leland 1980). Information asymmetries and opportunism can result in the breakdown of contracting processes in cases where there is a need to update sequentially contract terms to reflect changes in the economic environment (Goldberg 1976; Williamson 1976). Information problems can occur *ex ante* or *ex post*. *Ex ante* information problems occur during contract negotiation, whereas *ex post* information problems arise due to contingent updates and the need for contingent claims. In any event, when information does not arrive symmetrically across agents, private contracting can be seriously impaired or fail altogether (Wiggins and Libecap 1985).

Solutions to the information problem may be found only when the nature of the problem is properly identified in the first place. First and foremost, division of labor and specialization of knowledge must be considered a primary solution. There is consensus that division of labor economizes on information. The associated productivity comes not only from improvement in physical skills and more productive technology, but also from the greater productivity in the acquisition and utilization of information by each participant in the market. With specialization, each bit of information can be utilized more intensively. Arrow (1974, pp.38-39) posits that there are increasing returns to the use of information. Opportunities to purchase technological information at some cost may induce economies of scale, even where there are no economies of scale associated with the technology of physical production. Better information justifies a higher scale of operations and vice versa (Wilson 1975).

Second, given that information structures and incentive systems are closely interrelated (Dohan 1976), contractual arrangements may be designed in such a way that the various issues concerning information are considered.

Third, in the case of high cost market structures, Dohan (1976, p.448) suggests the following strategies to reduce costs:

- Use third parties as a source of expert advice.
- Restructure the market to reduce the quantity of information required for economic decisions.
- Employ non-economic institutions, such as introducing social norms of honesty, "playing by the rules," long-term personal relationships for generating accurate information independent of economic and other explicit incentive systems, and professional codes of conduct.
- Provide training and education that lower information costs (Dohan 1976).

In summary, useful information has value and this value may improve productive decisions, reduce the uncertainty and risks that economic agents face, and reduce the range of alternatives or opportunities available to the agents (Kwon et al. 1979). Table 4.2 provides a summary of the various issues concerning the problem of information.

Information is not the same thing as knowledge. Cartier (1994) notes that, although the stock of knowledge is continuously increased by research, society finds it a constant challenge to manage the "information overload". Therefore, one must guard against the situation of "drowning in information, but being starved of knowledge". Lastly, there has been a tendency to lump all information problems under "uncertainty", but this too must be avoided as this can be misleading (Hirshleifer and Riley 1992).

Table 4.2: Issues Concerning the Problem of Information

Problem category	Source	Impact	Possible solution
Information deficiency	Information incompleteness	Impairing contract negotiation	Contingent plans
	High cost of obtaining information	Impairing contract negotiation or causing contract process to break down	Technological change
Information asymmetry	Human behavioral problems, such as moral hazard	Information hold-out, Impairing contract negotiation	Economic instruments like contracts that induce correct incentives and economize on transaction costs

4.3 Transaction Cost Economics

In addition to property rights, transaction costs and information are of great concern to the new institutional economics. As a result of a seminal paper by Williamson (1979), the notion of transaction costs has gained increasing recognition, with many developments in the NIE centered around what is now referred to as "transaction cost economics" (TCE). While the previous section reviewed the literature on imperfect information, this section provides a brief overview of the literature on transaction cost economics.

4.3.1 Definition and origin of the concept of transaction costs

Based on Coase (1937), Williamson (1979) and others view the TCE as an extension of the neoclassical economic paradigm with a clear mission of probing into the nature of the firm.[1] Based on Arrow's (1969, p.48) view that transaction costs are the "costs of running the economic system", some economists have more recently defined transaction costs as the costs capturing and protecting property rights, and transferring them from one agent to another (Barzel 1997). These costs include "the costs of discovering exchange opportunities, negotiating contracts, monitoring and enforcing implementation, and maintaining and protecting the institutional structure" (Pejovich 1995, p.84).

Eggertsson (1990) attributes the originality of the concept of transaction costs to Coase (1937, 1960), who first explored "The Nature of the Firm" and then "The Problem of Social Cost". Coase (1988) summarized these respective contributions as follows:

> "Transaction costs were used in the one case to show that if they are not included in the analysis, the firm has no purpose, while in the other I showed, as I thought, that if transaction costs were not introduced into the analysis, for the range of problems considered, the law has no purpose" (p.34).

While Coase is credited with recognizing the importance of transaction costs for meaningful economic analysis, Williamson (1985, 1979, 1975) helped formulate the TCE as a distinct school of thought. Enlightened by Herbert A. Simon (1962, 1957), Williamson employed the concepts of bounded rationality, opportunism and contractual arrangements. The transaction-costs concept and approach were also inspired by the contributions of Stigler (1961) and Hayek (1937, 1945), and others working on the economics of information. It is primarily the addition to the neoclassical framework of positive costs of transacting that distinguishes the NIE from traditional microeconomics, with this addition changing the research agenda (Eggertsson 1990, p.14). Simply put, the recognition of transaction costs makes assignment of ownership rights paramount, introduces the question of economic organization, and makes the structure of political institutions a key to understanding economic growth.

---

[1] Williamson (1981) recognized the contributions of Coase (1937, 1960) and Commons (1951). He also acknowledged the contributions of legal scholars such as Llewellyn (1931) and organization scholars like Barnard (1938) (Williamson 1985, pp.4-7).

4.3.2 Sources and categories of transaction costs

Transaction costs arise when economic agents exchange ownership rights to assets and when exclusive property rights need to be enforced (Eggertsson 1990). The fundamental idea of transaction costs is that they consist of the cost of arranging a contract *ex ante* and monitoring and enforcing it *ex post*, as opposed to production costs, which are the costs of executing a contract (Mathews 1986).

Pejovich (1995, pp.84-87) lists the following as reasons why transaction costs may arise.

- Information about exchange opportunities is costly to obtain. This simply means that the costs associated with obtaining information must be treated as an input in production and exchange processes, and serves as the basis for decision-making by economic agents. The cost of obtaining information is the initial aspect of transaction costs (see Williamson 1985; Eggertsson 1990; Pejovich 1995).
- The costs of negotiating exchange can be substantial. Negotiation can be thought of as a process for achieving common understanding of the main attributes associated with the goods and services in question, and reaching agreement on the terms of obligations of the respective parties to a trade or contract.
- Exchange is costly to enforce, particularly in the case of contractual agreements that involve such things as warranties, post-purchase maintenance and repairs, and/or provision of services over time (e.g., cleaning contracts). A mechanism ("enforcement") is required to resolve disputes over the interpretation of contracts and performance standards for outcomes. Very often, monitoring and policing are needed in the process of production and exchange activities.

In short, transaction costs arise because of exchanges among economic agents. Exchange of property rights involves the following sorts of transaction costs: (1) The search for information about the distribution of price and quality of commodities and labor inputs, the search for potential buyers and sellers, and the search for relevant information about their behavior and circumstances is costly. (2) Bargaining is needed to find the true position of buyers and sellers. (3) Contracts need to be prepared. (4) Monitoring is required to ensure that the parties to a contract abide by its terms. (5) The enforcement of a contract and collection of damages when partners fail to observe their contractual obligations are a source of transaction costs. (6) Finally, property rights must be protected against third-party encroachment.

4.3.3 Bounded rationality and opportunism

Among the factors that affect the levels of transaction costs associated with institutional modes, bounded rationality and opportunism have been identified as two key behavioral assumptions that form the very basis of transaction cost analysis.

Neoclassical economics assumes that humans possess a "maximizing orientation" and a "strong form" of rationality (Williamson 1985, pp.44-45). In conventional economic models, contracting agents are assumed to be rational actors that maximize the joint benefits of the contract. The TCE departs from the conventional model by assuming that, while humans intend to behave rationally, there are limits to what is possible (Williamson 1985, p.30). In formulating and solving complex problems, and in processing information, humans are limited. They have a finite, albeit unknown, capacity for knowledge, understanding and reasoning, and they cannot foresee all possible future contingencies. This is the assumption of bounded rationality (see Simon 1991, 1962, 1957). Under bounded rationality, "the capacity of the human mind for formulating and solving complex problems is very small compared with the size of the problems whose solution is required for objectively rational behavior in the real world – or even for a reasonable approximation of such objective rationality" (Kostrisky 1993, pp.651-652). Hence, the TCE maintains that it is, perhaps, nearer to the truth than neoclassical economics to assume that humans behave only in a boundedly rational way, with Simon (1978) urging economists to expand their analyses to encompass procedural aspects of decision-making, paying attention to both "substantive rationality" and "procedural rationality".

The second fundamental behavioral assumption underlying the TCE states that people act in their own self-interest and often behave in an opportunistic way. Kostrisky (1993) points out that opportunism is prevalent among humans, but that the scope of opportunistic behavior is restrained by their bounded rationality. He also points out that the propensity for opportunism is ubiquitous, with the unforeseeability of future contingencies contributing to opportunism. Viewing opportunism as an effort to realize individual gains through a lack of candor or honesty in transactions, Williamson (1975) regards it as a somewhat richer version of self-interest than is ordinarily assumed in (neoclassical) economics.

While there is a great deal of agreement among economists about the validity of the bounded rationality assumption, there has been greater critique of the notion of opportunism, mainly because of its negative tone. For example, Cartier (1994) writes:

> "It is evident that laziness, cheating, absenteeism, pilfering and misappropriation, abuse and exploitation exist, and may be induced if the original contract were made under duress; but to postulate a general principle of shirking rests on a view of human behavior and a lack of objectivity which does not contribute to serious economic analysis" (p.186).

Indeed, Blaug (1983) proposes a more neutral view, believing that when exchange is frequent the behavior of the two parties in a contractual relationship may be reconciled by an "invisible handshake" of trust and loyalty. However, as noted in Chapter 3, this assumes that there is a great deal of social capital in the economy.

4.3.4 Incomplete contracting: negotiation costs and enforcement

To a large degree, relations among economic agents constitute a variety of social contracts, some formal and explicit, others informal and implicit. A traditional view is that no contract can be formed until clear and complete agreement is reached. Such a complete contract is to provide for all contingencies and comprehensively to specify the time, price, quantity and quality of performance (Kostritsky 1993).[2] Goetz and Scott (1985) explain that the perfectly contingent contract is a paradigm assuming highly rational actors capable of bargaining, at reasonable costs, to allocate explicitly the risks in future undertakings. The assumption underlying the so-called "strict" view is that the parties could and should express all of the material elements of the future exchange in the present agreement. Klein (1983) warns that aiming at a complete and fully contingent contract is simply unrealistic, a view echoed by Crocker and Masten (1991). The latter dismiss complete contracts as a "mechanistic approach", pointing out that such

---

[2] Kostritsky (1993, pp.629-630) observes that legal scholars tend to focus on an appropriate legal framework starting with initial bargaining because elements of uncertainty, moral hazard, and sunk costs have to be considered right from the stage of preliminary negotiations. He states further that achieving the optimal solution for the complexities of bargaining relationships demands the adoption of a legal default rule that substantively recognizes an implicit bargain, even in the absence of explicitly reciprocal communications.

contracts fail to appreciate the "richness of real-world contractual relationships and the laws that govern them" (p.96).

There has been a shift in research focus from complete to incomplete contracts as a result of changes in the perception of the nature of contractual relations (Murphy and Speidel 1991). It is now recognized that, when the parties to a contract have reached a bargain that is not fully contingent, the courts may intervene to resolve contractual incompleteness. As noted by Grossman and Hart (1986), and Hart and Moore (1990), ownership of assets gives the owner control and bargaining power in situations where contracts do not specify what has to be done. Contracts are incomplete because some terms are unspecified due to the costs of negotiation and information gathering and, simply, bounded rationality. The existence of incomplete contracts requires that, in a world of uncertainty, actions will have to be taken as called for by the particular situation (Simon 1991).

Kostritsky (1993, pp.627-628) maintains that bargaining is an essential element in the process of concluding a contract, and any bargaining model must account for the following: (1) how parties structure their relationships; (2) how they allocate risks and make choices; (3) what potential problems, including uncertainty, moral hazard and sunk costs, affect the bargaining process; (4) what goals contracting parties seek to achieve; and (5) how legal rules are likely to advance or hinder those goals. It is unrealistic to view contracts as a one-period phenomenon, as indicated by the fact that farmers and landowners often renew their sharecropping contracts (Allen and Lueck 1993). Given repeated contracting, economic agents gain experience (and information) over an extended period of time, modifying their behavior not only in their own interest but also out of consideration for a renewed relationship. This is why "relational" contracts have gained popularity, because they contain provisions that allow for readjustment in the allocation of risks depending on changing circumstances.

Transaction costs related to incomplete contracting can become a major barrier to concluding contracts. Negotiating costs are particularly high when a large number of agents are involved. Given informational barriers and uncertainty about the future, transaction cost economists conclude that comprehensive contracting is not a realistic organizational alternative when provision is made for a more realistic view of human nature, namely, that humans are boundedly rational and act in their self interest with guile. Recognizing limits on rationality helps explain why parties may initially fail to reach agreement. Because the costs of dealing explicitly with particular contingencies may be great, especially during preliminary bargaining, incomplete contracting is the common outcome.[3]

Finally, while factors such as bounded rationality and the problem of information constitute barriers to fully contingent contracts, resulting in incomplete contracts, opportunism tends to result in shirking, making the policing of contracts more difficult. Often, contract enforcement is costly because it attempts to curb deviations from contract terms (Kostritsky 1993). Allen and Lueck (1993) identified two issues that confront agents in a contractual relationship. The first is that contracts must ensure that the daily actions of the agent are in the principal's interest, and this problem can be dealt with in principle by providing the agent with appropriate incentives. The second issue is that contracts must be enforced so that gross violations do not occur. Features such as contract length and contract detail address these potential problems. Repeated contracting helps check the problem because violators will lose future contracts (Shapiro 1983). The familiar hypothesis that the principal and agent maximize the expected value of the contract only holds *ex ante*, "both have a long-term interest in effecting adaptations of a joint profit-maximizing kind" (Williamson 1985, p.63). *Ex post*, however, each party will focus on his or her individual interest and try to appropriate as much of the individual gain as he or she can on each occasion. Thus, it may be understood that incentive enhancing is possible through *ex ante* alignment, whereas hazard mitigation is mainly achieved through *ex post* governance of incomplete contracts (Williamson 1998a).

4.3.5 Framework for reducing transaction costs

Transacting costs can be large relative to gains because of natural difficulties in trading or they can be large for legal reasons (Demsetz 1967). Transaction costs may be reduced at various levels by the state, the firm and contractual individuals. Historically, the state has lowered transaction costs by establishing and maintaining standards of measurement and by introducing and maintaining a stable currency. The most notable achievement of the Chinese emperor, Shi Huang, was the unification of measurements and currencies in the year 221 BC. North (1968) documents how reduced piracy increased productivity in ocean shipping.

The impact of technical change on transaction costs is ambiguous. On the one hand, technical change can lower transaction costs by

---

[3] Kostrisky (1993, p.632) suggests that parties might prefer a default rule that minimizes costs by supplying the terms most parties would have wanted.

introducing new and effective methods of measurement, but, on the other, technical change is associated with more complex commodities, and hence higher transaction costs (Eggertsson 1990).

When transaction costs are low, private contracting is preferred as a solution to problems of production and exchange, but if transaction costs are high, contracting may be less successful (Williamson 1976; Goldberg 1976). To incorporate transaction costs into economic analysis, it is necessary to determine when private contracting will be effective and when it will not. Perhaps the most common means of reducing transaction costs lies in how contracts are negotiated and implemented. Pejovich (1995) observes that the law of contract allows each party to choose between performing in accordance with the contract or compensating the other party for damages. In addition to being an efficiency-enhancing provision, the law of contract reduces transaction costs by preventing opportunistic behavior. One of the important reasons for writing contracts is to guard against the hazards inherent to exchange "where one or both parties have invested in reliance, or relationship-specific assets, in support of the transaction" (Crocker and Masten 1991, p.69). Contracts promote efficiency by securing the distribution of quasi rents *ex ante*, thereby avoiding costly repetitive bargaining over the terms of trade and reducing the risk for each party of relying on the performance of the other (Crocker and Masten 1991; see also Klein et al. 1978; Williamson 1979; Shavell 1980).

Within the general framework of contractual relations, a number of schemes hold promise for lowering transaction costs. First, accepting the view that firms are complex sets of "explicit and implicit contracts" (Easterbrook and Fischel 1989), Kostrisky (1993, p.630) advocates the implementation of legal sanctions through a generalized "default" rule that permits implicit bargaining. The advantage of such a rule lies in reducing the costs of negotiating every detail of a contract. Rather than defining the full set of contract obligations at the outset, provisions may be made to allow for the determination in the future of some specific terms and duties. Where uncertainty about what will constitute optimal behavior at the time of performance may be significant, it is a good idea to leave aspects of that performance open to negotiation rather than constrain parties to specific but potentially inappropriate actions. For instance, long-term contracts often contain provisions for periodic adjustments of prices because relative price levels can change substantially over an extended period so as to render the originally agreed upon prices as inappropriate. Listing the advantages of less precise, "relational" contracts that leave terms to future negotiation, Crocker and Masten (1991) maintain that such agreements are considerably simpler to draft than contingent claims contracts. Indeed it is ideal to have agreements that remain flexible in the face of changing circumstances.

Second, apart from the adoption of legal measures, many economists favor economic instruments. The problem of transaction costs may be approached in terms of the principal-agent relationship, where the principal can limit divergence of interests by establishing incentives for the agent and monitoring the agent's activities. Thus, it may be necessary to include in a contract a reasonable level of details to make opportunistic behavior more difficult. As mentioned earlier, due to the problem of information, some scope for opportunism inevitably remains and, therefore, only limited success may be expected from planning in advance.

Third, with an understanding of the role of transaction costs, it becomes a legitimate concern to inquire about the level of transaction costs in a given institutional environment. One way of addressing such a concern is to examine the nature, characteristics and modality of various processes inherent in the institutional structure and to identify possibilities for reducing transaction costs. This means that attention should be given to transaction attributes because these attributes themselves take on significance (Furubotn and Richter 1984). Alchian (1984), Williamson (1985) and others have shown that the extent to which transactions are based on durable, firm-specific investments influences behavior. Similarly, the frequency of transactions and the uncertainty surrounding transactions help explain economic organization. The TCE logic suggests that transaction costs will be saved when the attributes of transactions are aligned with the characteristics of the economic agents involved in the contractual relationship. In other words, firms behave in a transaction cost economizing manner so that the choice of governance modes regarding specific activities conform with transaction characteristics. For instance, market oriented contracting usually prevails when nonspecific investments are involved. As asset specificity increases, market arrangements tend to give way to bilateral modes, and in the case of idiosyncratic investments that occur at frequent intervals, unified governance will be chosen (Williamson 1985). More recently, it has been recognized that lateral integration may be comparable to vertical integration in transaction cost economizing, and the choice of governance structures depends on the nature of transactions and circumstances (Groenewegen 1996). Ultimately, the TCE is concerned with the incorporation of institutional factors as explanatory variables. Nonetheless, economic efficiency is upheld as the most important explanatory variable for understanding and justifying the presence of markets and/or hierarchies (Williamson 1996). This aspect is further explored in Chapter 7 via an empirical study.

The TCE determines that output has to be viewed as a function of both input costs and transaction costs. Taking transaction costs as a separate variable in the selection of institutional arrangements is a prominent feature of the NIE. Randall (1975) suggests that a non-market mechanism may be justified in efficiency terms as long as the savings in transaction costs from its use exceed the gains from using the market. The TCE enables the determination of economic agents' responses to alternative institutional arrangements, and thus to evaluate whether and on what terms the arrangements should be restructured.

The new institutional economics is preoccupied with the origin, incidence and ramifications of transaction costs. The relevance of the organization of economic activities hinges on the existence, the level and the types of transaction costs (e.g., see Cheung 1989). Thus, rallying around the concept of transaction costs, the TCE scholars propose that economic institutions operate to minimize transaction costs at various levels through hierarchical arrangements, sequencial arrangements, contracts, and so on. Firms exist as an efficient mode of economic organization to take advantage of the lower levels of transaction costs, because many costs are saved in the processes of institutional restructuring that reduce the costs of information and opportunistic behavior (Coase 1937).[4]

4.3.6 Transaction cost economics: application

As a basic unifying theme in the NIE, the TCE is concerned with how contractual arrangements can deal with shirking and other motivational problems. For the TCE, transactions are the basic unit of analysis and contractual forms are an important subject matter (Williamson 1998a, 1998b).

In its early stage of development, the TCE was frequently a target of criticism for its tautological convenience (e.g., Fischer 1977), in spite of significant insights gained from studies of bilateral dependency (see Williamson 1975; Klein et al. 1978). In response to an appeal by Coase

---

[4] It is necessary to make a distinction between the concepts of information costs and transaction costs. Eggertsson (1990, p.15) provides an example: a lonely person on a desert island will encounter information costs as he goes about his "home production", but such an isolated individual does not engage in exchange and therefore will have no transaction costs.

(1972), and by Furubotn and Richter (1984), for more quantitative analysis within the TCE framework, a variety of empirical studies have been undertaken in the past two decades. Evidence suggests that the TCE approach has proved useful and vital as a distinct approach for comparing alternative organizational forms (Masten 1996). Progress in the development of methodologies and techniques for applying the transaction cost logic have been particularly noticeable, with studies covering a wide range of sectors, from automobiles to airlines and from natural gas to national defense. To a large degree, the increase in the number of empirical studies is attributable to the adaptability of TCE problem formulations to qualitative choice models. By the mid-1990s, on account of its established theoretical framework and its analytical capacity in handling a variety of real-world problems, the TCE had grown beyond the stage of conceptualization. Table 4.3 provides a sample of recent TCE empirical studies.

Table 4.3: Empirical Studies of Transaction Cost Economics

Sector	Study
Aerospace industry	Masten (1984)
Air force engine	Crocker and Reynolds (1993)
Airline industry	Phillips (1991)
Aluminum industry	Stuckey (1983)
Auto industry	Masten et al. (1989); Monteverde and Teece (1982a, 1982b)
Coal industry	Joskow (1985, 1987)
Electronics industry	Anderson and Schmittlein (1984)
Food industry	Frank and Henderson (1992)
Natural gas industry	Crocker and Masten (1988, 1991); Masten and Crocker (1985); Hubbard and Weiner (1991)
Petroleum industry	Barron and Umbeck (1984); Goldberg and Erickson (1987)
Railroad industry	Palay (1984); Phillips (1991); Pittman (1991)
Ship-building industry	Masten et al. (1991)
Silviculture/forestry	Wang and van Kooten (1999)
Tuna industry	Gallick (1984)

4.4 Contractual Relations in Forestry

Production and exchange involve contractual arrangements. From the perspective of the PR theory, these contractual activities exist not so much to accomplish the exchange of goods and services but to permit the exchange of bundles of property rights (Furubotn and Pejovich 1972). Meanwhile, contract terms are influenced by the access parties have to information, by the costs of negotiating, and by the opportunities for cheating (Simon 1991). Incentives and enforcement costs are both factors that determine optimal contract design, with the former being closer to the principal-agent approach while the latter clearly falling within the transaction cost approach. In this section, we briefly discuss contractual relations in forestry using British Columbia as our illustrative example.

A web of contractual relations exists in BC forestry. Some of the relations are horizontal in nature (with both the company and contractor performing the same tasks), while others are essentially vertical (with the contractor performing activities, such as silviculture, that the company does not). Forest product companies tend to form lateral contractual relations in which firms choose the scale and scope of their production. Since firms gain a comparative advantage from specialization, it is not uncommon for two firms to be located next to each other, but to specialize in the production of different products or to perform different stages in the production of a single product. However, in addition to the gains to specialization, there are transaction cost reasons for firms to be in a certain contractual relationship. For instance, when a re-manufacturing mill is located next to a sawmill, both mills may benefit from the proximity, but they do not necessarily have to be integrated into one firm. People with innovative ideas and specialized knowledge frequently start small secondary manufacturing businesses. Some of the lumber products coming from the sawmill can be readily used for secondary manufacturing products, such as finger-jointed products for wooden doors, while some lumber is best reserved as a commodity product with no further processing. There are clear gains from direct and stable contractual relationships.

In BC, an integrated forestry company typically has a hierarchical structure that not only links upwards into the government, but also downwards to contractors who undertake work in timber harvesting and/or forest regeneration. The company's need for wood may be satisfied from (1) wood cut by its own logging crews from the company's own licenses (e.g., TFLs and/or FLs) and private land if any, (2) wood cut by independent harvesting contractors, and (3) straightforward purchase from other sources. Some companies rely on only one or two modes of supply, while others rely on all three.

It is well known that forest companies have a special dependency relationship with independent contractors. Specifically, harvesting contractors usually are the owners of the machines they use, but sometimes they operate the logging companies' machines under some form of lease arrangement. It is not uncommon for contractors to be integrated with the partnering companies' overall operations, relying on the companies for services such as machine repairs and provision of fuel, for instance. The contractual relations between forest companies and contractors have been confirmed by legislation. However, as explained in Chapter 3, on account of the rigidity and uncertainty associated with BC's forest tenure system, often contracts between logging contractors and the integrated companies are characterized by short duration and a lack of renewability provisions. From a business point of view, a short-term non-renewable contract is of little value to a contractor because banks are less willing to provide needed financing to purchase machinery and equipment. In the BC Interior, in spite of legislation that requires forest companies to employ replaceable contracts of 3-5 years duration for up to 50% of their AAC, enforcement of the rule appears difficult. Locally known as "Evergreen" contracts, these replaceable contracts enable contractors to plan their equipment turnover more effectively and they are in a better bargaining position for loans with a reasonable interest rate. It follows that the contractor can work out an effective equipment amortization and depreciation plan, thus lowering costs. Evergreen contracts should, therefore, confer benefits upon the integrated forest company (licensee) because the contractor should be able to offer lower prices for logging timber. Whether this is the case is an empirical question that has not been investigated in the context of British Columbia.

Contractual relations between the Provincial government and the integrated forest companies, between the companies and (silvicultural) contractors, and even between the government and contractors are conspicuous insofar as forest regeneration is concerned. For one thing, as a condition of renewing tenures and to ensure adequate access to timber in the short term (to guarantee access to AAC), forest companies must demonstrate that they are taking steps toward regenerating logged sites on public land in a timely and acceptable manner. However, much of the regeneration is conducted by silvicultural contractors that are paid by the licensees to provide these services. The widespread use of contracting in silviculture indicates that information is not an obstacle in performance of forest regeneration, or basic silviculture, implying that vertical integration is unnecessary.

Sometimes the distinction between market communications and internal communications, and the criteria for choosing between the two alternative arrangements, are rather vague. Nevertheless, forest licensees and silvicultural contractors tend to specialize in acquiring and using differing types of knowledge. Silvicultural contractors acquire information about particular inputs, costs and general production techniques about which forest licensees have less knowledge. Forest licensees (integrated companies), on the other hand, specialize in timber harvesting and, perhaps, management. Silvicultural prescriptions themselves are a form of contract that specifies in great detail the silvicultural services to be delivered. Such prescriptions provide a great deal of information to diminish uncertainty and facilitate physical operations.

Economic agents interact with one another in a variety of different ways, with information made available to them through diverse signals. At one extreme, signals come in the form of market prices; at the other extreme are more complex hierarchical organizational relationships that involve relatively large information flows and negotiations that send a variety of signals. Within these limits are found all forms of signals that enable economic agents to conduct the everyday business of producing and consuming. In the remainder of this book, we discuss aspects of the contractual relations that prevail in British Columbia's forestry sector, focusing on the relationship between the large integrated, forest product companies and silvicultural contractors. Our analysis addresses forest-level activities that seek to correct the market failure associated with logging.

5 Organizations, Regulation and Policy Instruments

In this chapter, we provide a bridge between the preceding theoretical chapters and the ensuing analytical ones. We begin with an overview of the theory of the firm and organizations, followed by an explanation of issues pertaining to public regulation and control and its relevance to forest management. Then we highlight the significance of culture, conventions and norms as informal institutional constraints using forestry examples. The major policy instruments available to forestry decision-makers are then outlined in the context of British Columbia's forestry sector. Finally, we discuss linkages between sustainable forestry and the new institutional economics.

5.1 Theory of the Firm and Organizations

The traditional economic model of the firm generally neglects transaction costs and simply assumes that firms maximize profits. The existence of firms is not questioned and the rationale for contractual arrangements among firms received little attention (Scott 1984). Firms emerge and exist for economic reasons. Relying on internal structures and contractual arrangements, firms undertake production and are active in exchange. The corporate structure is necessarily an outcome of institutional arrangements, and the logic of such arrangements lies with a desire to economize on transaction costs (Coase 1937; Williamson 1975, 1979; Eggertsson 1990).

From the perspective of the NIE, the capitalist firm may be defined by a bundle of property rights, including (a) the right to receive the residual after all other inputs have been duly paid, (b) the right to revise or terminate the membership of the firm, and (c) the right to sell property as specified under (a) and (b) (Alchian and Demsetz 1972). Scott (1984) views the firm as an entity that has legal capability to unite a web of contracts among various suppliers of factors of production.

If the nature of the firm is said to economize on transaction costs (Coase 1937), the rationale for organizing production within the firm rather than through the market is at least threefold. First, in producing a product, different inputs must be used. While the firm faces the crucial problem of coordinating inputs in the interests of achieving technical efficiency, it has to guard against shirking by some inputs, mainly but not only labor (Alchian and Demsetz 1972). The firm is characterized by a hierarchical structure that entails one or more teams of employees. Furubotn and Pejovich (1972) point out that production should be seen as a team process and, during this process, the firm faces the cost of detecting the marginal productivity of cooperating inputs. The need to coordinate inputs and to make accurate assessments for achieving efficiency of team production justifies the existence of the firm and it is a firm's task to pay to each factor an appropriate amount depending on its contribution to output (Alchian and Demsetz 1972). Furthermore, production factors are integrated in various proportions and intensities in production. Simon (1991) argues that, the more intense is the interdependence among the factor inputs, the more advantageous it becomes to organize production within the firm instead of depending wholly on market transactions. Generally speaking, technical efficiency is partially a function of specialization, but specialization of tasks gives rise to an interdependence of the specialized functions. Production processes constantly unleash forces that call for improved and effective mechanisms for coordinating specialization. When the coordination becomes sufficiently complex, the coordinating function will tend to work best under an internalized organizational structure.

Second, firms are posited to be more efficient in utilizing knowledge and reducing uncertainty, which is a major reason explaining the existence of firms (Coase 1937). In order to reduce the inefficiencies arising from uncertainty, firms are expected to develop useful institutional arrangements that favor prompt processing of relevant information for production purposes (Simon 1962).

Third, firms have an advantage in the communication of orders and maintaining control. Modern corporations may be seen as institutional arrangements of a principal-agent relationship comprising structurally related but self-contained divisions. Corporations typically have in place a hierarchical management structure that specializes in

- enforcing orders and rules,
- monitoring production procedures, and
- promoting the flow of information.

The authority mechanisms available in a firm enable the coordination of employees' activities in ways that markets may not do as well because, within a firm, decisions in the forms of "constraints and information as well as orders" flow smoothly from one point to another (Simon 1991, p.32). As a result, the lines of authority in a firm ensure the observance of standards and rules, thus allowing individuals to know intimately their work environment, including the behavior of other actors.

The theory of the firm is often viewed as a unifying theory in the NIE literature. While Knight (1921) and Hayek (1937, 1945) made pioneering contributions to the issues of uncertainty and imperfect knowledge, Coase (1937, 1960, 1992) contributed substantially to the understanding of the institutional structure of production, especially the role of transaction costs. Of course, recognizing that firms exist to economize on transaction costs is in no way to discount the decisive role that market prices play in coordinating production. In its development, the theory has also received significant contributions from Alchian and Demsetz (1972) who emphasized the role of the firm in coordinating production factors. Klein et al. (1978) and Alchian (1984) identified the important role of asset specificity. A properly managed firm with an appropriate incentive scheme in place must induce the correct amount of relation-specific investment from employees. This point is most evident in the context of a firm that emphasizes specific human capital because specific human capital is highly valuable when the worker is employed at the current firm (Lazear 1989). Williamson (1975, 1979, 1981, 1985, 1988, 1998a, 1998b) has been a leading figure in the study of transaction costs – a notion central to the NIE.

Without doubt, a firm is in every sense an organization. As early as the 1960s, the firm was already recognized as "an organization characterized by searching, informational processing, satisficing, allocating mechanism" (Simon 1962, p.14). More recently, the theory of the firm has been extended to other organizational forms. Given the ubiquity of organizations and their dominance of the social as well as economic landscape, Simon (1991) views the world as having a large number of organizations that are interconnected by markets. He maintains that the modern industrialized society is, perhaps, more appropriately described as one comprising organizational economies rather than market economies.

Unlike many new institutional economists, Simon rejects the proposition that the pursuit of selfish personal goals should be taken as the only behavioral norm. He coins the term "enlightened selfishness" to describe human nature (Simon 1991, p.35), meaning thereby that, while an employee contributes to the success of an organization, she expects to be adequately compensated. While economic rewards indeed play an important part in securing adherence to organizational goals and management authority, the basis for a fair reward system to function properly is actually the ability to measure employees' contributions with reasonable accuracy. In other words, the effectiveness of a reward mechanism lies in an ability to trace accurately individual behaviors. Nevertheless, Simon recognizes that, the greater is the interdependence among various members of an organization, the more difficult it is to separate individuals' contributions to the achievement of the organization's goals.

Within the overall framework of promoting the attainment of organizational objectives, the challenge for an organization is typically twofold. The first is concerned with the management of workers and the second is, intriguingly, the management of managers. As far as managing workers is concerned, the main questions seem to be the following:

- Are the workers energized, motivated and working at their full potential?
- Is the work group a cooperative, supportive team?
- Is feedback regarding work performance being looped to the managers as well as supervisors of various levels promptly?

By and large, it boils down to the question of motivating people. Apart from economic motivations and rewards, Simon (1991) cites promotion, recognition, pride in work, and organizational loyalty as vehicles that an organization may employ to motivate its employees. Not dismissing the problem of shirking on the part of workers, as commonly discussed in the NIE literature, Simon emphasizes these traits as good indicators of successful organizations.

The issue concerning the behavior of managers has received considerable attention in the NIE literature in recent years. It has been recognized that one of the principal characteristics of modern publicly-held corporations is the separation of ownership and control. The distinction between management and ownership gives rise to a divergence of interests making it possible for managers to pursue their own interests instead of seeking solely to maximize the value of the organization or the wealth of the shareholders (Scott 1984). For instance, senior managers of large companies are generally entitled to significant fringe benefits, and pecuniary or non-pecuniary perquisites. It is often suggested that, if managers are also residual claimants to a company's profits (i.e., equity owners), the incentives for deviating from the corporate goal of maximizing shareholder wealth may be diminished, but this need not be true (Scott 1984).[1] Insights from organizational theory indicate that, although managers are responsible for identifying, evaluating and choosing alternatives, like ordinary workers they are also apt to shirk in terms of responsibilities and to deviate from corporate goals by pursuing their personal interest. Since the pursuit of self-interest is generally assumed to be the behavioral nature of all economic agents, including managers, the opportunistic behavior of managers may be mitigated by introducing well-designed contracts. Besides, appropriate control and monitoring has to be in place, for instance, by means of some mechanisms that fit the structure of the organization.[2] In the meantime, effective mechanisms should be implemented to reward wise decision-making, creative managerial performance and diligence. The purpose is to synchronize corporate objectives and personal career goals of all employees. In any event, monetary and material rewards and enforcement mechanisms are elements essential to the success of any organization (Simon 1991).

5.2 Public Regulation and Control

It is not uncommon for capitalist societies to have mixed economies in which the state is involved in production and exchange. However, when markets function well and transaction costs are minimal, government has little role to play, especially as far as production decisions are concerned. Capitalist firms are predominantly interested in maximizing profits. For instance, a private company will only undertake an activity if the value of the product of the factors employed is greater than their private cost. Since private companies are assumed to be less concerned with social cost, and when social cost is divergent from private cost, a social problem emerges, creating opportunities for government to intervene. Although state intervention is called for in the event of market failure, such as the presence of excessive and persistent monopoly power, government is expected by the public to make an effort in defining the scope and terms of state intervention

---

[1] Demsetz and Lehn (1985) found no difference in profits between corporations that were managed or controlled by owners and those with diffuse stock ownership. Simon (1991) believes that the absence of such difference may be attributed to organizational traits.

[2] Shleifer (1998) points out that politicians typically like to remain in power and enjoy the perquisites of their office, so a significant element of the goals of any government agency is to maintain political control.

and provide adequate justification. In spite of the usual argument that government intervention is likely to be desirable on welfare grounds, government action is unlikely to be effective unless it is taken on the basis of clearly stated social objectives with an understanding of the benefits and costs involved (Vickers and Yarrow 1991).

Government intervention is, perhaps, most conspicuous in the area of environmental protection. In many countries, the process of industrialization and agricultural intensification has resulted in an extensive range of environmental problems, resulting in, among other things, habitat loss and soil degradation. When negative externalities or spillovers are the result of activities on private land, the public may appeal to government to intervene in order to rectify the situation – for example, providing incentives to landowners to protect wildlife habitat or reduce noise and other pollution. Often it means imposition of regulations that infringe on existing property rights. In consequence, a conflict tends to develop over the question as to who has what and how much right to pollute. Economics offers little help on the normative side of the question, but it is capable, on the positive side, of identifying the benefits and costs of a certain course of action. After examining some of the issues of property rights restructuring, Bromley and Hodge (1990) conclude that alterations of existing property rights may be achieved via the use of economic instruments, such as taxes and subsidies, or by employing the heavy hand of command and control.

Government commonly exerts its influence in regulating quality by implementing minimum standards. Leland (1979) investigated the market of used cars and found that, due to the problem of asymmetric information for the seller vis-à-vis the buyer, some quality regulation may be useful in preventing potentially hazardous products from unduly hurting consumers. Introduction of new regulations represents imposition of restrictive measures that influence the choice of actions by economic agents. Actually, government need not be the only body that imposes regulatory standards. Many professional groups choose to impose requirements over their membership and set standards to ensure professionalism and to serve the purpose of quality improvement.

Regulation by government agencies on behalf of the public frequently finds its way into the land-use planning process. In the case of forestry, because forests have public good characteristics, especially when non-timber values are considered, it is difficult to rule out the need for public intervention. Sometimes government regulation is justified to protect the public interest or to resolve conflicts among economic interests. In particular, some form of public regulation may be justifiable under certain circumstances in which property rights are not clearly defined. Also, when timber harvesting results in the destruction of the forest resource base and leaves many non-timber values in jeopardy, public regulation may be introduced to restrict individual actions that have a negative impact on the well being of society.

International case studies have shown that government intervention is prevalent when forestland is publicly owned, and BC is an obvious case in point (Wilson et al. 1998; Wilson and Wang 1999). Until the early 1980s, the BC government was deeply involved in undertakings, such as the financing and performance of road building, timber cruising and reforestation. Since the late 1980s, there has been a change in the division of responsibility for forest management and resource development. At present, the forest industry is playing a performance role, while the government plays a regulatory and, to a lesser extent, a supervisory role.

Due to widespread public ownership of forestland, public sector infrastructure is highly developed in BC. From an institutional perspective, the organizational structure of the Provincial Ministry of Forests (MoF) constitutes the core of a large structure that radiates in all directions to connect forestry with the Province's economic, political and social system. Apart from the public planning process that operates at the administrative level both in the Victoria Headquarters of the MoF and in several regional centers, there are built-in interfaces and points of contact in the forestry institutional framework to enable participation, input and feedback from the general public. For illustrative purposes, if the MoF is described as the hub of a wheel, the various spokes consist of the administrative procedures, ministerial planning processes, public information system, data gathering, processing and reporting mechanisms. The rim of the wheel comes in contact with the biophysical and ecological world as well as with a multitude of changing social values. Most importantly, forestry legislation and established rules and regulations act as the axle on which the entire wheel turns and the axle is connected, in turn, with other organizations, either government or quasi-government, through various channels of communication. In this way, forestry administration performs as one of the wheels of the Province's institutional vehicle that governs the forest. Therefore, public control of the forest has found expression in virtually every aspect of forest management, especially on the legislative and administrative fronts. Modifying extant laws and introducing new ones are means by which social institutions are modified.

Table 5.1 provides a summary of the major forestry legislation pertaining to BC. The most recent effort at regulating forest practices in BC is the Forest Practices Code, which consists of legislation, regulations, standards and field guides that collectively or individually govern forest practices. The Code represents an amalgam of formal and informal institutions, with the Forest Practices Code of British Columbia Act (1994) establishing legislative powers, duties, rights and responsibilities pertaining to strategic planning and operational planning. The Act represents a first-level structure that establishes mandatory provincial and regional requirements for forest practices and sets compliance, enforcement and penalty provisions. It also specifies administrative arrangements by establishing a Forest Practices Board, and a process of independent audits and appeals.

Forest Practices Regulations that outline basic forest practices, and include a statement of broad principles, constitute a second-level structure, while the Forest Practices Standards comprise a third level. The latter expand upon the Regulations and provide for site-specific variability and detail that may include specific numbers and measurements. Field guides formulate the grass-root level of the package in providing guidance for implementing the Regulations and Standards. Many of the field guides are based on the established norms and some of these norms are constantly evolving and changing.

Designed to deal with the entire spectrum of forest practices relating to operational planning, forest health, soil conservation, recreation management, range management, silvicultural systems, forest road engineering, timber harvesting, forest renewal and forest protection, the Code is arguably the most comprehensive forest legislation in the world. The rationale of the Code is, apparently, a desire to simplify legislative complexities. It was claimed by the BC Ministry of Forests in the early 1990s that forest and range management activities in the Province were governed at that time by 6 national and 20 provincial pieces of legislation, totaling approximately 700 federal and provincial regulations and over 3,000 guidelines; many of the requirements in these documents were found to overlap and contradict each other. The Code has achieved a consolidation of the existing forestry legislation, but this has come with its own set of difficulties. In particular, the Code reduces flexibility, increases costs and, therefore, may represent an obstacle to forest certification.

Table 5.1: Major Forestry Legislation in British Columbia

Year	Act	Principal features	Remark
1865	Land Ordinance	Introducing granting of timber harvesting rights; introducing a royalty system requiring timber companies to pay fees for the volume of timber harvested	Timber leases emerged due to local government's desire to generate revenues for economic development; for a number of years, fee-simple Crown grants ran parallel to timber leases before the latter was established as a dominant approach.
1888	Land Act	Introducing a ground rental system, allowing for collection of fees by area of timber harvest	It marked forest industry's rising influence; while permitting long-term lease on large tracts of land, the Act required logging companies to operate a sawmill for each 400 acres of land under lease, to foster the growth of sawmilling industry.
1892	Amendment to Land Act	Permitting the government to auction timberland to the highest bid	The amendment resulted in an increase in government revenues from the forest industry.
1912	Forest Act	Creating the BC Forest Service; introducing the concept of forest reserves to formally protect Crown timberland from commercial exploitation	It ushered in a formal legislative framework for regulating BC's forest industry; it introduced a stumpage system by which fees charged to forest companies were based on both volume and value of wood cut.
1947	Amendment to Forest Act	Creating forest management systems	It endorsed 'sustained yield' as a new principle of forest management.
1978	Forest Act	Introducing the 'Evergreen' principle to allow licensees to continually renew their licenses	It was a landmark in the history of BC's forestry legislation in that licensees found more tenure security while government retained flexibility.
1978	Ministry of Forests Act	Upgrading the BC Forest Service to the Ministry of Forests	It established the Ministry and committed the government to improved forest management.
1994	Forest Practices Code	Consisting of legislation, regulations, standards, and field guides that collectively or individually govern forest practices	It was a package of formal and informal institutions with accountability and tougher enforcement being the core.
1994	Forest Land Reserve Act	Designating commercial forestland	It provided the forest industry with a stable land base.
1994	Forest Renewal Act	Creating the Crown corporation Forest Renewal BC	It introduced a 'Super Stumpage' system requiring forest companies to pay higher stumpage to fund reforestation on Crown land.

Consider two approaches for addressing market failure: one constitutes a detailed set of regulations while the other consists of a more general statement of the way forest management must proceed in order to address market failure, leaving significant leeway to field staff who are responsible for implementing the regulations. The former is process oriented, while the latter is outcome based. An example of the former is BC's Forest Practices Code, while Sweden's Forest Act (1994) is an example of the latter (see Wilson et al. 1998).

The benefit of a strict set of regulations, such as the Forest Practices Code, is that it requires forest companies to be responsible stewards in every stage of their operations, which is what many environmental groups prefer; its drawback, as already noted, is that it increases costs and reduces the flexibility of firms to adjust to market changes (it takes too long to obtain permission to harvest sites) and silvicultural needs (van Kooten 1999; van Kooten and Wang 1998). The Code has been criticized for its role in lengthening the paper trail between planning and actual harvesting (Gregory 1997). One Coastal company of considerable size reported an 83% increase in operational costs and the same company witnessed a fivefold increase in its harvest-related engineering costs. The increase in planning has not necessarily been a positive development from the perspective of the MoF because of the "avalanche of information" that needed to be processed. Existing staffing levels at the MoF were inadequate to deal with the extra paperwork required for approvals. Furthermore, despite BC's diversity, the Code does not allow for site-specific solutions, even though what works in one part of the Province may not work in another part.

The drawback of a more flexible system is that it affords the parties considerable latitude for dispute over what constitutes satisfactory performance, what constitutes a satisfactory outcome. An outcome or result-based approach is also likely to make it difficult for the public and the government to interfere with any intermediary steps, whether good or bad, that companies take, as long as the outcome is a desirable one. But this is true also for a cookbook approach, such as the Code; as long as a company is in compliance with the Code, activities must be accepted, whether these are considered good or bad.

5.3 Culture, Conventions and Norms

Although the NIE emphasizes understanding the crucial role played by formal institutional arrangements, such as contracts, property rights, laws, regulations, the firm and the state, it is also concerned with the role that culture, conventions and norms play. In recent years, these informal institutional constraints have been recognized as important elements for analysis. Informal constraints provide a framework for collective action and furnish an alternative mechanism in enforcing the rules of the game and facilitating transactions between economic actors (Nee 1998).

Leibenstein (1984) defines norms as an unwritten standard or convention that regulates human behavior. Demsetz (1967) points out that the customs and mores of a society provide an expression of people's expectations. According to North (1991, 1990), Alchian and Demsetz (1973), modern society tends to rely on both formal and informal institutional constraints to resolve conflicts over the use of scarce resources, because, while the behavior of individuals is subject to direct regulation by the state and other authorities, it is indirectly influenced by what they call "cultural indoctrination" (Alchian and Demsetz 1973, p.16). In slightly different terminology, Seitz and Headley (1975) use the term "social institution" in reference to socially sanctioned methods for guiding behavior. They further suggest that social institutions have two important functions, namely, reflecting the accepted procedures of doing things, and providing a certain stability and constancy in social behavior (p.640). Norms and conventions can be thought of as a form of social capital, just as important as natural and other form of human-made capital (physical and human).

Leibenstein (1984) identifies a number of economic issues that arise in connection with conventions. He indicates their possible economic significance and explains that conventions have value in and by themselves. A convention has search and coordination advantages, and a prisoner's dilemma-avoidance advantage. The latter helps reduce uncertainty because conventions set up a parametric situation where otherwise there might be a strategic choice problem. When exploring the nature of the relationship between informal and formal constraints, Nee (1998) explains that, being embedded in formal institutional arrangements and operating in the shadows of formal organizational rules, informal constraints can limit or facilitate economic action. By and large, however, studies on the effects of informal constraints and their relationship with formal ones are still in their infancy in the economics literature.

By stating that implicit norms may act as institutional constraints, one must bear in mind that many informal rules have transaction cost implications. For instance, it is usual practice when harvesting trees in BC for stump height not to exceed the diameter of the stump. Obviously, this rule makes it very easy for loggers and checkers to form on-the-spot judgements, thereby reducing measurement costs. The rule does not apply, however, to Pulp Leases because trees tend to be much smaller under Pulp Leases than under tenures such as TFLs or Forest Licenses.

Fundamentally, conventions and cultural norms are shaped by changes in human values that are affected, in turn, by resource availability, technology, life style, and so on. When forest resources were abundant and timber harvests were relatively small compared to the available forest stock, there was no concern about non-timber values. Further, when population pressure was low compared with available forestland, it was often the case that property rights were granted on a blanket basis, either fee simple or as tenures with relatively few restrictions. As time went by, it was only natural that more and more attributes associated with the forest were recognized; hence, pressure mounted to modify property rights to accommodate new demands. Urbanization also played a role in affecting human perception of the forest; folks living in cities where political as well as corporate decisions are taken increasingly influence modern society. Thus, urban values are imposed on forest management and policy. Unquestionably, demands for increased provision of non-timber products and services clashed with timber interests. In the process of providing for non-timber values, it is almost certain that some timber value will need to be sacrificed.

Values and perceptions are constantly changing, with changes in societal values and perceptions bringing about changes in the objectives of human activities. These, in turn, have an impact on institutional arrangements. Thus, BC witnessed an evolution of human attitudes toward forestry that may be characterized by four stages:

1. forests as a barrier to early settlement (late 18th to mid 19th century),
2. forests as a source of timber supply for sawmills (latter part of the 19th to mid 20th century),
3. forests as a source of timber and fibre (early 20th century to mid 1970s), and
4. forests as a multiple resource base (from 1970s onwards).

Institutional arrangements play a role in influencing as well as reflecting changes in societal values. In this respect, Pearse (1976) notes that "the new problem today is to rationalize forestry, as it is traditionally understood in the context of timber production, with the protection of the environment and other social values." Pearse felt that, from the point of view of forest managers, the most pressing challenge in contemporary times was to develop effective means of reconciling industrial forestry with other forest uses and social objectives to realize the full range of potential values. Recognition of recreational demands beyond the boundaries of parks began to have an important influence on forest management. This feature became increasingly prominent when the BC MoF officially incorporated forest recreation into its mandate in the late 1970s.

Changes in informal constraints also affect the way forestry activities are undertaken, as well as affecting the costs of doing business. For example, at the beginning of the 1980s, BC decided to switch to the metric system for measuring and reporting forestry statistics. This switch played a positive role in standardizing forest practices and promoting trade in forest products in international markets, except the US market.

5.4 Policy Instruments for Forest Management

There is a distinction between North's "institutions" and commonly perceived "policy institutions". The former refers to a wide range of social arrangements whereas the latter is focused more specifically on institutionalized establishments and instruments that serve the purpose of achieving certain social objectives or policy goals. Policy instruments can be deliberately chosen or designed to achieve desired economic objectives.

British Columbia again serves as a useful model for considering policy instruments in forestry. To provide some indication of the broad array of available policy instruments, consider that BC forest policy includes, among others, such things as forest tenures, timber supply control, yield control, timber utilization standards, industrial development criteria, and collection of stumpage fees and a wide range of other taxes. However, the most important policy instruments available to the provincial government may be classified into three broad categories: (1) forest tenures; (2) the control of timber volume available for harvest by forest companies via the determination and allocation of AAC; and (3) the determination and collection of stumpage fees. We briefly consider each of these instruments in turn.

5.4.1   Forest tenures

The structure of BC's forest tenure system and its effects have been studied by Pearse (1976, 1974), and Haley and Luckert (1998, 1990, 1986). As mentioned in Chapter 3, forest tenures have historically been used in the Province as a policy instrument not only for timber rights allocation but also to guide overall economic development. The whole pattern of present-day forest tenure types is reflective of the distribution of industrial facilities in an intertemporal and spatial sense. For instance, the relatively new forms of tenure and those that carry shorter duration, such as Pulpwood Harvesting Agreements, are typically found in the more remote areas of marginal timber since old leases and licenses are found mostly on readily accessible Coastal areas and near rail routes in the Interior.

Reliance on forest tenures as a policy instrument is attributed to the institutional role that these tenure arrangements can play. All forms of licenses are contractual agreements between the licensee and the Crown, with most of the terms and conditions of such agreements set out in the tenure document itself, while others are specified in the Forest Act. The license, which quite often serves as the cutting authorization, describes the surveyed boundaries of the particular tract of land in which harvesting activities are to be permitted. At a lower level, cutting permits are required, obligating licensees to submit a cutting plan that sets out specific features of proposed harvesting operations. Sometimes known as a logging plan, this document details logging techniques and the regeneration program to be undertaken, and it must be prepared and signed by a registered professional forester. In some licenses, development plans in terms of road building and manufacturing requirements need to be specified.

5.4.2   AAC, ACE and timber supply

If forest tenures were an instrument upon which the Provincial authorities relied heavily in the early days, say, until the 1960s, AAC has definitely become a tool of greater appeal in more recent times. AAC refers to the annual rate of timber harvesting specified for an area of land by the Chief Forester of the BC MoF. AAC applies to both timber supply areas and Tree Farm Licenses in the Province. The Ministry of Forests conducts a timber supply review at 5-year intervals. If the primary consideration is timber value, determination of AAC should be based on the Hanzlik formula (Pearse 1990):

$$(5.1) \quad AAC = \frac{V}{L} + MAI,$$

where *AAC* refers to the allowable annual cut, V is the volume of mature timber, L is the rotation age, and *MAI* is the mean annual increment, defined as the timber volume at optimal rotation age divided by the rotation age. Of course, AAC is determined not solely by biological and economic considerations but by political ones as well.

During the last two or three decades, virtually all stakeholder groups have accepted the saying that "AAC is the king of BC forest policy". In essence, AAC is rooted in the timber supply problem. The following factors are usually associated with the determination of AAC:

- Supply pressures arise from the so-called "fall-down" phenomenon, which refers to the fact that harvests from second-growth forests are necessarily lower than those from old growth, as is evident from the first term on the RHS of equation (5.1).
- Economic profit margins are shrinking because the Province uses utilization standards to get firms to harvest uneconomic timber.
- There is an upward trend in production costs.
- In recent years, markets have become more uncertain, partly due to new sources of global timber supply.
- BC companies often lack international competitiveness.

Recent studies have shown that production costs in the BC forestry sector have increased more significantly in real terms over the past two decades than the Province's major competitors in Europe, the United States and elsewhere (Wilson et al. 1998). The bottom line is that most of the remaining inventory in the Province is capable of yielding a reasonable return in good markets, but may be uncompetitive during times when global wood markets are weak. BC has become a marginal supplier, partly because of a failure of institutions that has weakened the forestry sector.

A concept that is intimately related to the AAC is the allowable cut effect (ACE). ACE refers to the immediate increase in today's allowable cut on assurance that higher timber yields are forthcoming from the new forest down the road. Schweitzer et al. (1972) summarize the conditions that have to be met in order for ACE to arise, whereas Binkley (1980) provides a rigorous analysis, from a timber investment perspective, of the mechanics of ACE as a policy instrument. As ACE is dependent on increases in timber volume resulting primarily from silvicultural operations, policies based on ACE are criticized for their effects in accelerating the liquidation of the old-growth forest. While it serves as a policy instrument to provide an incentive for private firms voluntarily to invest in silviculture on public forestlands in Canada, it appears that this instrument is rarely employed. Luckert and Haley (1995) ascribe this to the following:

- The extent of silvicultural operations that tenure holders are required to undertake is limited so that ACE-induced opportunities cannot emerge.
- The prevailing stumpage collection systems do not provide adequate financial incentives to tenure holders.
- The timber harvesting constraint is not binding, so one of the key conditions for ACE to arise is missing.
- It is too costly for firms to go through the administrative procedure of getting AAC increases approved.
- There is a great deal of uncertainty, especially from competing claims on public lands.

Forest tenures, AAC and ACE have been used, to varying degrees, as policy instruments in BC. After decades of exercise, the effectiveness of the tenure system has declined due to its rigidity arising from excessively long-term commitments of forestland and timber. Binkley (1997) argues that BC's tenures have been so attenuated and truncated that their real value is rather limited. The achievement of tenure consolidation in the late 1970s provided an opportunity for AAC to emerge as a major policy instrument. But, in recent years, the role of the AAC as the major policy instrument has diminished. For example, when licensee's AAC is adversely affected, compensation has customarily been made, usually in the form of access to timber elsewhere. However, the rising tide of environmentalism has resulted in greater allocation of forestlands for wilderness preservation, and the Provincial government is no longer capable of compensating forest companies simply because there is not much economic timber left for reallocation. Increasingly, the government is relying on other ways to intervene, and stumpage collection is one of them.

5.4.3 Stumpage fees

For a long time, the Rothery scheme for determining stumpage fees was employed in BC. Under the Rothery scheme, stumpage (S) is calculated as the difference between the selling price of timber (p) and operating costs (c), including an allowance for risk and profit taking (r):

(5.2) $S = p - c - r.$

Generally, loggers were permitted to recover their costs plus about 15% for profit and risk. In essence, the Rothery system was based on "cost-plus", and it merely gave the logger a percentage of the market price for profit and risk allowances.

The problem with the calculation of this formula was the lack of market information for calculating output prices and input costs. Output price for the BC Coast was derived from prices of log in the Vancouver log market, which is, at best, a residual log market. Firms sell excess logs or logs of species that they cannot use on the Vancouver log market. Since log exports are not allowed (in an attempt to keep secondary manufacturing in the Province), the prices of logs in the Vancouver log market are below their true value. For the BC Interior, the value of logs is determined from prices for wood chips and lumber, and a factor that converts logs into these two products. In both cases, costs are calculated from information provided to an accounting firm employed by the government to calculate c. The problem is that costs, c, are based on average values and can vary considerably from one company or site to another.

In 1987, as a condition for removal of a 15% federal export tax (imposed to satisfy US concerns with forest sector subsidies), the BC government introduced a comparative value pricing system, or "target rate of return pricing" system. The new scheme became controversial due to its complexity and underlying "waterbed" effect, which is related to the notion that costs are based on average values rather than actual ones. The equation for calculating stumpage under comparative value pricing is:

(5.3) $S = V + b (VI - AVI)$,

where V is the target rate set by the government for each forest region, b is a coefficient that is normally set to 1, VI is a value index that varies by stand and tree species, and AVI is an average value index – a weighted average for the forest region concerned. Target rates (for each forest region) are adjusted quarterly in response to market forces, as measured by two Statistics Canada price indices, for the Coastal and the Interior lumber markets. From an administrative standpoint, the formula is easy to adjust and simple to implement. Under the formula, better stands are charged higher stumpage. The system enables the government to use administrative means in setting an annual revenue target for allocation among timber harvesters. See van Kooten and Bulte (2000) for more details.

The comparative value pricing system was modified in 1994 with the introduction of the Forest Renewal BC (FRBC), a newly established publicly owned corporation whose purpose was to finance investments in silviculture. Known as "Super Stumpage", the modification enabled the government to collect larger sums of money annually as a means for financing FRBC.

The challenge of BC's forest policy is to promote efficient utilization of the forest resource base, while reconciling conflicts among interest groups. The challenges facing the Province are many. Among these are determining means for promoting sustainable forestry at a time when forest revenues are becoming stretched and government is desperate for revenues. In addition to revenue needs, particular problems of sustainable forestry include the inevitable "fall-down" in future timber supply, and the need for providing incentives for forest companies to invest in silviculture, something that remains dismally low.

5.5 Sustainable Forestry and the New Institutional Economics

Sustainable forestry is multi-faceted, charaterized by the need to make tradeoffs (Wilson and Wang 1999). In this regard, BC's forestry sector can be used to illustrate some relevant issues concerning sustainable forest development. In recent years, the Province witnessed an ongoing transition from the traditional emphasis on sustained timber yield harvesting to a new paradigm of sustainable forestry (although decision makers and the public are often unclear as to what that entails). There have emerged at least three new trends in BC forestry that impact upon the remaining chapters in this book. First, the legislative framework has been consolidated with an orientation toward sustainable forest practices and accountability. Second, the role of the MoF has altered from program implementation and management to resource stewardship, policy formulation and performance monitoring. Third, public decision-making has been decentralized considerably to the field level, and basic silvicultural responsibilities and forest nursery operations have been privatized.

Behind the practice of sustainable forestry is the notion that it may be possible to achieve simultaneously a sustainable and healthy forest resource base, a competitive forest industry and a vibrant forest-related economy. Attainment of these joint goals is in the interests of the government, the forest companies, forest dependent communities and the general public. The major objectives are:

- to realize the full potential contribution of the public forests to the economic and social well being of the citizens of British Columbia, recognizing the diverse values of the forest – commercial wood products, recreation and wildlife, domestic grazing and environmental-ecological values;

- to allow an efficient use of the forest resources to generate a fair share of the net benefits to all legitimate stakeholders;
- to maintain the health and vigor of the forest industry; and
- to improve the productivity of the resource base for future generations.

Unfortunately, that there are bound to be conflicts among multiple objectives is often downplayed or, even worse, ignored. For the most part, existing institutions are not well suited for dealing with conflicts in forestry, and there is a bias toward state intervention and against markets. As a result of the different stakeholders involved in policymaking, much BC forest policy amounts to little more than "muddling through", with great gyrating of policy to suit first one stakeholder group and then another. What is lacking is the political will to develop institutions that can deal with conflict in a consistent fashion – consistent with the general goals upon which society can agree. It has become rather difficult to attain the goal of sustainable forestry, because recent policies have increased the tradeoff between the economic and public good characteristics of the forest.[3]

Insights from the new institutional economics can be useful for guiding BC forest policy, as well as that in other regions. In the NIE framework, institutions are treated endogenously, and the neoclassical assumptions of full information and costless exchange are relaxed, and the consequences of positive transaction costs are recognized. The NIE does not reject marginal analysis and retains the centrality of markets and exchange (Simon 1991). It extends the tools of standard economic analysis to institutions, and analyzes institutions and the part they play in governing economic action (Nee 1998).

One question that can be addressed within the NIE framework deals with public versus private provision of the goods and services related to forests. It is important to make a distinction between public provision and public oversight. Thus, a public good can be privately provided as long as the correct incentives and institutions are in place. Shleifer (1998) and Hart

---

[3] As an example, consider the effect that the Forest Practices Code has on Forest Stewardship Council (FSC) certification. Existing forest practice codes are to be integrated as a requirement under FSC certification. However, as noted in the previous section, BC's Code is inefficient and, if included in certification, may threaten the economics of the commercial forest sector.

et al. (1997), for example, demonstrate that private provision of elementary and secondary education is preferred to public provision, but that the opposite is true for prisons. In both cases, the government pays the cost associated with the activity. Private provision is preferred whenever innovation (quality improvements) and cost savings are important and feasible (the case of schools), and corruption is not a problem (as it is with prisons). Public provision is often preferred when opportunities for quality improvements are limited and efforts to reduce costs adversely affect quality (Shleifer and Vishny 1998).

Given the extent of public ownership of forestland, and the degree of regulatory intervention to correct market failure, it is useful to consider whether the current system is up to the task of correcting market failure, and providing public goods, at lowest cost. Inefficiency in the provision of public goods can be costly to the economy and a threat to sustainable forestry. The current system has elements of public and private provision of not only public goods, but, to some extent, even of private goods, namely, logs for the wood processing sector. It would seem that there are better ways to organize the sector. In principle, there should be no difference in performance (measured both in terms of provision of public and private goods and services) between public ownership of forestland and private ownership, or between the current high level of public ownership and a mix of ownership that leans more toward private than now. Persistent intervention by government in the operations of forest companies tends to create an atmosphere of uncertainty, with companies expending more effort culling favors from government (e.g., ensuring future access to timber, or speeding up the regulatory process) than in marketing products. This results in an increase in transaction costs and makes the BC wood-processing sector less productive than might otherwise be the case.

The current study does not seek to address this larger issue of land ownership, and how the tenure system might be changed. Nor does it consider whether recreation, wildlife habitat and so on are better provided publicly or privately. Rather, we focus on one aspect of public goods, namely, provision of silvicultural services that correct market failure by providing more public goods (environmental or ecological services) than would otherwise be the case. In particular, in the next several chapters we consider factors that cause these activities to be performed by companies in-house versus contracting out. The analysis sheds some light on the issue of transaction costs, knowledge that can be used as an indicator of the role that private provision might play in future attempts to guarantee sustainable forestry.

6 The Silvicultural Contracting Sector

Oriented toward reforestation, silvicultural investments in BC began with nursery establishment in the late 1920s at selected locations on the Coast. Since then, silvicultural activities have evolved primarily in response to changes in the forest resource base, technological advances and shifts in societal values. Several decades of rapid forest development left behind large areas of not-satisfactorily-restocked (NSR) sites that contributed, in the late 1960s, to the emergence of a distinct silvicultural contracting sector in BC.[1]

During the past three decades, BC's silviculture sector faced a number of unique challenges. First, it struggled to expand delivery capacity in response to a dedicated public sector effort through the Forest Resource Development Agreement (FRDA) programs to regenerate the large area of backlog not-sufficiently-restocked (NSR) sites. Somewhat concurrently, the law was changed so that new logged-off sites had to be restocked (no such requirement existed previously). Second, the sector was born in an era of multiple use, and it matured as forestry shifted to encompass sustainable development as well as multiple use. This meant that, in addition to regenerating large NSR areas, silvicultural performance quality was also emphasized, in order to address multiple values. Third, because of predominant public ownership of forestlands and a complex tenure system, silvicultural activities have come to rely, to a great extent, on private action under public scrutiny, involving sophisticated institutional arrangements that blend public aspirations with private input. Given the objectives of rapidly restocking NSR land and enhancing the value and productivity of the forest resource base, the expansion in the scope and scale of silvicultural activities led to a policy package that the BC government adopted in 1987. As a result, forest companies operating under Crown licenses were given physical

---

[1] NSR land refers to productive forestland that fails to grow the minimum number of trees of desirable species to provide for commercially viable timber harvest at the end of a rotation.

and financial responsibility for planting all future logged-off sites on public land, according to pre-harvest silvicultural prescriptions, and managing the sites to a free-to-grow stage. A detailed chronology of major institutional and policy changes in BC's silviculture sector is provided in the Appendix at the end of this chapter.

Given the importance of understanding the institutional environment of BC's silviculture sector, this chapter provides a profile of institutional changes at the operational level, namely, the institutional arrangements that have emerged and the ways by which silvicultural activities are organized, particularly in terms of contractual relationships and arrangements. The information used in this chapter is based on separate surveys of BC's companies holding timber tenures on public land, nurseries, seed orchards and silvicultural contractors conducted by the authors in 1997. We begin, however, by outlining the general forms of contractual relationships in BC's silviculture sector.

6.1 Contractual Relationships in BC's Silviculture Sector

In BC, silviculture is a relatively small financial and employment component within forestry, although, in recent years, silviculture has gained greater importance within forestry, partly in response to public sector policy intervention. Each year, up to 20,000 non-union silvicultural workers are involved in a variety of silvicultural activities including tree planting, brushing and weeding, and forest seedling production. Because timber harvesting dominates forest management and technology, the role of silviculture remains small, making it a challenge to identify clearly the interconnectedness between silviculture and the other sub-sectors.

During the past three decades, the main feature of institutional restructuring in BC's silviculture sector has been the change in contractual relationships. Prior to 1967, when silviculture was confined to nursery work and small-scale tree planting, the BC Forest Service (BCFS) hired individuals directly to perform silviculture on Crown land (see Figure 6.1). After 1967, with an expansion in the scale and scope of silvicultural operations, the handling of an increasing amount of work became more costly. So, instead of directly hiring workers on an individual basis, the Provincial government began to assume the role of "principal" with the emergent silvicultural contractors as "agents". The rationale for such arrangements was to minimize transaction costs. Perhaps silvicultural contractors have lower costs because they possess specialized skills and knowledge, especially at the local level, that would be more difficult for government agencies to acquire and retain. Contractors can organize individual workers at less cost than the BC Forest Service, thus making it logical for them to serve as a level of management between the workers and the BCFS. Assuming contractors are more successful than the BCFS in minimizing the problem of moral hazard, transaction costs could be lowered by using silvicultural contractors.

The policy change that took place in 1987 necessitated new delivery arrangements. As a result of the change the existing relationship had to include the major licensees (e.g., holders of TFLs, FLs and Timber Licenses) within a BCFS-major licensees-contractors-workers model.[2] The reason for this new relationship had much to do with the rapid growth in the amount and type of silvicultural work and changes in expectations regarding the quality of silvicultural activities. The BCFS found it increasingly costly to stick to the old contractual arrangements, so a new "principal-agent" layer was inserted in the silvicultural contracting system that resulted in the further vertical integration of major licensees into silviculture. This change occurred because, from the standpoint of forest management, it provided a foundation for incorporating basic silviculture, which requires forest regeneration to take place soon after timber harvesting operations. Further, from an administrative and organizational perspective, the policy decentralized silvicultural decisions without altering the fundamental structure of the Province's existing forest tenure system. It effectively anchored the major licensees in the integrated forest management system in a compulsory fashion. The role of the BCFS, which became the BC Ministry of Forests (MoF) in 1979, included regulatory, administrative and, when necessary, punitive functions. Finally, the new approach improved economic efficiency by economizing on the transaction costs associated with the organization of silvicultural operations. By promoting decentralized contractual relationships, the new approach lowered the costs of contract negotiation, enforcement and information collection.

---

[2] Major licensees had used the services of silvicultural contractors in the 1970s for forest regeneration, but most costs were reimbursed by the BC Forest Service under the stumpage-credit system.

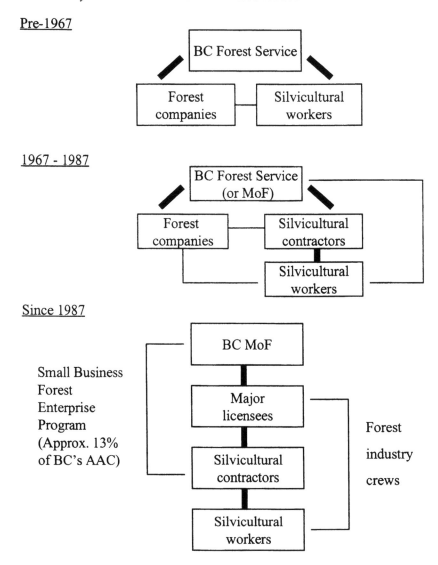

Thick lines indicate major relationships involving direct contractual relations on a frequent basis; thin lines indicate minor relationships and less frequent interactions.

Figure 6.1: Evolution in Contractual Relationship of BC's Silviculture Sector

       In essence, the contractual relationships in BC's silviculture sector are agency relationships. Conceptually, the MoF may be viewed as the first-level principal and the major licensees as the second-level principal.

Likewise, the licensee can be described as the first-level agent with the silvicultural contractor as the second-level agent. Thus, the principal-agent structure is, more comprehensively, a two-tier relationship with the MoF-major licensee comprising the first layer and the licensee-contractor forming the second layer. Pursuant to the provisions of the Small Business Forest Enterprise Program (SBFEP), the MoF also deals directly with silvicultural contractors. The SBFEP accounts for some 13% of BC's AAC and the MoF is responsible for silvicultural activity on the area harvested.

At a conceptual level, the principal-agent formulation characterizes the institutional and contractual reforms in BC's silviculture sector. Yet, it is the second-layer relationship that is essential because silvicultural operations hinge on the major licensee, which acts in a dual role as both a principal and an agent. In consequence, the licensee plays a central role in this new contractual relationship. In the remainder of this chapter, we describe contractual arrangements at the level of silvicultural activities in terms of seed orchards, nurseries and forest companies using data from the 1997 surveys. However, we begin with a description of the silvicultural workforce.

6.2 BC's Silviculture Contracting Workforce

Sources differ considerably in regard to the actual number of existing silvicultural contractors in BC. According to the *Canadian Silviculture Directory* (Canadian Silviculture Magazine 1997), there are 212 contractors in the Province. While the Western Silviculture Contractors Association (WSCA) reported a total of 62 full members and some 20 associate supplier members in early 1997, it estimated that the number of silvicultural contractors was upwards of 500 (Groves 1996). From the MoF, WSCA and other sources (e.g., the Council of Forest Industries of BC), we compiled a list of 140 active contractors to whom questionnaires were mailed. Although BC's silvicultural contracting covers a full spectrum of silvicultural operations, results from 52 responding contractors (response rate 37%) reveal at least three features. First, BC's silvicultural contractors tend to concentrate on basic silviculture – planting and brushing and weeding. Second, few contractors engage in incremental silviculture, which is defined as the silvicultural practices in established stands for enhancing stand value and yield. Finally, stewardship contracting, which is end-results based and involves multiple phases and multiple activities, is virtually non-existent in the Province.

According to the survey results, the average period that BC's silvicultural contractors have operated is 11 years, with WSCA members averaging 12.4 years and non-members 9.6 years. The silviculture contracting workforce is relatively young: the majority of the contractors surveyed have been in business for less than 15 years, and the two groups that have been around for 6-10 years and 11-15 years represent 37% and 29%, respectively, of all contractors. The overall young age of the contracting force is due to the emergence of a large number of contractors in the past decade or so. Many new contractors are not WSCA members.

Survey results confirm that BC's silvicultural contractors have a noticeable variance in the scope of activities. The intensity of engagement in silvicultural activities is as follows (in descending order): brushing and weeding, planting, spacing, and surveying. Comparisons between WSCA members and non-members provide no indication that the member contractors necessarily involve themselves more fully than non-members in silvicultural work. It has been found that contractors with more years of experience, regardless of the WSCA membership, demonstrate a greater degree of involvement in virtually all activities.

The survey included questions concerning contract length, payment scheme, employment, rate of returned workers and level of management in order to examine the performance quality of silvicultural activities and management efficiency. Compared with non-members, WSCA members tend to hire more workers and enjoy a higher degree of management efficiency in terms of the percentage of returned workers and the ratio of workers to supervisors (Table 6.1). Many contractors not only adopt piece wages but also other payment schemes, such as base wage plus bonus. In comparison, although non-WSCA members also use piece rates, they rely more on hourly wages. One reason for this difference is that, since WSCA members tended to have a longer operational history, they have experience with different sorts of incentive schemes. In this respect, it is possible that new contractors, lacking experience, opt for the hourly wage system for a period in an effort to reduce the risk associated with developing sector knowledge and a steady workforce. Management efficiency is clearly positively related to experience, and this is most noticeable when comparing the survey results for the pre-1987 and post-1987 sub-groups.

Table 6.1: Management of Silvicultural Contracting in BC (Weighted Average of 52 Contracting Firms)

Category	WSCA member Yes	WSCA member No	Entire Group	Contractor Pre-1987	Contractor Post-1987	WSCA member Pre-1987	WSCA member Post-1987
Number of managers	5	3.9	4.5	5	3.8	5.3	4.4
Workers hired in 1996	127	49	88	136	32	170	48
Returned workers (%)	66	49	57	61	55	68	63
Worker-manager ratio	26	11	19	26	9	36	8
Payment scheme (%)[a]							
- hourly wages	27	77	52	54	50	35	11
- piece wages	81	54	67	82	50	94	56
- base wage + bonus	12	15	14	18	8	12	11
- other (salary, etc.)	27	8	17	14	13	24	33
Contract length (days)							
- basic silviculture	66 - 67	73 - 88	69 - 77	67	79	55	94
- incr. silviculture	72 - 77	81	76 - 79	77	78	61	105
Ratio of workers to supervisors (proportion in parentheses)							
	1-5	1-5	1-5	1-5	1-5	1-5	1-5
	(12%)	(46%)	(29%)	(11%)	(46%)	(6%)	(22%)
	6-10	6-10	6-10	6-10	6-10	6-10	6-10
	(54%)	(34%)	(44%)	(63%)	(38%)	(59%)	(44%)
	11-15	11-15	11-15	11-15	11-15	11-15	11-15
	(35%)	(19%)	(27%)	(26%)	(17%)	(35%)	(33%)
Preference for[b]							
- Forest Service	15%	15%	15%	18%	13%	18%	11%
- Forest companies	100%	92%	96%	96%	96%	100%	100%

[a] Percentage of contractors using the method.
[b] Percentage of contractors making the indication.

In summary, BC's silvicultural contracting has been in existence for over thirty years. The survey shows the following. (1) Silvicultural contracting firms, especially the larger ones that have been in operation for a relatively long period, concentrate their efforts in basic silvicultural activities such as planting and brushing and weeding. (2) Contrary to expectation, contracting experience does not necessarily result in more contract days. (3) There is no evidence indicating that WSCA members win more contracts and/or obtain more secure silvicultural work than non-members.

The late 1990s witnessed a wave of consolidation of silvicultural contractors (Stolz 2000). Mergers take place as contractors seek to cut overhead costs, maintain longer seasons for their workers and avoid the more extreme forms of low bidding. Another trend is the gradual disappearance of small contractors simply because smaller contractors find it increasingly difficult to win contracts when the Province's total planting program shrinks in size.

6.3 BC Ministry of Forests' Silvicultural Contracting

According to the 1988 amendment to the BC Forest Act, the MoF has a mandate to deliver the basic silviculture obligations under the Small Business Forest Enterprise Program, or SBFEP. Virtually all silvicultural contracts under the SBFEP are awarded to independent silvicultural contractors at the MoF's Forest District level. In addition to the SBFEP silvicultural contracting, the MoF is involved in the management of FRBC's silvicultural projects. In these projects silviculture specialists with the MoF are responsible for silviculture contracting, site inspection and providing technical advice to practitioners.

Contractors who wish to be considered by the MoF for contracts usually are requested to submit a detailed résumé to a Forest District office in order to be included on a 'Select List'. An advertisement may appear on a local or industry newspaper.

According to the MoF's Integrated Silviculture Information System (ISIS) data base, contracts with the MoF for silvicultural activities on Crown land are undertaken by two categories of performers, namely, large forest companies and small firms. Small firms, which comprise independent contractors, are by far the largest group because they carry out over 85% of the MoF silviculture-related contracts. When major licensees have contracts from the MoF or FRBC sources, they usually sub-contract the actual work to independent contractors.

As far as individual activities are concerned, the most frequently occurring ones are (in decreasing order): surveying, planting, spacing and brushing. These four activities accounted for 73% of the total number of MoF silvicultural projects during the period 1995-97. As indicated in Table 6.2, between 1995 and 1997, there was an increase in brushing and site preparation contracts and a decrease in spacing contracts, but no discernible trend was observed for planting and surveying contracts. The ISIS reporting system was introduced in 1995.

Table 6.2: Silvicultural Contracts Funded by the MoF

Activity	1995		1996		1997		Total	
	Contracts	%	Contr'ts	%	Contr'ts	%	Contr'ts	%
Brushing	12	5	184	14	154	18	350	14
Juvenile spacing	48	21	257	19	123	15	428	18
Planting	36	16	290	22	170	20	416	17
Site preparation	16	7	164	12	89	11	269	11
Surveying	59	26	282	21	185	22	526	22
Other	55	24	172	13	130	15	357	15
Total	226	100	1,349	100	851	100	2,426	100

Source: The Integrated Silviculture Information System (ISIS), data maintained by the Forest Practices Branch, BC Ministry of Forests.

In 1996 the BC Forest Renewal Act was amended to require FRBC to establish a forest worker agency which would actively develop a process to match eligible BC forest workers with jobs arising through FRBC funded projects and to facilitate priority hiring for eligible BC forest workers.[3] Specifically, the Amendment requires that eligible BC forest workers who have experienced or are facing work reductions be given first priority in hiring for FRBC funded projects. This requirement has led to the creation of an agency, the New Forest Opportunities Ltd., which is expected to deliver Coastal silviculture activity funded by FRBC using a union-hiring hall style.[4]

6.4 BC's Seed Orchards

BC's seed orchard program arose from a perception of future timber shortages and a desire to secure a supply of high-quality seeds. As a result of an expansion in artificial regeneration, mainly by planting, an increase in demand for high quality seedlings to reduce timber shortfall generated enthusiasm for developing genetically improved seed (Hanson 1985).

The first seed orchard was established on the BC Coast in 1963 at Campbell River. During the 1960s and 1970s, the Forest Service and the forest industry established 25 orchards on the Coast, and, with the exception of one Sitka spruce (*Picea sitchensis*) orchard and one hemlock (*Tsuga heterophylla*) orchard, they focused on Douglas-fir (*Pseudotsuga menziesii*). In 1974, a seed production section was set up in the Reforestation Division

---

[3] BC Forest Renewal Amendment Act.

[4] Existing silvicultural contractors are concerned about the impact of this publicly-supported agency on the viability of their businesses and the sustainability of public spending on silviculture.

of the BC Forest Service. It was mandated: (i) to establish first-phase seed production orchards either by grafting of scions or use of seedlings from selected high-quality parent trees to produce regular supplies of seed with high germination vigor and wide adaptability; and (ii) to establish second-phase seed orchards from progeny-tested breeds of proven superior genetic quality. These two objectives were designed to reduce progressively, over the next 20 to 40 years, dependence on chance collection from wild stands (BC Forest Service 1974).

To improve coordination of government and industry efforts, two cooperative programs were formed: the Coastal Tree Improvement Council (CTIC), and the Interior Tree Improvement Council (ITIC). The two councils, formed in 1979 and 1981 respectively, have been responsible for making recommendations to the Province's Chief Forester regarding program objectives, strategies, agency involvement, and allocation of workload and research needs for future tree improvements in the Province. For instance, as a result of a CTIC recommendation, 10 of the initial Coastal orchards were either abandoned or withdrawn from intensive management because of their environmentally disadvantaged locations. Companies participating in the management of orchards were reimbursed for costs incurred through the credits-to-stumpage scheme under Section 88(1) of the Forest Act (1980).[5] The objectives of the Councils were twofold: (1) to establish programs to increase the levels of genetic gain through testing and breeding, and (2) to produce sufficient orchard seed (incorporating the highest available level of genetic improvement) to meet specific goals established for each species. Meanwhile, private orchards existed to produce seed primarily for private forestlands, and they have been managed and financed without government support.

Orchard planning is based on 37 seed-orchard planning zones. These boundaries represent a compromise between biogeoclimatic zones and subzone boundaries and administrative boundaries. Each planning zone projects long-term seed needs based on planting requirements for each forest species. The trend for the period between the late 1960s and mid-1980s was to establish and intensively manage seed orchards to produce seed of superior genetic quality for the major species used in reforestation. As of the

---

[5] Adopted in 1980, Section 88 of the Forest Act formalized the credit-to-stumpage practice. It enabled the MoF to reimburse timber licensees for approved forestry activities out of required stumpage payments. Silvicultural contractors benefited from Section 88 incidentally because, through this means of financing, timber companies were able to expand forestry activities many of which were undertaken by silvicultural contractors (see Appendix for more details).

early 1990s, the total area of seed orchards covered some 200 ha, with the MoF managing slightly more than half. Geographically, one third of the MoF's orchard area is in the Interior, but 82% of industry orchards are Coastal (BC Ministry of Forests 1992).

We conducted a survey of 16 seed orchards, with 13 responding (response rate of 81%). The forest industry's seed orchards are 10 years older (mean age 24 years) than MoF orchards (14 years). The average growing area for all seed orchards is 21.1 ha. The orchards have produced cones, on average, for 9 years. In aggregate, cone production ranges from 853 to 1,298 hectoliters per annum, for an average of 66-100 hectoliters per orchard.

The 13 orchards reported a total of 26 permanent employees, or an average of two per orchard. There are 10 professional and administrative staff, or just under one full-time equivalent person per orchard. Some 77% of seed orchards hire seasonal workers, but none hires more than 6 (Table 6.3). Three orchards, which are all operated by the MoF, use their own permanent staff to harvest cones. Workers are universally paid at a time rate. Survey results indicate that 77% of the orchards use their technical staff for supervising seasonal workers, while the rest (23%) rely on a combination of technical staff and hired people for supervisory work.

Some 92% of orchards provide some training, with 69% of those training their seasonal workers for less than half a day. Longer training (1/2 to a full day) occurs at only 31% of the seed orchards. No seed orchard provides training in excess of one day.

6.5 BC's Forest Nurseries

BC's first nursery for production purposes was established at Green Timbers near Vancouver in 1930 (Young 1989a). However, expansion in nursery capacity did not begin until the early 1960s (Young 1989b) because, up to the 1950s, only some of the most highly productive sites in the most accessible areas were considered for restocking (Sloan 1956). For instance, in 1955 approximately 7 million seedlings were available for planting in the Province, the majority being planted on the Coast. In 1961, seedling production was still about the same; two years later it had doubled. In 1963, BC had three major nurseries, producing 12.5 million trees for planting. With this rate of production and a planting density of approximately 1,000 trees per ha, only about 13,000 ha could be planted per year. By 1964, 23 million seedlings were produced. The estimated 1965 nursery capacity for seedlings in the Province reached 25 million (Sedlack 1965). At that time, nursery stock production was financed entirely by the government.

Table 6.3: Seed Orchard Management in British Columbia

	Number of orchards	Frequency (%)
Number of seasonal workers hired per year		
0	1	8
1 - 3	4	31
4 - 6	4	31
7 - 10	1	8
> 10	3	23
Period of employment for seasonal workers (number of weeks)		
< 5	3	23
5 - 8	3	23
9 - 12	1	8
> 12	6	46
Percentage of cones harvested by seasonal workers		
≤ 25	3	23
26 - 50	1	8
51 - 75	0	0
76 – 100	9	69
Ratio of seasonal workers to supervisors		
< 4	3	23
4 - 6	5	39
7 - 10	4	31
> 10	1	8

Since the late 1960s, planting accelerated, exerting increasing pressure on seedling production capacity. For instance, sowing requests for 1979 totaled 111 million seedlings, 11 million more than the nurseries could grow. The new situation forced the newly created MoF to explore the possibility of involving private nurseries to meet the increased demand for seedlings (Grant 1979). Quickly, more than one dozen were established. These included commercial operations producing stock for market sale and operations that were both owned and operated by forest companies.

Nursery management represents the greatest concentration of technology and investment in the forest growth cycle and rivals wood processing in capital and labor intensity (Gordon 1984). The nursery production cycle is short relative to many other forestry operations. Since nurseries are the first custodians of seed-orchard seeds, they have received increasing attention from silvicultural managers. Nurseries present a unique opportunity to multiply the effects of technology and research on wood yields (Gordon 1984). After several years of debate and preparation, the government decided to sell 9 MoF nurseries.[6] Located in several different regions, the nurseries for sale included the land, buildings and equipment needed for seedling production, and each was staffed by fully trained and experienced personnel.

Expressions of interest were solicited from the general public, but the MoF made it clear at the outset that the government reserved the right to negotiate an agreement directly with affected employees in the event a satisfactory proposal was received from those employees. If no acceptable employee proposals were identified, the normal public bidding process would apply. In any event, the government favored proposals that emphasized job creation and protection.

In mid-1988, 6 of the 9 nurseries were purchased by an employee group headed by one of MoF's top managers (*Vancouver Sun*, July 23, 1988, p.B8). The 6 nurseries involved a total of 100 jobs, with 47 of them being regular full-time jobs. The employees paid $5 million for the nurseries and they would give the government $3.9 million worth of seedlings and service charges over the next 5 years. The new company signed a four-year contract with the MoF for seedling production and a five-year contract for seedling storage. About the same time, two other nurseries were also privatized. Green Timbers – BC's very first forest nursery – was withdrawn from the privatization process partly in response to public opposition to privatization of the facility. Allington (1997) argues that the sale of government nurseries to the private sector marked a real transformation in BC silviculture, because the privatization encouraged innovative techniques. Prior to the privatization, the BC Forest Service was the sole supplier of seedlings and the overall system was not sensitive to market requirements.

Prior to October 1987, the MoF was financially responsible for growing almost all of the seedlings planted on Crown land. As a consequence of the changes in responsibility for funding reforestation in the Province, the administration of contracts, seedling morphological and physiological quality, nursery culture, pest management, shipping and cold storage became important to all licensees and nurseries due to changes in the supplier-customer relationship. Among other things, Bill 70, or the Forest Amendment Act (1987), created a forest industry-funded seedling market (Brazier 1991). The privatization of forest nurseries certainly served the purpose of promoting the development of tree seedlings production, because

---

[6] On November 12, 1987, the *Vancouver Sun* (p.B9) carried "... [an] invitation to apply for the purchase of 9 BC Forest Service nurseries." The nurseries produced 100 million seedlings a year.

allowing the private sector to grow seedlings meant the end of monopolistic supply of seedlings by the public sector in favor of greater competition among the private sector.

Since the early 1980s, production of forest planting stock in containers in BC has increased rapidly. Currently, of the some 220 million seedlings raised each year, over 90% are container-grown. There are many opportunities to save in regard to using container seedlings. For instance, compared with conventional seedlings, container stock is cheaper to transport since one can get more trees into the refrigerator and on the barges. Furthermore, on account of their small size, container seedlings are less expensive to plant. The principal species used in BC include spruces (*Picea engelmannii, Picea glauca* and *Picea sitchensis*), lodgepole pine (*Pinus contorta*), Douglas-fir (*Pseudotsuga menziesii*), western red cedar (*Thuja plicata*), hemlock species (*Tsuga heterophylla* and *Tsuga mertensiana*), true firs (*Abies amabilis*) and miscellaneous other species, including Ponderosa pine (*Pinus ponderosa*), western larch (*Larix occidentalis*) and yellow cedar (*Chamaecyparis nootkatensis*).

The change in 1987 from a single government buyer to a multiplicity of purchasers has resulted in a market-driven forest seedling industry. Market demands have increased the number of stock types from 8 in 1986 (Brazier 1991) to 35 in 1993 (Scagel et al. 1993). In terms of stock types sown, 1+0 containers have increased to dominate the market, 2+0 containers declined somewhat, bare-root seedlings continue to decline, and transplants increased during the late 1980s and early 1990s.[7] There has been a general trend from small containers to larger ones.

BC's nursery capacity presently exceeds demand. Three trends have been visible over the past 10 to 15 years: container seedlings have replaced bare-root seedlings; larger stock types have increased proportionally; and nursery production has shifted to greenhouses. These changes and Bill 70 created new facilities to meet the customer requirements of an increased number of clients (Brazier 1991).

A survey of 43 forest nurseries in the Province was conducted by the authors with 34 responses received (response rate 79%). Of the 34 nurseries, 4 are MoF nurseries, 6 are major forest companies nurseries, and

---

[7] Plug styroblock (PSB) is a commonly used container stock type. For a given species, a stock type name is comprised of nursery culture and growing seasons. For instance, 1+0 means one-year-old seedling, i.e., one year in container and 0 year in transplanting stage.

the remaining 24 are commercial ones (Table 6.4).[8] The MoF nursery at the Cowichan Lake Research Station is not included in our statistical calculations due to its focus on research. The MoF and commercial nurseries are larger in both area and production than nurseries operated by forest companies. Only half a dozen forest companies have their own nurseries because the planting programs of many firms are too small to support an independent tree nursery. Nurseries have been in operation for an average of 14-17 years, which corresponds with the time when the MoF decided to encourage private efforts in seedling production.

Table 6.4: Forest Nurseries in British Columbia

Nursery category	Number	Average years in operation	Average size (ha)	Total capacity (million)	Mean annual capacity (million)
MoF	4	36	340.0	36	12.0
Industry	6	15	14.6	29	4.8
Commercial	24	14	30.1	240	10.0
Overall	34	17	64.0	305	9.0

The three MoF production nurseries currently produce 25 million seedlings, but, since the MoF needs to make 45 million seedlings available for planting, some 20 million seedlings are contracted out to private growers. The selection of private nurseries is done on a rating basis handled by a nursery contract review board. The formula is a weighted average of 60% quality of seedlings and 40% ability and contract price.

The MoF nurseries have the largest permanent staff and technical personnel and do not hire seasonal workers to the same extent as private nurseries (Table 6.5). Regardless of nursery category, temporary workers are invariably hired for labor-intensive jobs such as thinning, weeding, lifting and packing. The MoF nurseries tend to contract out activities such as lifting, maintenance, and so on. Several industry nurseries also contract out some activities, but the commercial nurseries do not contract out at all.

---

[8] The BC MoF identified two categories of private nurseries. Private tree seedling nurseries under contract to the Ministry, for direct payment of seedlings destined for Crown land, are categorized as commercial nurseries. Private nurseries operated by forest companies that harvest on Crown land are called industry nurseries.

Table 6.5: Forest Nursery Management in British Columbia

Nursery category	Permanent employees	Technical staff	Intensity of seasonal hiring (%)		
			< 10	11 - 20	> 20
MoF	10	9.3	33	33	33
Industry	6	2.4	17	17	67
Commercial	9	4.7	8	25	17
Overall	8	4.7	12	24	24

Normally, the period of employment for seasonal workers is around 3 to 6 months. With a few exceptions, seasonal workers are from local communities. Some exceptions occur with the forest industry nurseries. As far as unionization is concerned, the MoF nurseries are 100% unionized and forest industry nurseries are largely unionized. Of the commercial nurseries, unionization is generally not a factor except for a few relatively large nurseries. Time rate is the predominant payment method for seasonal workers. However, some one third of the nurseries have also adopted a piece-rate system, or production bonus schemes.

It has been found that, due to their relatively greater permanent and technical staff component, the MoF nurseries can afford to let one person supervise fewer seasonal workers; the ratio of supervisor to workers is considerably lower in both commercial and forest industry nurseries (Table 6.6). As far as training is concerned, up to 90% of the nurseries provide some form of training to seasonal workers. Although training typically lasts half a day at the beginning of every employment season, private nurseries tend to spend a little longer on training than the MoF nurseries, perhaps because the MoF nurseries employ a higher ratio of supervisors to workers.

Table 6.6: Supervision of Nursery Seasonal Workers

Nursery category	Responsibility (%)		# of seasonal workers supervised (%)		
	Technical staff	Tech. + hired	10	11 - 20	20
MoF	33	67	7	0	3
Industry	83	17	7	33	0
Commercial	75	25	1	63	7
Overall	73	27	4	52	4

6.6 BC Forest Industry's Silvicultural Contracting

Given the nature of institutional reforms in the BC silviculture sector, major forest licensees are a key component of silvicultural decision-making and delivery. A list of forest companies was developed using the MoF annual reports and information from the Council of Forest Industries of BC and the affiliated industry associations. In total 117 questionnaires were sent out to companies or major divisions of companies, and the response rate was 88% (i.e., 103 completed surveys). About two-fifths of the companies (or their divisions) operate on the Coast.

Survey results indicate that 44% of the major licensees have separate silvicultural divisions, some divisions appearing in the 1950s. However, most firms did not establish separate silvicultural divisions until the 1980s or 1990s. All major forest companies now have separate silvicultural divisions.

Only 45% of the respondents operate with an AAC exceeding 500,000 m^3, while 59% indicated that they have some form of area-based tenure, such as TFL or private land. However, a considerable number of licensees (41%) do not have any area-based tenures, having only volume-based Forest Licenses.

The majority of licensees have few permanent silvicultural staff. The survey results indicate that only 14% of the licensees have more than 10 permanent silvicultural staff, while companies with more than 2 registered professional foresters or administrative staff account for a mere 30% of all firms.

Forest companies generally do not directly hire a large number of seasonal workers, with only 37% of licensees hiring 10 seasonal workers or more each year. For those companies that do hire seasonal workers, the work period is relatively short. Only 46% of the respondents provide longer than 3 months of silvicultural work, with many forest companies in the

Province providing less than 3 months of silvicultural work. Only one third of the respondents report that they have basic silvicultural contracts longer than 3 months. Some 65% of the major licensees surveyed reported that incremental silviculture work was available at their operations. Monitoring of individual performance is done either by managers of a firm or by hired checkers and evaluators. Silvicultural workers are paid an hourly rate (41%), a piece rate (25%), or a salary (34%).

Up to 93% of the respondents indicated that they had a "preferred contractor," with only 35% indicating that they relied on "low bid." Yet, silvicultural contracting appears to be quite competitive. Nearly 80% of the respondents reported that 4 to 7 contractors were available to them, whereas 17% of the companies indicated that there were less than 3 contractors available in their region; two companies even reported that they each had more than 7 contractors to choose from.

The survey results also suggest that there is some mobility among silvicultural contractors. One third of the companies hired less than 30% of their contractors from the local community, and another one third relied on between 30% and 70% of contractors from the local community.

As a result of in-person interviews prior to mailing out questionnaires, 5 determinants for selecting contractors were identified – low bid, good reputation, successful relationship in the past, whether the contractor was unionized, and employment for the local community (Table 6.7). It turns out that companies put a great deal of weight on previous experience and reputation as main criteria for selecting contractors. This is consistent with Dohan's (1976) finding that it is preferable for contracts to be awarded according to past experience and other criteria for potential efficiency, rather than according to low price bids.

Table 6.7: **Ranking of Determinants for Sivicultural Contractor Selection**

Determinants	Percentage indicating
Successful relationship in the past	91.3
Good reputation	77.7
Employment for local community	61.2
Low bid	52.4
Union issue	4.9

When asked to rank contract negotiation on a 5-point scale (1=low, 5=high), the majority of the respondents rated it as moderately complex. An escape clause that allows contracting parties to terminate an agreement or re-negotiate is usually included in silvicultural contracts. Re-negotiation (usually on an annual basis) is quite common, with 60% of companies having re-negotiation provisions in their contracts. Forty percent of the companies choose to negotiate with their partners on an *ad hoc* basis; (re-) negotiation of contract terms takes place upon a request from one of the parties. Negotiation is the predominant form (96%) of dispute resolution, followed by arbitration (7%) and litigation (3%). Given the confrontational and costly nature of the latter two ways of handling disputes, they are only reported by several large Coastal companies.

Silvicultural activities are either contracted out or performed in-house within the corporate structure. Some firms adopt both forms at the same time. The choice of specific contractual forms is the subject matter of Chapter 7.

In summary, survey results from BC's silviculture contracting industry suggest three general conclusions. First, a network of contractual relationships exists in the BC silviculture sector. Largely vertical in nature, this relationship reflects the "MoF-Major Licensee-Independent Contractor" hierarchy that characterizes BC's silviculture institutional matrix. Second, firms, whether a seed orchard, a nursery or a forest company, choose appropriate contractual arrangements for various silvicultural activities that reduce transaction costs. Thus, firms contract out straightforward and labor-intensive activities, while opting for in-house delivery of those operations that require a high level of technical skill and the use of specialized equipment. Third, with the exception of some FRBC programs, silviculture expenditures in BC remain largely aimed at site preparation, planting, brushing and other basic silviculture activities.

Appendix: Chronology of Major Events and Policies Regarding BC's Silviculture

1912 Passage of BC's first Forest Act; creation of the Province's Forest Branch

1923 Amendments to the Forest Act, introducing seed tree regulations

1924 The first cone was collected for seed, followed by experimental planting at the Shelbourne Nursery in Victoria the following year

1925 Establishment of Forest Reserve Account to provide fund for planting

1927 Initiation of experimental harvesting in favor of reforestation

1930 Establishment of BC's first production nursery at Green Timbers in Surrey; the nursery was closed in 1999 after playing a key role for seven decades in BC's reforestation efforts

1932 Planting of logged-off land on West Thurlow Island

1936 Beginning of operational planting by the Forest Branch

1937 Mulholland's appeal for more efforts in reforestation

1938 Huge forest fire at Campbell River, destroying 31,000 ha of forests; in response, the Forest Branch accelerated reforestation program by planting 4,050 ha each year and this policy marked the beginning of production planting in BC
      Tree planting initiated by predecessor companies of MacMillan Bloedel

1945 Release of the first Sloan Royal Commission report, which set the stage for sustained yield management of BC's forests

1946 Establishment of Silviculture Fund

1947 Expansion of nursery capacity on the Coast and first production from the Duncan forest nursery

1947-8 Introduction of cut control regulation and establishment of area based tenures such as Forest Management Licenses and Farm Woodlots, which enhanced commitment to forest regeneration

1950 Supply by government of free seedlings for replanting of denuded privately owned forestland

1953 Denuded private forestland subject to Forest Service examination and planting of NSR private forestlands encouraged

1956 Release of the second Sloan Royal Commission report, calling for artificial regeneration in the Interior; building of a seed extraction plant at Duncan; initiation of a seed registration program; Forest Management Licenses renamed Tree Farm Licenses

1958   Organization of the Plus Tree Board; commencement of a genetically improved seed production program; pilot plantations in the Interior; establishment of small nurseries at Ranger Stations in the central Interior

1964   Forest Act amended to permit payment as compensation for post-logging silvicultural treatments by stumpage offset or by funds appropriated by the Legislature

1967   First production of seedlings from a forest nursery at Red Rock, close to Prince George; swelling of planting program beyond the Forest Service in-service capacity, and planting contracts being advertised for competitive bidding, marking the beginning of the separation of silviculture as a distinct industry from the forest industry

1971   Interior exceeded Coast in artificial regeneration for the first time in BC's history

1972   Forest Act amendment, urging all tenure holders to be responsible for post-logging reforestation

1975   Initiation of the biogeoclimatic ecosystem classification project, which was not completed until 1994, and this system has provided the foundation for silvicultural decision-making in the Province

1976   Release of the Pearse Royal Commission report

1978   Passage of a new Forest Act, Ministry of Forests Act, and Range Act, the above three Acts providing a new framework for the management, protection and conservation of BC's forest and range resources, replacing the Forest Act of 1912 and the Grazing Act of 1919

Timber Sale Harvesting License replaced by newly created Forest License; FL together with TFL and Timber License holders being required to submit a management and working plan with explicit regeneration commitment

1979   Intensive Forest Management Subsidiary Agreement was signed between federal and provincial governments as a cooperative support to silviculture. It was expected to terminate on March 31, 1984, but was extended for one additional year and expired on March 31, 1985

1980   Credit to Stumpage Regulation, under Forest Act (Section 88), was approved and ordered. Section 88 of the Forest Act became the principal means of financing forest management activities undertaken by forest tenure holders. It allowed the Ministry to reimburse licensees for approved activities, such as planting, by deducting the cost of activities from the stumpage the licensee would otherwise pay to the government

1980-1 White Paper on the Growing of Tree Seedlings, a significant policy decision concerning nurseries in that: (i) production from the Ministry of Forests nurseries would be constrained to about 100 million seedlings per year; (ii) all production above this level required to meet the five-year program goals would be achieved through the development and expansion of private nurseries, and (iii) the Ministry would pay for the cost of producing seedlings in private nurseries that are used to restock Crown land. As a result of this policy, in 1980-81 the Ministry approved 4 nurseries to be developed by the forest industry (licensees), and 7 commercial nurseries were allocated production

1981-2 The Duncan Seed Center facility became inadequate to meet future program needs, so planning for a new facility was begun during the year

1982 Western Silviculture Contractors Association established

1983-4 Shifting of more forest management responsibilities to TFL holders was proposed in an MoF discussion paper

1984-5 To improve cost-effectiveness, a large 2+0 container seedling program was initiated since some sites required larger planting stock, which could compete successfully with other vegetaion; seedlings of this type were intended to replace more costly transplanted seedlings on brushy sites

1985 The MoF *Five-Year Forest and Range Resource Program, 1985-1990* proposed substantial increase of planting to reach 200 million seedlings per year

1985 Provincial and federal governments signed the first Canada-British Columbia Forest Resource Development Agreement (FRDA I), $300 million, which emphasized the regeneration of 738,000 ha of good and medium sites of accessible forestland denuded prior to 1982

1986 Forest Stand Management Fund was established to fund silviculture and related activities to enhance the Provincial forest resource base. Matching contributions to this fund were anticipated from the federal government, forest industry, municipalities and forestry sector trade unions

A new seed center was established at Surrey, replacing the one at Duncan

A Memorandum of Understanding between the Ministry of Forests and Lands and the Ministry of Health on Minimum Standards for Silviculture Camps was reached

Canada signed with the United States a softwood Memorandum of Understanding (MOU) in which the Canadian government proposed to lift the US 15% duty and establish a 15% export tax on all softwood lumber exports to the US; it was agreed that this tax could be eliminated if provincial governments took "replacement measures" to raise stumpage fees to the equivalent level of the export tax

1987   BC government announced major policy changes via amendments to Forest Act, i.e., Bill 70:

- cost and responsibility for basic silviculture up to a free-to-grow condition was shifted to the industry (on Timber Sale Licenses the Crown would continue to carry out the silviculture work with funding from the Small Business Forest Enterprise Account)

- a new stumpage system, namely, the comparative value pricing system, was introduced, and an increase in stumpage was implemented

- the TFL program was proposed to expand from 28% to about 66% of the Provincial AAC to provide the industry with more tenure security

- 5% of major licensees' timber harvesting rights were reallocated under the SBFEP

Pre-Harvest Silvicultural Prescription was implemented and major licensees were obliged to prepare PHSPs for approval prior to harvesting

1988   Small Business Forest Enterprise Program and its Account were established

Introduction of a silviculture regulation, which outlined the contents for a PHSP and the requirements to meet basic silviculture obligations

Privatization of 8 government forest nurseries, with the Crown retaining 3 only

1990   Initiation of the Silvicultural System Program to investigate alternatives to conventional clearcutting and to identify their ecological, operational and socio-economic implications and opportunities

1991   FRDA II was signed—$200 million for 4 years, covering the fiscal period 1991-92 to 1994-95, and the primary objectives of the agreement were to conduct incremental silviculture (spacing, pruning, fertilization) and to fund initiatives in communications, extension, research, small-scale forestry, product and market development and economic and social analysis

Release of the Forest Resources Commission's report *The Future of Our Forests* that contains recommendations on silviculture and many other forest related aspects

1992 Establishment of the Commission on Resources and Environment (CORE)

National Forest Strategy formulated; the provincial, territorial and federal governments, as well as industry, labor, First Nations and environmental groups signed the Canada Forest Accord, committing to the concept of sustainable forestry

Announcement by the BC government of a Protected Areas Strategy, the goal being to achieve 12% of the Province under protection by the year 2000

1993 Establishment of BC 21 – the Forest Worker Development Program to promote local forestry contracting and offer opportunities for contractors to train workers in safety, quality and work skills

1994 Passage of three pieces of legislation:
- Forest Renewal Act
- Forest Practices Code of British Columbia Act
- Forest Land Reserve Act

Silviculture Regulation replaced by the Silviculture Practices Regulation, which established requirements for administrative penalties, improved soil conservation and maximum densities for all conifer species

Forest Renewal BC Plan was announced in April 1994. Forest Renewal BC, a new Crown agency, was established in the same year by the BC Forest Renewal Act. Forest Renewal BC's funding was derived from increases in stumpage and royalties paid by companies to harvest timber on Crown land. On May 1, 1994, stumpage rates were increased to begin generating this revenue

1995 The Forest Practices Code of British Columbia Act came into effect

1996 BC Forest Renewal Act amended to assign priority hiring to displaced forest workers on all FRBC funded projects

1997 On June 19, Premier Glen Clark announced the Jobs and Timber Accord, aiming at creating 39,800 new jobs by 2001; 5,000 of these jobs were expected to come from forest renewals

Established pursuant to BC Forest Renewal Amendment to deliver government silvicultural activities in the Coastal region, the New Forest Opportunities Ltd. acted as a union-only hiring hall for FRBC-funded silvicultural activities, except for basic tree planting

1999   Silviculture Workers Association of BC changed its name to the Canadian Reforestation Environmental Workers Society (CREWS)

* This chapter is based on an article (*The Forestry Chronicle* 74(6): 899-910) entitled "Silvicultural contracting in British Columbia" by S. Wang, G.C. van Kooten and B. Wilson; permission to use the article was granted by the Canadian Institute of Forestry.

7 Contracting Out or In-house Delivery?

Silvicultural activity has generally been studied as an investment decision problem (Reyner et al. 1996; Thompson et al. 1992). The evaluation and selection of silvicultural projects are dictated by a set of economic efficiency criteria, with funds allocated to investments that promise the greatest expected discounted net benefits over the specified project life. Rooted in Faustmann theory, this capital budgeting approach has dominated economic analyses of stand-level forests. However, the limitations of the conventional approach in guiding forest planning and management have been increasingly recognized. As mentioned in Chapter 3, efforts aimed at augmenting the approach have been made along at least three lines: (1) incorporating non-timber values into the standard economic analysis (Hartman 1976; Calish et al. 1978); (2) elevating the unit of analysis from the stand to the forest level, which led to debates on whether zoning can reconcile conflicts between dominant and multiple uses of forestland (Sahajananthan et al. 1998; Vincent and Binkley 1993), and on the role of the allowable cut effect in the harvesting of old-growth forests and regeneration (Schweitzer et al. 1972; Binkley 1980); and (3) including silviculture as a component of ecosystem management with attention to inter-regional and inter-generational considerations (Martin 1994; O'Hara and Oliver 1992).

While the conventional approach focuses on economic efficiency, it says little about how economic efficiency is implemented in practice and the role of institutional arrangements in bringing about efficiency. New institutional economists have investigated both the role of property rights and transactions costs, and how these relate to economic efficiency. Stating that economic behavior is influenced by differences in the structure of the property rights underlying the relationships among economic agents, the PR approach points out that agents respond to incentives in their performance of economic activities (Alchian and Demsetz 1973; Demsetz 1967). Since incentive schemes vary from one property rights regime to another, and property rights differ in dimensions measurable by identifiable attributes (such as comprehensiveness, duration, transferability, *et cetera*), the efficiency of economic activities can be analyzed by examining property rights for their incentive implications (see Haley and Luckert 1986). As mentioned in Chapter 3, Luckert and Haley (1993), and Zhang (1996), investigated forest tenure issues in BC's context.

Related to property rights theory, and yet distinct from it (see Williamson 1985, 1996), the TCE approach is concerned with firms' organizational behavior. Much of the analysis in the TCE literature is based on the argument that economic institutions develop to minimize the costs of transacting, either within firms or through market contractual arrangements that lie outside firms' organizational structures (Coase 1937; Williamson 1979, 1985, 1996). Recalling Chapter 4, the transaction costs literature has identified three characteristics of transactions that have important impacts on whether transactions are conducted within a firm. *Specificity* of physical and human assets dictates governance choices in contractual relations; an activity's *frequency* of occurrence is a crucial aspect determining how transactions are arranged; and *uncertainty* underlies the different capacities of alternative governance structures in responding effectively to disturbances in the institutional and physical environment (Klein et al. 1978; Alchian 1984; Williamson 1979, 1985, 1996; Joskow 1988; Masten et al. 1991). The TCE reasoning insists that firms behave in a transaction cost economizing manner so that the choice of governance modes regarding specific activities conforms to transaction characteristics. For instance, there is greater reliance on market contracting when investments have been made in assets of a general nature. As asset specificity increases, market contracting (with many parties) tends to give way to bilateral modes that involve two contractual parties. When assets are sufficiently specialized and activities to be performed occur at frequent intervals, reliance on contracts may give way to unified governance or in-house delivery (Williamson 1985).

Meanwhile, it is also quite common that private firms as well as public agencies choose to contract out distinct projects or assignments that are easily compartmentalized. Dohan (1976) found that products or services that are exceedingly technical and special in nature are typically contracted out on a "cost-plus" basis. The choice between private and public provision has been studied by Hart et al. (1997). When posing and answering the question whether the mode of provision matters even when the government pays, Shleifer (1998) argues that if the government has full knowledge in what it wants the producer to make, then it can put its demands into the contract, or a regulation and enforce this contract. In this case, the difference between in-house provision and contracting out disappears.

Use of the TCE approach in forestry is rather limited. Leffler and Rucker (1991) examined timber-harvesting contracts from the perspective of transaction costs and the efficient organization of production. Thomson and Lyne (1993) analyzed transaction costs identified as constraints to land rental in South Africa, while Goedecke and Ortmann (1993) looked into the structures of transaction costs in the context of labor contracting in South African forestry. In the remainder of this chapter, we apply the TCE approach to analyze contractual arrangements in BC's silviculture sector. We begin in the next section by presenting a theory of silvicultural contracting. An analytical model is presented in section 7.2, while the data and empirical results are provided in section 7.3.

7.1 A Theory of Contractual Choices in Silvicultural Operations

As noted in Chapter 4, the performance of economic activities relies on contracts, and contractual arrangements depend crucially on the incentive structures embodied therein. At an operational level, contractual modes have direct bearing on economic efficiency, particularly from the perspective of transaction costs. The TCE approach is characterized by a contracting orientation with transactions as the unit of analysis, and the TCE approach is concerned with the transaction cost implications of different governance structures (Williamson 1985).

Recalling earlier chapters, the predominant public ownership of forestlands (some 95%) and reliance on the private sector for operational activities characterize BC's forestry sector. As a result of the sweeping policy changes introduced in 1987, forest companies' involvement in forest management has extended beyond the stage of timber harvesting to include silviculture. Emphatically, forest companies are required by law to reforest after logging. The companies have three options regarding the manner in which the harvested site may be reforested. First, they could do it in-house by directly hiring labor and providing both management and supervision themselves. This is equivalent to the fixed wage contract in farm management. Alternatively, they could contract out the silvicultural work for a fixed lump sum payment. In this outsourcing contract that is equivalent to the rental contract in farm management, independent contractors who are not forest tenure holders by assumption hire silvicultural workers and provide supervision. Given the fact that silvicultural contracting market is highly competitive (i.e., with a perfectly elastic supply of contractors), the payment will be competed to the level at (or marginally above) the contractor's opportunity income. Finally, a forest company and a silvicultural contractor could make a share contract in which the former provides management, the latter supervision, and the output is shared. But, in the case of BC, sharing of output of silviculture has not taken place.

Silvicultural programs are comprised of activities that can be viewed as distinct transactions. Silvicultural activities may be described by identifiable (measurable) attributes, such as the needed level of technical skill, the degree of specialized equipment and tools employed, the frequency of the activity, and the degree of uncertainty in controling performance quality. Then, forest companies' organization of silvicultural operations can be examined by investigating whether existing silvicultural governance structures match the attributes of activities. Based on the TCE logic, we propose the following theory regarding the contractual mode for the performance of silvicultural activities:

> Silvicultural activities that tend to be performed in-house are those that are complex to manage, have a low degree of seasonality, and involve highly specific physical assets, and require high levels of human skills; contracting out occurs otherwise.

Several explanations are in order. To begin with, the most salient features that distinguish silvicultural activities from other (forestry) activities include the following. (1) Seasonality. For obvious reasons, silvicultural activities are not year-round operations and the window of opportunity in terms of timely performance being narrower for basic silviculture than for incremental silviculture. (2) Temporal and sequential dependence. As a rule of thumb, silvicultural activities are carried out in a sequential order, and they are tied to harvesting operations in the case of basic silviculture. (3) The difficulty of defining a tangible 'final product'. This basic distinction underscores a number of differences that persist in production processes and in the assets employed in the silviculture sector. First, the equipment and tools used in many silvicultural activities are not idiosyncratic in that they are not specific to a particular activity. In the case of basic silviculture, physical assets are generally unspecialized, inexpensive and tend to be much less relationship specific, and are not site or location specific. As a matter of fact, most of the physical assets used tend to be portable and mobile to permit employment at various locations.

Second, regarding human assets, except for a few activities, the skills, knowledge and experience required of planters and spacers do not demand extended apprenticeships, and, generally speaking, the skills are not specialized to forestry. Third, future forest crop is subject to random fluctuations because of such factors as pests and weather. In BC, large forest companies are better able to cope with uncertain situations. Hence, the likelihood of integration is expected to increase with increasing uncertainty. Finally, differences in the types of silvicultural activities influence the circumstances that give rise to opportunism and that determine the level of organization costs. Silviculture mainly involves organizing and coordinating a variety of relatively low-technology, labor-intensive activities. The requirement for highly technical, engineering-intensive activities takes place at the stage of preparing pre-harvest silvicultural prescriptions, which invariably are handled by company employees, often with a registered professional forester status.

In examining the issue of basic silviculture versus incremental silviculture, several propositions are offered: (1) the greater the total value of company-specific assets, the greater the likelihood of vertical integration in the form of an internally oriented vertical arrangement. According to this logic, since tree planting is not distinctive and asset specificity is low, therefore, outsourcing via market contracts is common for tree planting; (2) basic silviculture tends to be performed by contractors whereas incremental silviculture may be implemented in-house, or through special contractual arrangements; (3) since desirability of integration (or coordination) increases as work load increases, we expect to see more 'special arrangements' as more activities of higher-level silviculture increase; and (4) firm size is an important factor. Large companies are able to achieve economies of scale in acquiring and utilizing management skills; so, scale economies are likely to play an important role in virtually all integration decisions. Since large firms have greater ability to aggregate inputs, large-sized forest companies tend to maintain their own silvicultural crews or directly hire silvicultural workers.

To summarize, the choice of contractual forms depends on the types of activities, characteristics of the firms, contractors and workers. It is posited that activities that tend to be contracted out are those with the following features: high degree of seasonality in work scheduling, high degree of seasonality in labor demand (e.g., college students looking for summer jobs), and high intensity of work (e.g., tree planting is quite demanding physically). In contrast, activities that tend to be performed in-house are those that are less seasonal and require greater care and knowledge of production or a higher level of training. Finally, it must be noted that the above theorizing explicitly abstracts from risk considerations. This is not to say that risk factors are non-existent in silvicultural contracts. However, due to the fact that risk is a crucial factor that determines share contracts, and farm-management-type share contracts are rare in BC's silviculture sector, it is believed that ignoring the risk factor is, partially, justified.

7.2 Modeling Contracting out or In-house Contractual Modes

BC's restructuring of silvicultural arrangements provides an opportunity to test the applicability of the TCE analytical framework. In choosing how economic activities are to be performed, the TCE emphasizes dimensions of specificity, uncertainty and frequency. Hence, a forest company would be more likely to exercise control over an activity, by (vertically) integrating it into its hierarchical structure, if that activity requires specialized physical assets and human input, and complex management. The rationale is that companies will want to carry out activities in-house if contracting them out gives rise to higher transaction costs. Our research problem is to test the hypothesis that companies choose to undertake some silvicultural activities internally and/or contract out others to independent contractors as a means of minimizing transaction costs. The choice of contractual mode depends on organizational characteristics (company size and other distinguishing features), as well as on activity attributes that include the specificity of physical assets, human technical requirements that go along with the activity/asset, frequency of activities, and uncertainty in controlling performance quality.

Following Masten (1996), Majumdar and Ramaswamy (1994), and Masten et al. (1989), suppose G^1 and G^2 represent alternative contractual arrangements for performing a specific silvicultural task. The preferred alternative G^* that is actually chosen is determined as follows:

(7.1) $$G^* = \min [C^1(G^1), C^2(G^2)],$$

where C^1 and C^2 are associated transaction costs corresponding to contractual arrangements G^1 and G^2, respectively. The levels of transaction costs determine contractual choices, and transaction costs can be related to the observable transaction characteristics and firm attributes:

(7.2) $\qquad C^j = c(\beta'X^j) + e^j, \quad j = 1, 2, ..., n,$

where transaction costs are a function of the matrix X of observable firm characteristics and activity attributes that affect organization costs; β is a vector of parameters; and j identifies the firm (observation). The error terms are given by e.

The variables used in the model are explained in Table 7.1. For the choice between the contractual forms, "outsourcing" and "in-house" performance of silvicultural activities, the dichotomous choice model can be estimated using probit regression (see Maddala 1983; Greene 1993). In that case, the dependent variable, y, takes on the value 0 for contracting out (to an independent silvicultural contractor) and 1 for in-house performance of the activity. However, many BC forest companies do not rely solely on in-house or outsourcing for performance of silvicultural activities – the choice is not necessarily binary as many firms both contract out silvicultural activities *and* perform them in-house. Hence, the binary probit model needs to be extended to accommodate multiple choices – contracting out, in-house and a combination of these. In that case, an ordered probit model needs to be used (see Maddala 1983; Greene 1993), with $y = 0$ if the firm contracts out the activity, $y = 1$ if the firm is engaged in both contracting and performing the activity in-house, and $y = 2$ if the firm performs the activity solely in-house.

Table 7.1: Variable Description

Dependent variable	
y (probit)	0 = contracting out, 1 = in-house performance of activity
y (ordered probit)	0 = contracting out, 2 = in-house, 1 = combination of both
Independent variables	
TCE attributes	
– technical skill	5-point scale from 1 to 5, 1 is low and 5 is high
– frequency	5-point scale from 1 to 5, 1 is low and 5 is high
– uncertainty	5-point scale from 1 to 5, 1 is low and 5 is high
– physical asset specificity	5-point scale from 1 to 5, 1 is low and 5 is high
Firm characteristics	
– AAC	0 for ≤ 0.5 million m^3, 1 otherwise
– Company category	1 = company with stocks publicly traded, 0 = otherwise
– Silvicultural division	0 = firm does not have, 1 = firm does have
– Region	0 = BC Interior, 1 = BC Coast (Vancouver Forest Region)

The explanatory variables are divided into two categories, activity attributes and firm characteristics. Four TCE attributes are identified. (1) Technical skills refer to the specificity of human skills required to perform the silvicultural task. It is generally the case that basic silvicultural activities like planting, brushing and weeding require lower levels of skills than incremental silviculture activities like spacing, pruning and so forth. Specifically, brushing is the process of using a power saw to cut down trees, fireweed, ferns and anything else that interferes with the growth of planted or desirable natural trees on a block. Weeding, also known as weed whacking among silvicultural workers, is similar to brushing. It involves knocking down fireweed on freshly planted blocks some 3 - 6 weeks after planting, to give seedlings a chance against the weeds. Pruning involves using a handsaw to cut off the branches within, say, 3 meters of the ground. Although it does not require sophisticated tools, good pruning demands a great deal of skill and training on the part of the worker. Finally, spacing is the process of cutting down 5 to 15 year-old trees to make room for desirable species and to let the timber trees grow. Involving the use of a chainsaw, spacing is usually more difficult to learn than brushing. More detailed explanations of specific silvicultural activities are provided in Chapter 8. (2) Frequency refers to the rate of occurrence of an activity and time interval between activities (e.g., tree planting occurs only during certain months of the year). (3) Uncertainty indicates the degree of complexity in controlling performance quality. (4) Specificity of physical assets indicates the types and levels of up-front investment required, the re-employability of the equipment and tools involved, and whether the equipment and tools used are specialized or standard by nature. Based on ratings by industry respondents, all TCE attributes are measured on a 5-point scale, with 1 referring to low and 5 to high specificity, uncertainty, *et cetera.*

Firms are characterized by several variables. A firm's (or operational division's) AAC is used as a dummy variable for a firm's commitment to silviculture, with 0 for an AAC of half a million m^3 or less and 1 for AACs greater than half a million m^3 (see Table 7.1). Although AAC may be indicative of company size, this is not always the case. We also employ a company category variable, set equal to 1 for companies whose stocks are publicly traded and 0 otherwise. While the AAC dummy is primarily linked to the resource base, the "stock-traded" category variable is likely a better indicator of company size. The two variables are not the same because some companies may be large, with publicly traded stock, but have less AAC as they are involved more heavily in wood processing. Both variables are hypothesized to have a positive effect on a firm's decision to adopt in-house contractual forms. Our reasoning is the following. Companies with higher levels of AAC have a larger commitment to regenerate logged-off sites; hence, they are subject to a greater degree of public scrutiny for compliance with relevant regulations. In essence, their "size in the woods" makes them a target for environmental groups. Therefore, companies will likely want to rely more on in-house performance of silviculture to secure compliance and performance quality. The same is true of companies whose stocks are publicly traded, because their behavior, including silvicultural performance, involves an issue of credibility.

A dummy variable for the existence of a separate silvicultural division is also included as an explanatory variable. It is hypothesized that the variable is positively related to a firm's decision to undertake silviculture in-house, based on the rationale that there tend to be more opportunities to save on organizational costs if a relevant institutional structure is in place within a firm.

Finally, a regional dummy variable is included to distinguish between firms or operational divisions in the BC Interior (=0) or on the Coast (=1). To some extent, this variable captures forest tenure as the Interior is dominated by Timber Supply Areas (where volume-based tenures such as FLs prevail), while the Coast is characterized by TFLs and private lands (area-based tenures). Because tenure arrangements are institutionally stronger on the Coast (e.g., TFLs versus FLs), we expect that more silvicultural activities are conducted in-house on the Coast than in the Interior. We do not use an explicit tenure variable due to the exceptional complexity of the Province's tenure system.

7.3 Empirical Results

A mail-out survey of BC's forest companies (or their operational divisions in the case of large companies) was conducted by the authors during the spring of 1997. Prior to this, in-depth personal interviews were conducted with 5 companies, with this information used to construct the subsequent mail survey. A total of 117 questionnaires were sent out, each accompanied by a cover letter explaining the purpose of the survey. The response rate was 88% (103 responses).

Survey results indicate that, measured by AAC, a large number of BC's forest companies (or operational divisions in the case of large companies) are relatively small in size because only 45% indicated that their AAC exceeded half a million m³. Some 44% of the major licensees have separate silvicultural divisions, and the earliest such divisions appeared in the 1950s. However, most firms that chose to have separate silvicultural divisions did not do so until the 1980s or the 1990s, which coincided with the government's major policy changes. In terms of geographic distribution of respondents, 40% of firms operate on the Coast and the remainder in the Interior. Silvicultural activities are either contracted out or performed in-house, although some firms adopt both forms at the same time. A summary of activities and contractual forms is provided in Table 7.2, while the four transaction-cost attributes of major silvicultural activities are presented in Table 7.3.

Table 7.2: Silvicultural Performance in BC by Contractual Form (%)

Activity	In-house	Contracting out	Both
Cone collection	14.3	77.4	8.3
Seedling production	8.5	78.0	13.4
Site preparation	23.1	52.7	24.2
Planting	12.7	63.7	23.5
Brushing and weeding	6.1	77.6	16.3
Spacing	8.5	80.5	11.0
Pruning	7.0	87.7	5.3
Thinning	7.0	88.4	4.7
Fertilizing	8.8	85.3	5.9
Surveying	36.1	24.7	39.2

Table 7.3: Transaction Cost Attributes of Silvicultural Activities (Mean on 5-point scale)

Activity	Technical skill		Frequency		Uncertainty		Physical specificity	
	Mean	SE	Mean	SE	Mean	SE	Mean	SE
Cone collection	2.35	0.12	2.23	0.11	2.24	0.11	2.92	0.17
Seedling production	4.54	0.09	4.52	0.12	1.78	0.09	3.94	0.13
Site preparation	3.78	0.10	4.03	0.13	2.00	0.10	2.96	0.12
Planting	3.54	0.09	4.75	0.06	1.90	0.10	3.03	0.13
Brushing and weeding	2.90	0.10	3.77	0.11	2.38	0.12	2.60	0.11
Spacing	3.23	0.09	2.98	0.13	2.08	0.10	2.26	0.11
Pruning	2.74	0.11	1.90	0.12	1.96	0.11	3.06	0.14
Thinning	3.48	0.12	1.93	0.13	2.36	0.12	2.63	0.13
Fertilizing	3.10	0.15	1.50	0.10	2.49	0.15	3.05	0.17
Surveying	4.39	0.08	4.83	0.05	1.90	0.09	2.24	0.13

With 103 of 117 questionnaires returned, and given 10 silvicultural activities (see Table 7.2), 1,030 observations are potentially available.

However, the number of observations is only 697 for three reasons. First, we asked respondents to report only silvicultural activities in the most recent time period, so many firms indicated that they had engaged in only several of the activities. Second, some firms did not provide answers about one or more TCE attributes, although the corresponding activity did take place, thus rendering the entire observation unusable (this was the case for 11 of 103 responses). Finally, 7 respondents were corporate-level managers. Since their operational divisions also responded, only observations from these were used to avoid double counting.

LIMDEP Version 7.0 (Greene 1995) is used for the probit and ordered probit regressions. For the probit, three sets of explanatory variables are considered – TCE attributes alone, firm characteristics alone and the two sets of explanatory variables together (see Table 7.1). The reason for so doing is to examine the effects of TCE attributes and firm characteristics, first in isolation from one another and then in a combined fashion.

The probit model results are presented in Table 7.4. In terms of goodness of fit criteria, the likelihood ratios are all high and statistically significant. The four TCE variables are statistically significant in most instances. Specifically, a positive (negative) sign on an explanatory variable indicates that higher values increase (decrease) the probability that an activity is performed in-house. The findings generally confirm the TCE theory to the effect that those activities requiring a high level of technical skill, occurring with a high frequency, having a high degree of uncertainty, and demanding specialized physical assets tend to be performed by the firm itself (i.e., in-house). Of the four firm characteristics, the AAC and "stock traded" category dummy variables are statistically significant and have the expected positive signs. The separate silvicultural division variable turns out to be insignificant. The reason is probably due to the structure and composition of such a division at the firm level. Interviews with industry representatives indicated that many companies indeed had separate silvicultural divisions in place. However, in some cases, it was a division with one or two people, say a forester and a technician. Thus, the existence of such a division, and its limited size and lack of resources, seemed to account for the division's failure to play an institutional role in bringing about more in-house performance of silvicultural activities. As noted above, the sign of the coefficient on the regional dummy variable was predicted to be positive. However, the regression results do not support the hypothesis that stronger tenure arrangements would lead to greater in-house performance of silvicultural activities.

Initially, we divided our sample according to whether activities involved basic or incremental silviculture. However, a Chow test and a Goldfeld-Quandt test indicated that the two sub-samples were generated by the same process, so, separate regressions were unnecessary (see Kennedy 1992). This provides support for the notion that BC is still at the basic silviculture stage, and that it cannot be viewed as a jurisdiction that has progressed to a stage where incremental silviculture is also important, as mentioned in Chapter 6 above.

The results of the ordered probit regression are presented in Table 7.5. The likelihood ratio test statistic, or χ^2 value, indicates that the ordered probit model is statistically highly significant, and the general TCE hypotheses are confirmed.

It turns out that the technical skill variable is highly significant, as are the other TCE attributes variables. Concerning firm characteristics, the AAC and "stock traded" category variables are statistically significant, having the hypothesized positive signs; the silvicultural division variable and the region dummy variable are statistically insignificant. It should be noted that, in our ordered probit model, the coding of the dependent variable, i.e., 0, 1 and 2, reflects only an order or ranking. In other words, the difference between a 0 and a 1 cannot be treated as equivalent to the difference between a 1 and a 2. Furthermore, the sign of the coefficients must be interpreted with caution. When an estimate is positive, this means that the probability that $y=0$ must decline and that probability that $y=2$ must rise, but the direction of the change in the middle choice ($y=1$) is ambiguous (see Greene 1993; Kennedy 1992; Maddala 1983).

The NIE is concerned with questions such as when activities will be carried out through the market and when they will be carried out within firms. In-house delivery and contracting out are alternative means for carrying out silvicultural activities. In other words, the allocation of activity as between market-based contracting out and corporate hierarchy inclined in-house delivery should not be taken as given. In-house operations tend to avoid duplication and reduce the amount of paperwork required to conduct business. There are advantages in specialization. Silvicultural contractors can do a better job in basic silviculture. Also, the focus and line of business encourage specialization in knowledge and management.

Table 7.4: Contractual Choice for Silviculture in BC, Probit Results[a]

Variable	Estimate	Asymptotic t-statistic[b]	Elasticity at means
TCE attributes			
Technical skill	0.1615	3.388***	0.656
Frequency	0.1638	4.034***	0.713
Uncertainty	0.0802	1.610*	0.193
Physical asset specificity	0.0741	1.892**	0.250
Constant	-2.0878	-8.273***	-2.449
N = 697			
χ^2 : 51.16 (4); critical value = 13.28 (0.01 level)			
Pseudo R^2: 0.410			
Correct prediction: 68.6%			
Firm characteristics			
AAC	0.2198	2.129**	0.104
Company category	0.1816	1.628*	0.135
Separate silvicultural division	0.0207	0.217	0.012
Region	-0.1398	-1.237	-0.049
Constant	-0.6863	-6.405***	-0.788
N = 697			
χ^2 : 9.58 (4); critical value = 9.49 (0.05 level)			
Pseudo R^2: 0.374			
Correct prediction: 69.3%			
TCE attributes plus firm characteristics			
Technical skill	0.1692	3.524***	0.690
Frequency	0.1611	3.898*	0.705
Uncertainty	0.0892	1.754**	0.216
Physical asset specificity	0.0747	1.875**	0.253
AAC	0.1579	1.469*	0.077
Company category	0.2577	2.228**	0.196
Separate silvicultural division	0.0291	0.282	0.018
Region	-0.1909	-1.617*	-0.068
Constant	-2.3206	-8.433***	-2.735
χ^2: 61.27 (8); critical value = 20.09 (0.01 level)			
Pseudo R^2: 0.418			
Correct prediction: 69.0%			

[a] Dependent variable: 0 = contracting out, 1 = in-house.
[b] *** significant at the 0.01 level, ** at 0.05 level, * at 0.1 level.

Table 7.5: Contractual Choice for Silviculture, Ordered Probit Results[a]

Variable	Estimate	Asymptotic t-value[b]
Technical skill	0.1893	4.349***
Frequency	0.1199	3.026***
Uncertainty	0.0653	1.384*
Physical asset specificity	0.0594	1.562*
AAC	0.2355	2.746***
Company category	0.1718	1.801**
Separate silvicultural division	0.0445	0.816
Region	-0.1495	-0.033
Constant	-2.1106	-7.626***
MU (1)	0.6173	11.782***
N:	697	
χ^2:	58.20 (8)[c]	
Pseudo R^2:	0.614	
Correct prediction:	69.2%	

[a] Dependent variable: 0 = contracting out, 2 = in-house, 1 = combined.
[b] *** significant at the 0.01 level, ** at 0.05 level, and * at 0.1 level.
[c] Critical χ^2 value = 20.09 at 0.01 level.

The TCE approach is, by and large, an extension of the neoclassical economics approach. Rather than replace the conventional analysis, the TCE approach augments it by drawing attention to organizational modes, with emphasis on contractual relations. It argues, in essence, that the costs of transacting should be incorporated into the analysis of the total costs of economic activities. By directing investigators' attention to the fact that contracting practices and contract provisions tend to vary in a systematic and predictable manner with the attributes of transactions so that some costs of transacting may be reduced, the TCE logic implies that neither pure market-based institutions nor vertically integrated firms necessarily prevail. The choice is often dictated by the nature of the transactions involved.

This chapter demonstrates the applicability of the TCE approach to silvicultural contracting in BC. It assumes that firms make decisions about whether to contract out or perform an activity in-house on the basis of the activity's transaction costs, with the aim of minimizing these costs. Empirical results confirm the general validity of the TCE theory, and transaction cost economizing behavior is evident from the choice of contractual forms by forest companies. For the purpose of synchronizing the attributes of various silvicultural activities with firm-specific characteristics, companies choose to contract out straightforward and labor-intensive activities, while performing in-house those operations that require a high level of technical skill and the use of specialized equipment. When predicting what activities will be contracted out or undertaken in-house, one therefore needs to examine the transaction cost attributes of the activities in question and the characteristics of the firms involved. One policy implication is that if the Province wishes to encourage forest companies to expand their hiring of workers to do more in-house silvicultural work, measures that may be considered include extending the work period and reducing seasonality of work, and raising technical specifications and quality standards. Conversely, standardization of technical requirements and reduction of uncertainty surrounding management and quality control will provide more opportunities for independent silvicultural contractors.

* This chapter is based on an article originally published as "Silvicultural contracting in British Columbia: A transaction cost economics analysis," *Forest Science* 45(2): 272-279. © Society of American Foresters, 5400 Grosvenor Lane, Bethesda, MD 20814-2198. Reproduced with permission.

8 How to Hire and Pay Silvicultural Workers?

Since Coase (1937) first explained that firms economize on transaction costs, increasing attention has focused on organizational structures in order to understand the rationale behind firms' contractual arrangements. As discussed in earlier chapters, transaction costs may be lowered through the selection of appropriate contractual forms that match the physical attributes of the activities undertaken and the institutional characteristics of production units and agents. At the firm level, production of a good or service occurs either by contracting out the activity or doing it in-house. Generally speaking, activities tend to be performed in-house if they are complex to manage, requiring high levels of human skill, occur frequently, and/or involve highly specific physical assets.

With outsourcing, payment schemes vary with different contractual forms, but lump-sum payments upon completion of certain tasks are the usual method for paying contractors (Figure 8.1). When contractors hire workers, or when firms perform the activity in-house by hiring workers directly, there are at least two options for paying them – according to their accomplishments (a piece wage) or on the basis of time spent working (a wage or a salary). The means by which workers are compensated falls under the realm of contractual arrangements and organizational structures, and different payment schemes have distinctive transaction cost implications (Spence 1975; Roumasset and Uy 1980; Williamson 1980).

Contracting out has over the past two decades become more prominent in BC's silviculture sector. Previously, in Chapter 6, we examined the historical forces that shaped the patterns of silvicultural contracting in BC, while, in Chapter 7, we used a TCE approach to analyze the relationship between organizational structure and the choice of firms either to contract out silvicultural activities or perform them in-house. However, we neglected the relationship between organizational form and the method used to compensate workers for performing silvicultural activities when these are conducted in-house (and not by contractors). In-house performance of silvicultural operations by forest companies and their woodland divisions is not uncommon. Since firms are assumed to pick contractual arrangements to economize on transaction costs in every aspect of organizational management, it is worthwhile to examine the conditions under which firms use different payment schemes. Research findings indicate that, notwithstanding other differences, contractual arrangements can be reduced to the choice and design of payment schemes, because appropriate reward systems induce optimal effort from workers (Datta et al. 1986).

The objective of this chapter is threefold. First, we provide an overview of the processes by which independent contractors and, to a lesser extent, forest companies, bid on silvicultural contracts, hire workers and organize operations. Second, we highlight some of the salient features of the theory of payment schemes relating to BC's silviculture sector, explaining the logic of the prevailing payment methods from the TCE perspective. Finally, we develop a simple model to test several transaction cost hypotheses using data from a 1997 survey of BC forest companies.

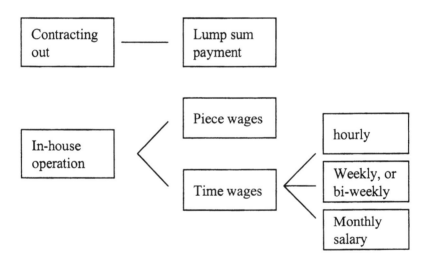

Figure 8.1: Contractual Forms and Payment Schemes

8.1 Organization of Silvicultural Operations

Recalling that, until the late 1960s, the BC Forest Service (which became a Ministry in 1979) was solely responsible for organizing and financing reforestation activities on public forestland. With the rapid expansion of harvesting operations, the burden of reforesting an increasing area of logged-off sites compelled the Forest Service gradually to release its reforestation responsibilities to the large, integrated forest companies and to an emerging silvicultural contracting force. As a result of sweeping policy changes in BC's forestry sector, full responsibility for post-harvesting regeneration was transferred to the private sector in 1987.

8.1.1 The contract bidding process

A silvicultural contract is an agreement entered into by a silvicultural contractor and the organization that pays for the project, such as a forest tenure holder or a Ministry of Forests (MoF) district. In the case of a tree-planting project, among other things, the contract includes the following:

- the size and location of cut-blocks to be planted,
- the species and density of trees to be planted,
- planting specifications such as the appropriate techniques for tree handling and root media,
- procedures for assessing the quality of planting,
- dispute settlement mechanisms,
- planting schedule, and
- safety, camp and other employee regulations.

BC's contractual arrangements for silvicultural activities entail a mixture of an open "low-bid" system and a system of "invitational tenders from preferred contractors". For open bidding contracts, when projects are available for bidding, interested contractors have an opportunity of viewing the cut-blocks to be planted before submitting a sealed bid. Depending on who is responsible for silviculture, the MoF or the licensee (i.e., the tenure holder), contracts are generally awarded to the lowest bidder. Obviously, the "low-bid" approach tends to attract new entrants who may seek to win contracts by underbidding, but subsequently may shirk their responsibilities in order to realize contract goals. During the early 1980s, the "low-bid" system resulted in a high turnover rate of contractors, leading to frequent defaults in payment to workers and bankruptcy of contracting firms. As a result, a set of enforceable contract rules has been adopted. The most important one is the requirement that the successful bidder must put down a minimum security deposit of $10,000, which the contractor loses in the event that (a) the contractor fails to start the contract, (b) the planting quality fails to reach a minimal standard, or (c) the contractor fails to complete the contract. On account of the security deposit, contractors will want to ensure satisfactory performance of the contract, because losing the deposit will have adverse consequences, such as less future work, bad reputation and so forth. In the event that the lowest bidder does not accept the contract, the next-to-lowest bidder is offered the contract, and so on. It should be noted that contractors receive a list of all the bidders and prices, so they can see where they stand in the competition (Stolz 2000).

Most tenure-holding companies do not use an open-bid approach. The transfer to forest companies in 1987 of physical and financial obligations for silviculture, along with the mandatory requirement for the attainment of a free-to-grow status, has promoted the use of different approaches to choosing a silvicultural contractor, such as "select bidding", "preferred contractors" and "direct negotiations". Specifically, forest companies generally invite a few reputable, independent silvicultural contractors to view cut-blocks and bid on a project. They select the contractor who offers the best combination of low price and quality work. This approach does not guarantee that the lowest bidder will necessarily be awarded the contract. Occasionally, a so-called "direct award" contract is employed. It occurs when a forest company sets the price and asks a contractor whether it is interested in the job, or, alternatively, when the company offers a contractor a job, asking the contractor to view the cut-blocks and propose a price. The "direct award" contracts are the least common among the various contract types.

In recent years, the BC MoF has modified its bidding approach to include requirements for non-price qualities. Under what is known as a "proposal bidding" approach, contractors are asked to bid on contracts and explain why he/she is best suited to undertake the project. This involves demonstrating that the contractor can (a) maintain adequate camp and safety standards; (b) finish silvicultural contracts with 100% payment to workers and a 93% minimum job-quality performance; and (c) use mostly experienced planters. This makes it difficult for new entrants as proof of these requirements is based on an established record of performance. The result of this new approach, known as "the lowest qualified bid", is that contracts are no longer always awarded on a low-bid basis, but may be awarded on the basis of other contracting features deemed desirable.

8.1.2 Hiring workers: payment schemes and management

After a contractor agrees to undertake the silvicultural operations specified in a contract, he or she is responsible for hiring, supervising and paying silvicultural workers, and providing accommodations, safety equipment and transportation for the workers. The contracting firm is subject to Provincial regulations regarding its operations and employees, such as minimum wage laws, safety, camp and transportation standards, terms of employment, payment, dismissal and so on.

A large proportion of tree planters consists of university students, whose summer vacation begins just when the planting season gets underway in most places (late April, early May). Most tree-planting contractors therefore do the bulk of their hiring at universities during February and March. Stolz (2000) lists physical fitness, mental stamina and desperate need for cash as three most important qualifications for a tree planter. Generally, contracting firms prefer to hire people who have familiarity with tree planting, have realistic expectations and an understanding of the working environment, will work for at least two planting seasons, and want to make serious money (i.e., work hard). In other words, planting companies do not want to hire those who are simply looking for "a new experience" or have a desire "to improve the environment". After all, silvicultural activities are business undertakings. Unless they have experience, those graduating the following year are unlikely to be hired by established contracting firms, because they are unlikely to be available the following planting season.

A typical summer planting season lasts two months in BC, usually May and June, averaging 42-45 days of actual planting. This indicates the seasonality of tree planting. Tree planters usually work for 4 days before getting one day off. The 4-day-on, one-day-off scheme is believed to work better than other schemes because it helps keep planters more focused and physically fit (Shand 1999).

All seasoned contractors know that getting new workers off to a quick, productive start is a first priority in silvicultural operations. Experience plays an important role in silvicultural work. For instance, as far as manual release of seedlings is concerned, production rates for experienced workers average about 0.2 ha per day, while that of novice workers averages half that rate (Fiddler and McDonald 1990). There are opportunities for a silvicultural worker to improve productivity and technical efficiency.

In a planting job, questions that the planter needs to think about include: Should I carry all materials (seedlings, etc.) at once, or make runs?

Should I move materials into my block before planting, or return to the cache for them? A cache is where seedlings are stored on the block under a tarp. Some of these questions involve ergonomics issues. For instance, a seemingly simple choice of shovel types may have direct bearing on the planter's health as well as his/her pay.[1]

Similarly, the way in which trees are planted may not be as simple as it first appears. It is counter-intuitive that the conventional "line planting" is not common with experienced workers. The reason is that "line planting" generates a "dead walk" – moving through open land without planting or travelling through planted areas instead of planting. Some useful tips for minimizing "dead walk" include (Stolz 2000; Shand 1999):

- planting in the shape of L – planting along one side of a block, and then across the back, to "fill" the land in an "L" shape;
- area planting, which involves planting small sections of land that are defined by natural borders, such as fallen trees, stumps, brush and rock, this method being highly efficient for smaller seedlings; and
- back-filling, which refers to planting the part of the block away from the cache/road first.

Tree planters have to pay for most things, mainly camp and equipment costs. Camp costs average $23-27 per day, more specifically, $20-23 per day in bush camps, $25-30 per day in logging camps, and $8-15 per day in hotels (where no food is included). Full set-up costs for equipment and gear for novice workers amount to $600-800; this includes camping gear, such as a tent, tarp and sleeping bag, and planting gear, such as boots, shovels, planting bag and raingear. According to Shand (1999), in some cases, silvicultural contractors provide new gloves and spikes at no extra cost to the planters. The rationale is that, if the planters are allowed to use their own gloves and spikes, they are not likely to change them often enough. In many logged-off sites, sharp corks constitute a concern from the perspective of safety. Planters do get hurt and, when injury occurs, the Workers' Compensation Board may be involved. With new spikes, planters are definitely more productive because they are less likely to fall.

Prior to the 1970s, the BC Forest Service used hourly wages to pay tree planters, but piece rates were adopted when the Forest Service began to

---

[1] Stolz (2000) discusses the advantages in using a "D-handle shovel" versus some other types.

engage silvicultural contractors. Contracts were awarded according to a "low-bid" system and implemented on an area basis, with contractors paying piece rates to their workers. By the early 1980s, planters received an average $0.15-0.20 per tree, depending on the terrain (Davis-Case 1985). However, this rate has not increased much over the years, in spite of the implementation of the Forest Practices Code that has resulted in the adoption of higher standards and the use of larger seedlings in some areas.

While piece rates remain the dominant modes of payment for planting activities, time-based wages are also common. As noted earlier, when the Forest Service was still involved in reforestation, crews were hired on an hourly wage basis. Today the BC MoF employs silvicultural contractors, which use both piece rates and time-based wages. In the latter case, a variety of pay periods are used, with bi-weekly or weekly being most typical (Lousier et al. 1989). Upon an employee's request, the contractor may make proportional advance payments, with the balance settled 2 to 4 weeks after project completion or at the end of the planting season. Tree planters are paid in advance a minimum of $250 per week, and then receive their pay on a piecework basis (Shand 1999). New contractors tend to rely more on time rates to gain knowledge and experience, often switching to piece rates at a later point in time.

Intriguingly, forest companies in BC, many of which are well established, use time rates as well as piece wages to pay silvicultural crews. They rely on piece rates considerably less than do the silvicultural contractors (Table 8.1). We believe that the greater scope of silvicultural activities that the companies undertake enables the use of a variety of payment methods to lower transaction costs.

When payment is made on the basis of piecework, it is the number of trees planted that counts. Consequently, excessively large-sized seedlings are unpopular with planters for the simple reason that fewer trees of large size can be planted within a unit time period. When planting is paid by the hectare, while it is generally still true that fast planters get more pay, the speed of walking and the area covered are important. The area walked is particularly important for checkers of tree survivals. Under hectare planting, workers have every incentive to plant as few trees as possible by employing the trick of wide spacing. They will want to walk as fast as they can to cover as many blocks as possible within a certain period of time (Shand 1999). For some activities that do not involve machinery or tools, piecework is highly popular. Because piecework stimulates production, activities such as manual release are believed increasingly to be on a per-tree basis (Fiddler and McDonald 1990).

Table 8.1:   Payment Schemes for Silvicultural Workers in BC (Responses to a Survey)

Payment method	Silvicultural contractors	Forest companies
	% indicating use[a]	
Hourly wage	51.9	40.8
Piece rate	67.3	25.2
Salary (other time rates)	17.3	34.0
Number of respondents	52	103
Number contacted	139	117

Source: Wang (1997).
[a] May not add to 100% as payment schemes are not mutually exclusive.

As far as tree planters' wages go, prices for MoF contracts tend to be similar across the board due to the practice of open market bidding. The benchmark wage for experienced planters on BC MoF contracts is about $200 per day. Good planters will likely average more, for instance $220 per day, to make up for slow times. New planters average about $120 per day in their first month of employment. However, forest companies that use select bidding or direct-award contracting invariably offer higher prices than those who work on MoF contracts. Compared with other provinces (e.g., Ontario), planters earn more money in BC, in spite of the relatively higher levels of skill requirement and greater variability of terrain (see Table 8.2). According to Stolz (2000), high-income planters in Canada prefer to work for small contractors in BC's southern Interior or on the Coast. Compared with those that primarily take contracts from the MoF, the contractors that have established good working relationships with private clients and experienced planters tend to provide higher-paying jobs.

Specifically, people are usually paid less for brushing than for planting, around $14 per hour versus $25-30 per hour for planting (Shand 1999). As compensation for brushing is on a per ha basis, brushing almost never pays as well as planting. However, it is physically much easier. Some silvicultural workers undertake brushing to take a break from planting while continuing to earn some money. As a general rule of thumb, a brushing contract that pays below $250 per ha is not worthwhile considering from a silvicultural worker's perspective (Stolz 2000). Spacing and pruning are also paid on an area basis, and workers tend to earn more in these tasks than in brushing activities.

Table 8.2: Daily Earnings of Tree Planters in BC and Ontario ($)

Planter type	BC	Ontario
Novice planters	150 - 175	120 - 150
Veteran planters	200 - 250	170 - 200

Source: Stolz (2000).

Generally, for independent contractors, 45-50% of the bid price goes to the planters and the non-planting workers as wages. This percentage is usually higher for forest license holding companies, where 60% goes to wages (Wang 1997). Other components of the cost of a planting contract include: 15-20% for the use of vehicles for transportation, 6% for support staff, 15-17% for office overhead costs, insurance and miscellaneous items, and 8-10% for profit (Stolz 2000). While silvicultural workers pay a certain percentage of their earnings into the Canada Pension Plan and Unemployment Insurance, in addition to personal income taxes, contracting firms are required to match their employees' contributions and also pay a fee to the Workers' Compensation Board. Obviously, an employer must have adequate knowledge about his/her employees' hourly and daily pay rates. Also important are the daily costs of pension contributions and workers' compensation, health and dental plans. However, for contractors that use piece rates to pay silvicultural workers, the issue of holiday pay and overtime pay is not relevant, as these are the concern of the individual workers.

The size of a firm is a useful indicator of company attributes. Generally, large contracting firms tend to hire a larger proportion of new planters. Stolz (2000) reveals that the owners' lack of personal contact with the planters, slow response to planter problems and poor bids are the hallmark of many large contractors. In comparison, medium-sized firms usually have a fair number of experienced planters and pay reasonably well. However, small contracting firms are the cream of BC's planting contractors; they are the ones that hire mainly recommended experienced planters and usually have long-term agreements with local tenure-holding forest companies. The main features that characterize contracting firms are summarized in Table 8.3.

Table 8.3: Silvicultural Workers' Perspectives of Contracting Firms

Contractual aspects	Characteristics of a "good" contractor	Characteristics of a "bad" contractor
Hiring pattern and worker composition	Hiring 60 - 100% experienced planters and having mostly returning workers, with a large proportion of older workers	Hiring mostly inexperienced planters and having very few experienced and/or returning workers, with a large proportion of younger workers
Work scheduling	4 days on/one day off (4 and 1), or 5 and 2, and 8.5 hours/day to maximize productivity and prevent burnout	Irregular schedule and more than 4 days in a row, e.g., 6 and 1, 12 and 2, and longer than 8.5 hours/day
Bonus and deduction rule	Not deducting more than 5% of pay (this is just to cover possible quality fines) if one leaves the contract before it ends	Using a bonus system for planters who stick around, and deducting pay if one leaves before the contract ends
Contract client and bidding system used	Working for private (i.e., non-Ministry) clients for higher bid prices that use either select bid or direct award approaches	Working mostly for the Ministry instead of forest companies for contracts awarded to the lowest bidder
Camp costs requirement	Not offering free camp costs, which is usually associated with higher piece wages	Offering free camp costs, which almost certainly means lower piece wages for the planters
Management style	Helping interested applicants to get in touch with experienced planters for equipment advice and recommendations about the firm	Making no effort in putting new recruits in touch with returning workers
Contract clause	Making available formally prepared employment contract with sufficient details	Contracts of employment being either non-existent or poorly prepared

Source: Adapted from Stolz (2000) and Shand (1999).

When a tree-planting contract is awarded, the price paid the contractor is generally the original bid price times the assessed quality as expressed in terms of a percentage. For instance, if a contractor bids at 20 cents per tree and gets 90% quality, the contractor will be paid 18 cents per tree. This rule affects planters' pay in that contractors pay their planters according to the quality of planting performance. This is understandable since, by assumption, workers have no incentive to care about the quality of planting and will do the minimally acceptable job possible. Ultimately, quality is evaluated by the MoF or the forest tenure holder that oversees the contract. The MoF or forest company either hires checkers or uses its own staff to plot some gridded lines on a map of the planted block and then walk through the site. On the basis of the specifications stipulated in a contract, density, spacing, and root media and position aspects are assessed. Root media and position are major quality aspects in BC. Fundamentally, quality calculation is the number of satisfactorily planted trees divided by the number of plantable spots.

Tree planting is an activity that generally does not involve a high level of technical difficulty. However, there are some important considerations, such as picking the right type of soil and spot, digging a good hole, closing it properly, and so on. Of course, gimmicks vary from region to region and even from one site to another. Seasoned planters all know that, as a planter, one aims to plant trees of adequate, rather than perfect, quality, simply because the more perfectionist a planter is, the fewer trees he/she plants (Stolz 2000). Since the minimum necessary for full pay is 93% in the case of the MoF jobs, experienced planters will try to stay slightly above that quality level. Planters have been found to "show boat at the front", with trees along the road nicely spaced and attractively planted to impress the contract checker, while trees planted further from the road not up to the same planting standard. (Shand 1999).

Like any other social activity, tree planting has its codes of behavior. A typical crew consists of a foreman and 8-12 workers. By ignoring crew etiquette, a person invites problems and even hatred from other members. Some of the recognized bad behavior includes intruding on another's block to plant, especially when that person has saved his/her best land for last (Cyr 1998). Some illegal acts, such as stashing (burying or throwing away seedlings) and over-claiming planting, will result in the planter being fined and fired. In a contract job involving the MoF, stashing means destroying the government property, which will likely result in prosecution in addition to being fired.

8.2 Methods of Rewarding Silvicultural Workers

In this section, we examine the factors causing some forest companies to use a piece-rate system and others to rely on wages (or salaries) to compensate workers for identical silvicultural activities. It may be argued that the payment scheme chosen reflects an attempt on the part of managers to minimize transaction costs. From principal-agent theory, it is known that, in the absence of appropriate monitoring, piece rates allow the agent to shirk in terms of quality, whereas time rates encourage shirking in terms of quantity (Stiglitz 1975; Lucas 1979). Thus, Datta et al. (1986) found that, in practice, one would observe less wage contracts (a) the greater is the labor-intensity of the activity, (b) the harder it is to detect shirking, and (c) the greater is the agent's marginal gain from shirking. Fundamentally, it is a moral hazard problem and one solution is that, in choosing a payment method, the principal seeks to minimize agent (employee) payoffs while providing adequate incentives to avoid shirking (Bardhan and Singh 1987; Braverman and Stiglitz 1986).

Alchian and Demsetz (1972) define shirking in terms of its effect on other workers, implying that the marginal product of one worker is affected by the effort of another. If shirking occurs, it is difficult to determine the value of a worker's marginal product, because it is also affected by the performance of other workers. In the case of silvicultural work, shirking occurs because reduced effort and diligence on the part of workers negatively affects the anticipated "output" and "quality" of the forest ecosystem. Again, it is difficult to determine a worker's true marginal value product, although it rises as shirking is diminished.

Shirking may exist in any wage contract and can be costly to prevent. Piece-rate contracts are preferred to hourly wages if monitoring output costs less than enforcing input (Cheung 1969), while such contracts also reveal productivity differentials among workers more clearly than any other payment scheme (Cheung 1983). However, with piece rates the worker is inclined to be "sloppy" and produce products of inferior quality, that is, exploit opportunities to shirk on quality. Thus, piece rates may be less desirable if the physical attributes of the product are such that it is relatively costly to police a specified standard. The root of the problem lies with high information costs. It is necessary to recognize that firms lack the ability to control agents' effort levels on the one hand and observe output on the other, unless excessively high costs are incurred.

In farm management, two abilities are crucial – the ability to supervise labor and the managerial ability to make production decisions based on technological know-how and market information (Vandeman et al. 1991; Vaupel and Martin 1986; Eswaran and Kotwal 1985). As silvicultural activities are labor intensive, labor supervision in silviculture is of crucial importance because silvicultural output is very sensitive to the quality of effort. Many silvicultural activities are characterized by the fact that the quality of effort applied cannot be easily ascertained until after the work has been completed. The inherent moral hazard problem of shirking implies that the labor hired and the supervision effort applied to reduce shirking jointly form an effective input into the silvicultural investment activity.

Labor is a crucial input in silvicultural investments, but the firm does not have direct control over the effort (denoted by e) and the diligence (q) with which hired labor performs its task – the quantity and quality aspects, respectively. The firm has direct control over (1) the number of workers hired, (2) the level of supervision that can (perhaps) affect e and q, and (3) the method for paying workers. Most principal-agent models focus on (1) and (2), neglecting (3) entirely. For example, Alchian and Demsetz (1972) consider both shirking by workers and by their supervisor; only if the supervisor can capture the residual value of labor's output does the supervisor have the least incentive to shirk. Roumasset and Uy (1980) use a constrained optimization model, with firms maximizing expected profit by choosing the number of workers and the level of supervision, subject to the choice by workers to maximize utility as a function of effort and diligence (see also Laffont 1989). Supervision enters the constraint since both effort (the quantity aspect) and diligence (the quality aspect) are assumed to be concave functions of the level of supervision (S).[2]

In the choice of the specific means of rewarding workers, transaction cost logic suggests that pecuniary compensation and supervision are a necessary but not sufficient condition for rational production. The reason is that a firm does not know a worker's cost of effort function due to the difficulty in measuring it. Of course, actions that the worker takes may reveal information about that function. The firm can use that information in subsequent periods against the worker. As a result, the worker attempts to disguise $C(E)$, leading to inefficiencies. Nevertheless, there is a high price associated with cheating and cheaters may be severely punished. A cost-effective approach is that firms pick payment schemes that match the identifiable attributes of the activities, because transaction costs are minimized when proper payment schemes are adopted in conjunction with appropriate levels of compensation and supervision.

Clearly, the choice of payment method depends on the characteristics of activities. For a given activity, if both quality (performance) and outcome are easy to monitor, one would expect to observe the use of hourly wages. This is the case where divisibility and separability are high in terms of job composition or job components. Workers are hired just to "do the job." In this case, agents (workers) may shirk on quantity, but it will not be costly for the principal to detect such behavior because the outcome is obvious. Assuming a competitive labor market, shirking is likely to disadvantage workers if the amount of work that the average worker is expected to do has already been established.

---

[2] Mathematically, $e = e(S)$, with $e'(S) > 0$ and $e''(S) < 0$, and $q = q(S)$, with $q'(S) > 0$ and $q''(S) < 0$.

For an activity that comprises distinct intermediate processes, if these are easily compartmentalized and quantified, one expects the use of piece rates. As long as the performance outcome is verifiable, the scope for shirking on quality is limited. Workers doing routine work are more easily supervised and can sometimes be rewarded on a piecework basis (Simon 1991). Quite often, quantity is easier to observe than quality. The problem with incentive contracts that are based on output quantity is that they induce the worker to go for speed and to ignore quality. If quality can be observed, the worker can be compensated appropriately for quantity and quality. If quality cannot be observed, payment by input solves the quantity/quality problem. When the worker is paid, say, by the hour, and is merely instructed to produce goods of a given quality, he has no incentive to deviate from that instruction. Since compensation in this case is based only on input, there is no desire to rush the job and quantity may suffer. However, in this case, it should be relatively easy (inexpensive) to find a method of monitoring effort related to quantity (Lazear 1986, 1989).

When the final outcome is not readily observable and difficult to quantify, one would expect the use of a (monthly) salary scheme, with workers having little incentive to shirk on quality, although they may shirk on quantity. In this case, since quality is a primary concern, the salary system is more advantageous to the principal than any other payment method. As noted earlier, where marginal products of individual workers are not easily separable, salary is invariably used as the method of payment.

Both time wage and piece rates are incentive contracts. Piece rates induce workers to sort themselves so motivated, productive workers select to work for firms that use piece rates. Firms offering piece rates can, on the other hand, discourage less productive workers from selecting them by charging for the use of capital (see discussion in previous section). Salaries (or hourly wages) that pay on the basis of an imperfect measure of effort attract lower-quality workers (Lazear 1989). Therefore, all other things constant, high-quality workers choose to work at firms that pay piece rates and low-quality ones choose firms that offer salaries (Lazear 1986). Therefore, the difference in quality across firms that this selection bias causes implies that a movement towards greater use of output-based incentive contracts will increase total sector output.

Historically, in BC's silviculture sector there was a need to promote a high level of production in terms of quantity; as a result, basic silviculture was emphasized. Even as recently as the early 1990s, silvicultural investment focused on the rapid regeneration of backlog NSR lands in the Province. Since efforts at reducing regeneration delay were the primary concern, emphasis was placed on the quantity of trees planted rather than subsequent stand performance (quality). The demands of basic silviculture are relatively low in terms of technical requirements, and this tends to promote the use of piece rates that encourage shirking with respect to quality. Although responsibility for regeneration was transferred from the public to the private sector during the 1980s, quality issues also became more important as there was increased emphasis on the environment. In recent years, BC's forest companies have increased the performance of enhanced silviculture in response to environmental regulations and certification efforts. As a result, although forest companies still outsource many activities to silvicultural contractors, they undertake many others in-house, choosing different means to pay workers hired directly.

Within BC piece rates are used more in basic silviculture than in incremental silviculture. This is due to standardization of operations through silvicultural prescriptions (formerly known as pre-harvest silvicultural prescriptions) and a series of punitive rules, such as the so-called "85%" clause (where full payment is not made until the survival rate of seedlings exceeds 85%). This quality level has been raised to 93% in recent years. When silvicultural activities expand in scope and scale, increased complexity and uncertainty require the integration of activities, with the benefits of adopting a salary system becoming more prevalent. Under such circumstances, contracts take on a longer term so as to mitigate opportunistic behavior, and internal structures of a firm tend to be relied upon to a greater extent.

8.3 Empirical Evidence from a Survey of Forest Companies

Transaction cost economics holds that firms economize on transaction costs by designing contractual arrangements to match the attributes of production activities and firm characteristics. A simple econometric model is used to test empirically the hypothesis that forest companies' characteristics influence the choice of specific payment methods. The focus is on firm characteristics due to the lack of available information on the attributes of activities, which are expected to be quite standard across firms and throughout BC (mainly because of government environmental regulations).

The data for the study were obtained from a 1998 survey of forest companies. Only companies with forest tenures were included in the survey, because, since 1987, only such tenures required the performance of silvicultural treatments as a condition of logging public lands. Companies operating on lands directly managed by the Ministry of Forests (characterized by short-term cutting rights) are excluded from the survey because, in these areas, silvicultural treatments are the responsibility of the MoF, which employs silvicultural contractors. Questionnaires were sent to 117 forest companies (for large companies the survey was sent to the operating division), with 103 completed surveys returned for an 88% response rate.

The dependent variable in the models is type of payment scheme. In the first model, the dependent variable is binary, taking on a value of 1 if an hourly wage or salary is used and 0 if a piece rate is employed. For dichotomous dependent variables, both probit and logit regression methods are generally used. The probit model assumes a normal cumulative density function (see Maddala 1983; Greene 1993) and is used in this study. In the second model, the dependent variable is polychotomous but ordinal in the sense that the piece rate provides the least opportunity for shirking with respect to quantity and performance speed, while the opposite is true for the salary scheme; the hourly wage lies somewhere in between these. Thus, an ordered probit regression is used to examine the effects of the explanatory variables on the choice of payment schemes.

The explanatory variables are all dummy variables and they are the same for each of the regression models. They are as follows.

1. A dummy variable is used to distinguish various company types, with 1 for companies whose stock is publicly traded. This dummy variable is used as an indicator of company (as opposed to operating division) size.
2. The level of harvest available to a forest company in any given year, its AAC, is represented by a dummy variable, with 1 used to represent an AAC exceeding 0.5 million m^3. The choice of 0.5 million m^3 as the threshold is because that level of AAC tends to separate small forest operations from large ones, based on our knowledge of the actual situation in BC. Our survey results indicate that some 45% of the divisions surveyed operate with an AAC exceeding 0.5 million m^3.
3. For a company that conducts silvicultural activities, a dummy variable taking on a value of 1 is used if more than 10 workers are hired annually. The use of this benchmark was based on suggestions made during in-person interviews of industry representatives during the pre-test component of the survey.
4. A dummy variable for the length of silvicultural work (=1 if greater than three months, =0 otherwise) is also used to distinguish between basic

and enhanced silviculture. Basic silviculture refers mainly to replanting of logged-off sites, while enhanced silviculture requires such things as thinning, pruning and other activities that enhance the quality of a stand or the environment. If a company is primarily engaged in basic silviculture, the length of silvicultural work will generally be less than three months.

5. Finally, a region dummy variable is used to distinguish between firms operating on the BC Coast (=1) and in the Interior (=0). The BC Coast constitutes a temperate rainforest (with no distinct period where the ground is frozen), whereas the Interior is much drier with a more continental climate and distinct boreal-like climate. Thus, harvesting conditions and the size of logs differ between the two regions, as do the tenure arrangements, which are different in the Interior (with greater reliance on short-term logging contracts) than on the Coast (where long-term forest management agreements are in effect).

In spite of their usefulness, dummy variables have their limits. Specifically, while the company type and BC region dummy variables are purely qualitative, the other three are artificially-constructed benchmark variables. While multiple dummy variables could have been introduced to get around this problem, it would have an adverse impact on the available degrees of freedom.

The results of the probit and ordered probit regressions are provided in Tables 8.4 and 8.5, respectively. In interpreting the results of the probit model, a positive (negative) sign for an explanatory variable indicates an increase (decrease) in the likelihood that time wage is used by the forest company to reward silvicultural workers. However, in the ordered probit model, the signs of the coefficients must be interpreted with caution, bearing in mind that the coding of the dependent variable indicates only an order or ranking (see Maddala 1983; Greene 1993). Based on the χ^2 statistics at the given level of significance, the ordered probit model provides a better explanation than does the probit model. In general, however, the results from both models conform to TCE theory.

The regression results indicate that the larger forest companies tend to rely more on wages, and especially salaries, than do smaller ones. The latter are more likely to opt for the piece rate payment scheme. Evidence for this is provided in both Tables 8.4 and 8.5 by the positive effect on time-based payment methods of companies whose stock is publicly traded. It is also evident from the positive correlation between time-based payment schemes and whether a company (or its division) is found on the Coast, as

Coastal firms and operations tend to be larger. Further, the more workers that a company hires directly, the more likely that a piece-rate system is adopted. The results also indicate that, as the length (duration) of silvicultural work increases, the greater is the chance that forest companies rely on a salary scheme.

Table 8.4: Payment Schemes for Silvicultural Workers: Probit Results[a]

Variable	Estimate	Asymptotic t-value[b]	Mean of variable
Company type (1=stock traded, 0=otherwise)	0.6322	1.790*	0.73
AAC (0 if ≤0.5 mil. m³, 1 if > 0.5 mil. m³)	0.0234	0.072	0.45
Silvicultural workers (0 if ≤10; 1 if >10)	−0.8922	−2.595**	0.37
Duration of work (0 if ≤3 months, 1 if >3 months)	0.3846	1.138	0.48
Region (1=BC Coast, 0=BC Interior)	0.5419	1.677*	0.35
Constant	0.2554	0.816	
N = 103			
χ^2: 19.07 (5); critical value = 15.086 (0.01 level)			
Pseudo R^2 = 0.459			

[a] Dependent variable: 0 = piece wage; 1 = time wage.
[b] ** significant at 0.01 level, * at 0.1 level.

Table 8.5: Payment Schemes for Silvicultural Workers: Ordered Probit Results[a]

Variable	Estimate	Asymptotic t-value[b]
Company type (1=stock traded, 0=otherwise)	0.6921	2.276*
AAC (0 if ≤0.5 mil. m³, 1 if > 0.5 mil. m³)	0.2922	1.069
Silvicultural workers (0 if ≤10; 1 if >10)	−1.0769	−3.691**
Duration of work (0 if ≤3 months, 1 if >3 months)	0.8321	2.991**
Region (1=BC Coast, 0=BC Interior)	0.2366	0.871
Constant	0.1736	0.593
MU (1)	1.440	7.292**
N = 103		
χ^2: 19.07 (5); critical value = 15.086 (0.01 level)		
Pseudo R^2 = 0.459		

[a] Dependent variable: 0 = piece wage; 1 = hourly wage; 2 = salary.
[b] ** significant at 0.01 level, * at 0.05 level.

A key policy implication of these results is that large BC Coastal operations have a market incentive to underwrite incremental silviculture. These same companies have borne the brunt of environmental protests (both domestic and international) and are the ones most likely affected by current certification efforts. As a consequence, these companies are relatively more interested in enhanced silviculture. Furthermore, given the better yields of the Coastal region, enhanced silviculture is generally more profitable on the Coast than in the Interior region (see Thompson et al. 1992; Benson 1988). Abstracting from the uncertainty inherent with the public ownership of BC's forestlands, policy in pursuit of sustainable forest management can capitalize on this characteristic.

The transaction cost model suggests that rewarding of basic silviculture will take the form of piece rates, while remuneration for enhanced silviculture will take the form of time-based payments. This is because it is easier to monitor basic silviculture (there are opportunities for shirking on quantity, but this is relatively easy to monitor), while quality is important for enhanced silviculture and this is more difficult (and costly) to monitor. The regression results confirm these observations. As the nature of forestry in BC changes, with greater emphasis on environmental performance, it will be necessary to emphasize the training of skilled silvicultural workers, who focus on quality and are responding to a wage or salary structure. This is quite different from the current situation – a less highly-trained workforce that emphasizes quantity over quality.

According to transaction cost economics, firms seek appropriate contractual forms that minimize the costs of organizing, information gathering and performance monitoring. Selection of payment methods is an important aspect of contractual arrangements. The payment schemes that forest companies in BC have used for silvicultural activities have generally confirmed the transaction cost theory. The results indicate that decision makers at the management level of a firm or government agency should be aware of the need to synchronize attributes of activities with characteristics of production units. This will complement the purpose of saving transaction costs to achieve optimal economic efficiency. It is also apparent from the results that public sector intervention to stimulate or regulate additional silvicultural investment would benefit, in efficiency terms, from a careful assessment of the existing silvicultural market characteristics.

* A portion of this chapter is based on an article (*Forest Policy and Economics* 1(May 2000): 71-79) entitled "Remuneration for silviculture in British Columbia: insights from transaction cost economics" by S. Wang, G.C. van Kooten and B. Wilson; with permission from Elsevier Science.

9 Silvicultural Investment and Institutional Restructuring

In the early days of forestry development in British Columbia, reforestation received little attention. Compared to Europe and other places where forest culture has evolved over several hundred years, if not longer, forest management, particularly forest renewal, is a fairly recent phenomenon in BC. In this concluding chapter, an assessment of silvicultural investment in BC's public forestlands is provided and conclusions are drawn. We begin in section 9.1 with an overview of the principal institutional features of the silviculture sector, followed in section 9.2 by a profile of the Province's silvicultural investments.[1] In section 9.3, we discuss the major institutional obstacles to adequate silvicultural investment. Then we make recommendations in section 9.4 on how to restructure BC's institutional framework to encourage greater efficiency in the choice and manner in which silvicultural activities are carried out. Finally, we conclude with some general observations.

9.1 Institutional Features of BC's Silviculture Sector

Given the predominance of public ownership of forestlands in British Columbia, the relatively short history of the development of silvicultural programs bears out a prominent characteristic, namely, the necessity of integrating private initiatives into the undertaking of production and management activities on public land. As a result of a series of reforms since 1987, the institutional structure of BC's silviculture sector has acquired the following features:

---

[1] Section 9.2 of this chapter is based on a paper entitled "Silvicultural investment in British Columbia: economic efficiency and employment" by S. Wang and B. Wilson in B. Slee and I. Hughes (eds.) *New Opportunities for Forest-Related Rural Development* – Proceedings of IUFRO Group 6.11.02 Symposium, August 1999, University of Aberdeen, pp.395-401.

- The BC Ministry of Forests (MoF) is bound by legislation to administer the Province's silvicultural programs on public land.
- The major forest companies or licensees – those holding TFLs, Forest Licenses, Timber Licenses, *et cetera* – are required by law to undertake basic silviculture to the free-to-grow stage after timber harvest, and their silvicultural performance must adhere to approved pre-harvest silvicultural prescriptions and comply with relevant standards.
- Direct government involvement in silvicultural operations has been sharply reduced, with the Small Business Forest Enterprise Program the primary program still in the hands of the MoF.
- Most planting material production facilities are now privately owned, with up to 90% of the seedlings used for planting each year supplied by some 40 commercial and industry nurseries.
- While basic silviculture is the responsibility of the integrated wood products companies (on TFL lands) or the MoF (on TSA lands), the majority of silvicultural activities are contracted out to smaller firms specializing in silviculture.

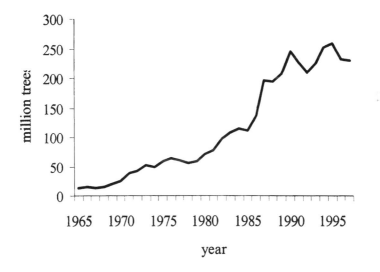

Figure 9.1: Tree Planting on BC's Public Forestland

The wide scope of silvicultural operations in British Columbia, ranging from seedling production to fertilizing and surveying, is testimony to a transition from old-growth to second-growth harvesting and management. In terms of scale, the increase in the number of seedlings planted is indicative of an accelerated growth of the silvicultural industry, particularly beginning in the early to mid 1980s (see Figure 9.1).

The expansion of silvicultural programs necessarily brings about changes in institutional arrangements. As far as physical arrangements are concerned, the BC Forest Service was at first the only player involved in the reforestation of denuded public lands. Beginning in the 1970s, the single player gradually gave way to an umbrella with the Forest Service as the focal point in coordinating and/or monitoring of silvicultural investment, with silvicultural activities involving forest companies, silvicultural contractors and workers. As a result of the policy changes of 1987, a stratified structure emerged that realigned the relations among the various players in a vertically connected chain. The development of silviculture and changing relationships among an increasing number of players has had financial implications. Basic silviculture is now paid for by major licensees (the large wood products companies), with incremental silviculture financed largely by specially earmarked programs, such as the Forest Resource Development Agreement (FRDA) during 1986-1996 and, more recently, Forest Renewal BC.

The above trends are open to different interpretations. One way is to view them from an institutional perspective. As the scope and scale of activities exceeded the capacity of the BC Forest Service to deliver silvicultural programs, it became necessary to decentralize physical delivery at the operational level. The privatization of 8 government nurseries in 1988 was a case in point. However, decentralization was accompanied by intensified legislative regulations and administrative controls. The outcome is a specialization of productive functions and vertical integration of management relationships. Prior to the 1980s, the BC Forest Service acted as a testing ground for new developments in silviculture. The introduction of containerized seedling production techniques in the early 1970s was an example. As the scale of operations grew, a need for specialization arose. When the management capacity of the Forest Service was exceeded, it became more economical for the Forest Service to promote division of labor by having the private sector undertake some of the operations. Thus, new institutional arrangements emerged to facilitate a transfer of obligations from the public to the private sector. For instance, the BC Forest Service contracts may have served as a training ground for contractors who subsequently worked with the tenure-holding forest companies. Contractors who work with the major licensees are mostly those that have "graduated" from the Forest Service contracts and already "know the ropes"; they are largely the "crème de la crème" of contractors (Davis-Case 1982). The institutional changes since 1987 have altered the role of the Ministry of Forests, from that of an implementing body to that of a regulatory agency.

Given the increase in the scope and scale of silvicultural activities, the government lacks the ability to continue implementing silvicultural projects. Neither can the government monitor the quality of silvicultural performance in a discriminating fashion, without incurring formidable costs. Very simply, the MoF is too far removed, institutionally, from the forest. The forest companies face a similar difficulty but to a lesser extent because they are closer to the forest, generally being involved in logging operations and overseeing everyday management. As expectations and standards rise, complexity also increases, resulting in a shift toward more in-house operations.

The MoF has now been relieved of responsibilities for direct involvement in physical operations (except in the Small Business Forest Enterprise Program) to become more specialized in administering and monitoring silvicultural programs. Meanwhile, the major licensees have become more specialized in managing forest operations in a manner that unifies harvesting and silviculture planning, leaving much of the physical silvicultural work to independent contractors. In essence, BC's institutional reforms have brought about two fundamental changes. One is a change in the institutional environment and the other a realignment in contractual relationships. While evidence of the former is the emergence of a new legislative and policy framework that has taken into account public aspirations for enhanced silvicultural products and practices, the latter finds expression in the establishment of a new relationship with respect to silvicultural performance.

9.2 The State of BC's Silvicultural Investment

BC's silviculture sector did not fully emerge until the 1970s for two reasons. First, there was a concern about future timber supply, a concern that had previously driven silvicultural investment in other countries, most notably Sweden (see Wilson et al. 1998). Second, and perhaps more importantly, there was (and still is) increasing recognition that harvesting entails externalities associated with reduced biodiversity, scenic amenities, and so on. Failure to adequately regenerate forests after logging resulted in market failure. The initial driving force behind the expansion in the scope and scale of silvicultural activities was the need to bring large areas of not satisfactorily restocked, or NSR, lands to an acceptable stocking level. Prior to silvicultural investments to reduce NSR area, these areas were increasing as a result of logging and/or natural causes (fire, disease or insect infestation) and the failure of stands to reestablish to commercial potential on their own.

In spite of the inherent natural regeneration capabilities that all forestlands possess, one trend of the past three decades in BC has been an increased use of nursery-grown seedlings for forest regeneration. The number of seedlings planted annually on public land increased to well over 200 million in the mid-1990s from about 13 million three decades earlier (Figure 9.1). Although for many years harvested area exceeded planted area, in recent years the area planted has surpassed the area that is harvested (Figure 9.2). This is the outcome of mandatory reforestation legislation and dedicated government funding to reduce the NSR area.

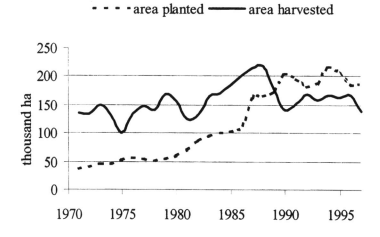

Figure 9.2: Area Planted versus Harvested on BC's Public Land

In addition to basic silviculture (tree planting), incremental (or intensive) silviculture is also practiced, but on a limited scale. Incremental silviculture refers to stand tending treatments, such as site rehabilitation, conifer release, juvenile spacing, pruning, fertilizing and commercial thinning, that are undertaken to maintain forest health, increase timber yield and improve timber quality. As shown in Table 9.1, among the three principal stand-tending activities, spacing increased most dramatically in the past two decades. In comparison, pruning was virtually non-existent until the beginning of the 1990s and fertilization remained fairly stagnant during the period.

Table 9.1:   Incremental Silviculture on BC's Public Land (Average Annual Area, ha)

Period	Spacing	Pruning	Fertilizing
1982-1985	9772	0	1444
1986-1989	24748	0	13033
1990-1993	42315	2757	6009
1994-1997	45740	7525	9900

Source: Calculated from BC Ministry of Forests annual reports.

In financial terms, silvicultural expenditures devoted to BC's public forestlands increased steadily from the early 1970s to the 1990s. As shown in Figure 9.3, measured in 1994 constant Canadian dollars, total expenditures reached $263 million in 1987 compared with the $20 million spent in 1971 – an annual growth rate of 17.5%. After the 1987 policy changes that resulted in the transfer of financial obligations for basic silviculture to the private sector, total silvicultural expenditures on BC's public forestlands continued to grow (until the early 1990s) thanks to sustained expenditures made by the Ministry of Forests and increased expenditures by forest companies. In 1990, private expenditures significantly lagged behind those by the public sector, but by 1997 private sector expenditures were nearly 80% more than those of the public (Canadian Council of Forest Ministers 1999). As discussed in previous chapters, forest companies use their employees to manage various aspects of tree planting, but most of the work is handled by silvicultural contractors with whom the companies have well-established relationships. All planting is checked by the company's division foresters and audited by corporate staff foresters. The results are subject to inspections by the MoF.

Silvicultural expenditures on BC's public forestlands have largely been funded from stumpage charges. As the nominal steward of the Province's forest resources, the Ministry of Forests collects stumpage fees. The proportion of silvicultural expenditures charged against the MoF's revenues has averaged about 30% for the past three decades. From the beginning of the 1980s to the mid-1990s, the Canadian federal government was involved in BC's forestry development. The Intensive Forest Management Subsidiary Agreement, which was signed in 1979, served as a vehicle for the federal government to provide assistance to silvicultural activities in BC. This program paved the way for the much larger FRDA programs. Implemented in two phases, FRDA I (1986-1990) pooled a total of $300 million from the federal and Provincial governments, which emphasized the regeneration of good and medium sites of accessible forestlands denuded prior to 1982. FRDA II (1991-1996) mobilized a further $200 million shared between the federal and Provincial governments. The primary objectives of the second phase were to conduct incremental silviculture and to fund initiatives in communications, extension, research, small-scale forestry, product and market development, and economic and social analysis. The mid-1990s saw the completion of the FRDA programs and the beginning of Forest Renewal BC, or FRBC, which derives its funding from additional stumpage charges. In the first three years of its implementation, the FRBC funding that went to silviculture was small relative to the expenditures made by forest companies. Since 1997, FRBC has increased its financial allocations to silviculture.

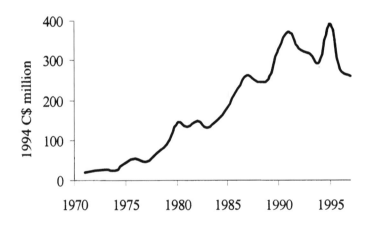

Figure 9.3: Silvicultural Expenditures on BC's Public Land

Clearly, BC's forest companies tend to focus on basic silviculture, which is characterized by quick post-harvest planting of desired tree species to achieve rapid full stocking. Planting is usually followed by brushing and weeding. This volume maximizing strategy is consistent with projected future demand for BC forest products. It is no secret that the majority of BC's forest companies are highly suspicious of the notion that future markets will show significant differential pricing associated with higher quality wood (such as knot-free timber of large diameters). The reason is that manufacturing can now create many of the characteristics associated with high quality timber, using timber of much lower quality. Although silvicultural regimes vary according to costs and benefits, and their timing, silvicultural treatments aimed at creating specific stand conditions and products at harvest too often focus on a hypothetical harvest age.[2] In practice, it is difficult to predict actual harvest timing at the stand level – the level at which silvicultural treatments are prescribed. Consequently, prevailing corporate strategies seem to favor differentiating future products through strategic investments in conversion facilities rather than attempting to spend heavily on developing the timber resource today for unknown markets of the future (TimberWest 1996). This is one reason why many companies keep their silvicultural expenditures to a bare minimum.

9.3 Obstacles to Intensive Silvicultural Investment

In assessing the efficiency of BC's silvicultural expenditures, especially in intensive or incremental silviculture, economic theory needs to be brought to bear. To begin, BC's silviculture sector is characterized by under-investment. Under private ownership, profit-seeking forestland owners invest in silviculture when they are convinced that profitable opportunities exist. With an understanding about the value of the lumber or fiber associated with mature forests, investors will only commit financial resources in anticipation of future benefits. This rule is not the case in British Columbia due to the predominance of public ownership and lack of tenure – benefits may not accrue to the investor. Zhang and Pearse (1996) found empirical evidence suggesting that willingness to invest in silviculture is positively correlated with the security of tenure. Public ownership and insecure forest tenures create investment disincentives (Luckert and Haley 1993). As noted in Chapter 3, forest companies treat silvicultural expenditures as a cost of doing business, the price for permission to harvest mature public timber. Since the aim is to acquire and maintain timber harvesting rights rather than investing in forest renewal, it is only natural for firms to minimize silvicultural expenditures. By law, tenure holders are responsible for ensuring reforestation, but, when it is financially unattractive

---

[2] Silvicultural regimes certainly have an effect on future crops, which, in turn, will influence the economics of harvesting. Recognizing that harvest cost is inversely related to harvest intensity and tree size, one US study suggests that harvesting profitability is near zero when removing trees averaging less than 20 centimeters in diameter at breast height (Kluender et al. 1998).

to undertake silviculture, forest companies refrain from committing all but the minimum required resources.

There are additional problems that suggest intensive, and even basic, silvicultural investments may not be worthwhile. Due to BC's predominant public ownership of forestland, consistent, coherent and explicit objectives are difficult to maintain. At times, the purpose of silvicultural expenditures is to increase AAC through the allowable cut effect; at other times, silviculture is used as a means for creating jobs. Other than the effort in reforesting NSR lands, BC suffers from a lack of focus and direction in its silvicultural programs (Drushka 1999).

Many tree species in BC have a long rotation cycle and the Province has a disadvantage in terms of forest growth compared to its major competitors (Wilson et al. 1998). The long gestation period (around 60 years on the Coast and up to 100 years in the Interior) and the relatively low mean annual increment give rise to a great deal of uncertainty, thereby encouraging companies to minimize up-front costs and delay spending as close to timber harvest as possible. Organization theory suggests that uncertainty can be reduced by delaying the commitment to specific actions from the time planning begins until the time when action is called for (Simon 1991). This logic is applicable to silvicultural investment because it makes financial sense to delay activities whose results have a high degree of uncertainty. Using the capital budgeting approach, Benson (1988) arrives at a similar conclusion. He argues that Canada, including much of BC, should concentrate on forest regeneration and limit investment in incremental or intensive silviculture.

Of intensive silvicultural activities, juvenile spacing is often considered a promising mechanism for ensuring that future stands will have high economic values. This proposition is based on the premise that juvenile spacing will result in larger log sizes, reduced harvesting, handling and conversion costs, and greater market opportunities. However, using current spacing costs and a range of macroeconomic pricing outlooks, it is difficult to find empirical evidence confirming that spacing operations generate a reasonable rate of return on investment. As a matter of fact, a number of major forest companies in BC share the view that there are only two real opportunities for value-adding stand management practices in addition to high-quality basic silviculture, namely, selective late-rotation fertilization and genetic improvements (Binkley 1997).

To summarize, silvicultural expenditures on BC's publicly-owned forestlands are often made to secure access to standing public timber rather than as an investment in forest renewal. The prevailing institutional setting in the Province tends to dissuade private sector investment in silviculture. The free-to-grow requirement in BC represents a minimum quality standard for regeneration. Currently, the best that the major licensees would choose, or accept, is basic silviculture. Anything more than that will mean a commitment to location-specific performance over a relatively long time span. Given the forest tenure structure and overall institutional set-up, it is logical for each licensee to commit to the minimum length of time but to aim for the maximum space. In other words, a rational firm would choose to minimize its effort in regeneration along the temporal dimension in order to be able to cover a larger area and thus meet the minimum regulatory requirement. Incremental silviculture has, thus far, been program driven, having been turned on and off in the past two decades according to the availability of funds and political will. The relatively short duration of forest tenures and uncertainty resulting from tenure renewal, transfer of cutting rights and possible future limitations that are arbitrarily imposed on tenure rights by the government discourage private companies from investing in silviculture beyond that required by law.

9.4 Need for Institutional Restructuring

The essence of institutional reform in BC's silviculture sector is decentralization. Over the past three decades, BC's forestry sector has experienced a privatization drive characterized by

- a transfer to the private sector of forest nurseries, which resulted in a competitive tree seedling market,
- downloading to major forest tenure holders of financial and physical responsibility for forest regeneration, and
- contracting out to the private sector of publicly financed services that were previously performed by the Ministry of Forests.

Not only have obligations been decentralized, decision-making has also been decentralized. In comparison, power and control were considerably concentrated at the level of the MoF prior to 1987.

Since 1987, there have been two opposing forces at play. On the one hand, the complexity of silvicultural operations has increased; on the other, systematization and institutional restructuring have made the rules governing and evaluating the processes and products of silvicultural activities clearer, making the actual implementation of silvicultural work easier than before. Transaction costs have been reduced in some aspects (e.g., in contract writing due to diminishing uncertainty in the institutional environment), but have increased in other respects, such as monitoring and policing (e.g., increased auditing). The overall net effect on total organization costs is ambiguous, with the direction being a function of the relative strengths of those opposing forces. The outcome is, of course, an empirical question. Nevertheless, the transaction costs facing the forest companies have definitely increased because they have been required to undertake more planning, management and supervision, which means higher overhead costs.

According to Williamson (1996, 1979), the problem of economic organization is to devise contract and governance structures that have the purpose and effect of economizing on bounded rationality, while simultaneously safeguarding transactions against the hazard of opportunism. Given BC's predominant public ownership of forestlands, the scope for institutional restructuring is limited, unless government is willing to reconsider its role as the primary forestland owner. Therefore, the following suggestions may be useful.

First, initiatives might be taken to promote multiple-period, long-term contracts. The contractual relationships in BC's silviculture sector are highly interdependent, and institutional reforms have heightened this interdependency. Prior to the mid-1980s, silvicultural performance was characterized by single activities, such as reforestation, so dependency was weak. But since the late 1980s, silvicultural activities of all kinds have increased. When the final product of basic silviculture (i.e., free-to-grow forests) is based on performances involving a host of agents, individual contracting is costly in terms of the time cost incurred by both parties. New circumstances call for multiple-activity, multiple-period contracts. From a TCE perspective, long-term contracts promote economic efficiency because they diminish opportunism by reducing uncertainty. Of course, for long-term contracts, problems of enforceability hamper the ability to spell out all possible contingencies in advance. So, it is important to build into long-term contracts the necessary escape clauses that provide for re-negotiation and modifications when the need arises.

Multiple-period, multiple-activity contracts, which are also known as end-result contracts (ERCs), reduce contract preparation and administration costs by consolidating contracts and streamlining use of administrative personnel (Wright and Rideout 1990). This means that activities whose outcomes depend on concerted multiple-stage efforts can be consolidated and undertaken, based on outcome performance contracts instead of task completion contracts. Such a change in contractual form has the potential to reduce transaction costs. ERCs enable one to consolidate activities into the ERC structure, expanding the range of contractual activities and judging performances based on results instead of specialized tasks (Wright and Rideout 1990). This approach makes it possible for the independent contractors to take initiative and apply all their skills and knowledge to advance the achievement of the licensee's objective. In addition to potential cost reductions, ERCs encourage innovation on the part of agents and promote relations between contractual parties.

Second, because forest companies are required to undertake basic silviculture that encompasses a range of activities, a higher degree of inter-dependency incidentally promotes sequential collaboration. Also, silvicultural investment involves sequential co-ordination of the timing of inputs. Since BC's silvicultural activities have moved away from reliance on one-time contracts toward multiple-period contracts, the interdependency has become mutual and sequential in nature, correlating positively with the duration and extent of operations. Provincial authorities may consider necessary steps to foster the type of incentive contracts that allow a sharing of both investment costs and returns between the licensees and the public landowner. The applicability of one contractual form over another also depends on natural conditions. For instance, in areas where regeneration is reliable, the risks of ERCs are manageable because potential problems can be identified and addressed. Failure to produce results can be traced to an activity or to natural conditions such as drought. In contrast, in areas where regeneration is difficult, it may be hard to determine if fault is due to the contractor, the forest company or government agency or, simply, nature (Wright and Rideout 1990).

Third, it may be necessary to encourage small contracts in terms of dollar amounts and work sites. In BC, two recent phenomena that have significant policy implications for silviculture are worth noting. One is the increasing differentiation of wood products, calling for greater attention to product quality while providing opportunities for niche markets. The other is that, at the forest level, single use has given way to multiple use and stand management is being replaced by landscape management. As a result, location-specific operations become increasingly important. With the leveling-off of regeneration programs, in terms of the number of seedlings being planted each year, smaller scale contracts are trendier, and silvicultural contracts will likely move into other activities such as incremental silviculture.

Fourth, when it comes to contracting procedures and payment schemes, it is evident that there is a need for change. For instance, the insistence of the MoF on awarding contracts on the basis of the lowest bid is likely to be advantageous to new contractors. Since BC is moving in the direction of more and more enhanced silviculture, the chances of winning contracts and maintaining contractual relationships will depend, increasingly, on the quality of performance in addition to the ability to make competitive bids. Therefore, one would expect an increase in the use of "preferred contractors" and a shift toward time wages (especially salary schemes) instead of the popular piece rate system. After all, contract type, duration and payment schemes are reflections of dynamic contractual relationships. The "low-bid" system may be incompatible with long-term contracts, and it does not foster stability.

Lastly, in recent years attitudes toward tree species have undergone significant changes. In the mid-1980s, some one dozen coniferous species were planted on BC's public forestlands; but, 10 years later, over 20 coniferous and deciduous species were used in the planting program (Bartlett 1996). Studying aspen (*Populus tremuloides*) and other hardwoods is now a significant component of contemporary research pertaining to second-growth forests. Technological progress and evolving markets present opportunities for commercially using aspen that once was regarded as a weed species of little value. In response to growing public demand for sustainable forest practices, "close-to-nature" silviculture is increasingly practiced. This favors variable retention, natural regeneration, mixed stands, and a higher proportion of broad-leaved trees. As societal values and demands for forest resources change, governments have to change tenure specifications, which results in changes in the associated costs to tenure holders. Changing policies influence future expectations of tenure holders, which, in turn, further influence investment decisions. Although natural regeneration may be an effective silvicultural prescription, planting plays the role of encouraging specific species to match the species to the ecosystem.

In summary, the institutional structure of BC's forestry sector has developed in response to the socio-economic needs of the time, evolving along with alterations in the political-legislative landscape, shifting societal values, advancing technologies, and the dynamics of the resource base. The evolution of silvicultural institutions has proved to be a process of systematization, punctuated by reforms that brought about dramatic changes in, among other things, contractual relationships. For instance, the policy change of 1987 that brought major licensees into the vertical contracting structure for silviculture bears witness to an ongoing integration process and new transaction-cost-economizing arrangements. A process of specialization has accompanied this integration process. BC's silviculture sector is now vertically integrated and many of the transactions that were previously organized and implemented by the MoF are now directly negotiated at the operational level. The requirement for pre-harvest silvicultural prescriptions serves the purpose of infusing greater credibility into silvicultural practices that are otherwise fraught with high transaction costs.

Financial returns to most silvicultural activities in BC are low, but risks are high (Thompson et al. 1992). The reasons are varied but are primarily due to long rotation ages and relatively short and insecure forest tenures. The present institutional structure for silvicultural activities in BC provides the raison d'être for independent contractors to undertake silvicultural contracting. Because of the competitiveness of BC's contracting industry, and the nonspecific nature of the silvicultural activities and their seasonality, outsourcing makes economic sense, not only on the grounds of saving production costs but also on the grounds of reducing transaction costs. However, an obvious asymmetry exists between major licensees and silvicultural contractors. Most contractors are small firms or individuals. In contrast, major licensees tend to be large companies with considerable bargaining power. Also, the high competitiveness of the contracting industry compromises even further the bargaining position of individual contractors.

The institutional structure of BC's forestry sector dictates the program-based nature of incremental silvicultural activities. Therefore, earmarking FRBC funding is of great importance to successfully implementing incremental silvicultural projects. Furthermore, launching incremental silvicultural programs is a far cry from creating permanent silvicultural jobs. Having workers space plantations, prune trees and fertilize stands for up to 9 months a year is difficult to arrange, both physically and biologically. In the event that this difficulty is overcome, a sufficient number of economically viable and environmentally sound projects will have to be identified. Concrete arrangements in personnel recruiting, performance supervision and quality assessment need compatible organizational structures. Since nearly half of BC's major licensees have a separate silviculture division, either at the corporate or operations level, management of enhanced silviculture is more effective and efficient if forest companies are permitted some latitude in their choice of contractual forms, including the freedom to work with their preferred contractors. However, BC's silviculture sector is characterized by the presence of a competitive silviculture contracting force, uncertainty about tenure security and lack of incentives for forest companies to perform silvicultural activities in-house. It is simply cheaper to contract out rather than to preserve a year-round silvicultural crew under most circumstances. This is because, to occupy workers fully, a company may have to integrate a variety of activities that use related skills and can be employed elsewhere during slack periods.

9.5 Final Remarks

The philosophical underpinning of this book is grounded in the new institutional economics. The NIE is, by and large, an extension of the neoclassical economic approach. Rather than replacing the standard microeconomic analysis, the NIE augments it by drawing attention to the importance of institutions and emphasizing organizational modes and contractual relations. Along with resource endowments, technology and preferences, institutions are one of the main pillars of an economy (Feder and Feeny 1991). As a result, the NIE has grown to become a vital field in economic thinking (Furubotn and Richter 1984).

The NIE framework enables the examination of firms' contracting orientations. In the context of British Columbia's forestry sector, this book investigates the relevance of the NIE and the applicability of the TCE approach by examining firms' choice of contractual forms, the organization of labor, and the payment methods that firms adopt. The research demonstrates the relevance of the NIE, especially the transaction cost economics, to the general field of forestry. Our findings indicate that transaction cost economizing behavior is clearly observable from the choice of contractual forms that firms make. Empirical evidence confirms that governance structures tend to align with transaction attributes and firm characteristics so that some costs of transacting can be saved. For the purpose of synchronizing the characteristics of various activities with the transaction cost attributes of alternative organizational arrangements, firms evidently choose to contract out straightforward and labor-intensive activities, while performing in-house those operations that require a high level of technical skill and the use of specialized equipment. Ultimately, neither pure market-based institutions nor vertically integrated forms need to prevail. The choice of governance mode should be dictated by the nature of the transactions involved. Emphatically, transaction attributes as well as firm characteristics are subject to change under the influence of institutional circumstances that are in a state of flux.

So what does the future hold for forestry? As sustainable development has become an important principle, forestry is being redefined to meet a broad range of economic, environmental and social expectations. Different segments of society have different aspirations toward the forest.

Specifically, forest companies aim for profits; forest workers and forest dependent communities rely on the forest for jobs; the government views the forest as an important source of revenue. Other major stakeholders such as the Aboriginal people, city dwellers and civic groups have their respective interests and goals with respect to the forest. There exist a wide variety of institutional arrangements that economists and forest managers need to look into. It would be erroneous to assume that all institutional arrangements are of an efficient nature. Likewise, it would be a mistake to assume that forestry exists in a world largely free of institutional influences. The complexity of forest management at large, and silvicultural investment in particular, calls for expanded research into the role of institutional forces.

More recently, two global trends deserve attention, one being largely internal to the forestry sector and the other having originated from outside of the forestry circle. On the one hand, the growing prominence of forest certification requires companies to make greater efforts than before in convincing consumers that their products are derived from well-managed forests. To achieve this, a certified chain of custody needs to be demonstrated and, incidentally, the economics of sustainable forest practices becomes all the more important.

On the other hand, changing forest practices have been accompanied by growing influence of the so-called 'new economy', which is characterized by the popularization of information technology. This has resulted in an acceleration of the flow of information regarding the management of the forest product supply chain. To be successful, forest companies will have to respond to new circumstances by re-organizing their productive and managerial activities in order to improve economic efficiency. According to Williamson (1996), changes in the institutional environment trigger 'shifts' in production and organizational parameters, giving rise to the need to redesign governance structures. The emergence of e-trade as a modern way of doing business is crisscrossing with the unfolding of a variety of forest certification schemes, resulting in transformation of the existing forestry paradigm. Firms will face enormous challenges in altering their organizational and contractual arrangements accordingly so as to reposition themselves in the new institutional environment.

References

Acheson, J.M. 1994. Welcome to Nobel Country: A Review of Institutional Economics. In: J.M. Acheson (ed.) *Anthropology and Institutional Economics*. Lanham, MD: University Press of America, pp.3-42.

Akerlof, G.A. 1970. The market for 'lemons': qualitative uncertainty and the market mechanisms. *Quarterly Journal of Economics* 84(3): 488-500.

Alchian, A.A. 1961. *Some Economics of Property*. RAND D-2316. Santa Monica, California: RAND Corporation.

Alchian, A.A. 1965a. Some economics of property rights. *Il Politico* 30: 816-829.

Alchian, A.A. 1965b. The basis of some recent advances in the theory of management of the firm. *Journal of Industrial Economics* 14(December): 30-41.

Alchian, A.A. 1984. Specificity, specialization, and coalitions. *Journal of Institutional and Theoretical Economics* 140(1): 34-49.

Alchian, A.A., and H. Demsetz. 1972. Production, information costs, and economic organization. *American Economic Review* 62: 777-795.

Alchian, A.A., and H. Demsetz. 1973. The Property Right Paradigm. *Journal of Economic History* 33(1): 16-27.

Allen, D.W., and D. Lueck. 1993. Transaction costs and the design of cropshare contracts. *RAND Journal of Economics* 24(1): 78-100.

Allington, R. 1997. From survival of the fittest to selection of the fittest to survive – a brief history of North Island silviculture. *Business Logger* 7(9): 23-25.

Anderson, E., and D.C. Schmittlein. 1984. Integration of the sales force: an empirical examination. *RAND Journal of Economics* 15(3): 385-395.

Apland, J., R.N. Barnes, and F. Justus. 1984. The farm lease: an analysis of owner-tenant and landlord preferences under risk. *American Journal of Agricultural Economics* 66(3): 376-384.

Arrow, K.J. 1969. The organization of economic activity: issues pertinent to the choice of market versus nonmarket allocation. In: *The Analysis and Evaluation of Public Expenditure: The PPB System,* vol. 1. U.S. Joint Economic Committee, 91st Congress, 1st Session, U.S. Government Printing Office.

Arrow, K.J. 1974. *The Limits of Organization.* New York: W.W. Norton Co.

Arrow, K.J. 1985. The economics of agency. In: J.W. Pratt and R.J. Zeckhauser (eds.) *Principals and Agents: the Structure of Business.* Boston, Mass.: Harvard Business School Press, pp.37-51.

Arrow, K.J., and A.C. Fisher. 1974. Environmental preservation, uncertainty, and irreversibility. *Quarterly Journal of Economics* 88: 321-319.

Bardhan, P., and N. Singh. 1987. On moral hazard and cost sharing under sharecropping. *American Journal of Agricultural Economics* 69(2): 382-383.

Barnard, C.I. 1938. *The Functions of the Executive.* Cambridge, Mass.: Harvard University Press.

Barron, J.M., and J.R. Umbeck. 1984. The effects of different contractual arrangements: the case of retail gasoline markets. *Journal of Law and Economics* 27: 313-328.

Bartlett, K.J. 1996. *Just the Facts: A Review of Silviculture and Other Forestry Statistics.* British Columbia Ministry of Forests. Victoria, B.C.

Barzel, Y. 1997. *Economic Analysis of Property Rights.* Second Edition. Cambridge, UK: Cambridge University Press.

Bechmann, R. 1990. *Trees and Man: the Forest in the Middle Ages.* New York: Paragon House.

Becker, G.S., and G.J. Stigler. 1974. Law enforcement, malfeasance, and compensation of enforcers. *Journal of Legal Studies* 3: 1-18.

Benson, C.A. 1988. A need for extensive forest management. *The Forestry Chronicle* 64(5): 421-430.

Berns, G.L., H. Bovenberg, E. van Damme, F. van der Duyn Schouten, F. van den Heuvel, T. van de Klundert, N. Noorderhaven, and H. Weigand. 1999. *Economisering van de samenleving* (The Economisation of Society). Tilburg, NL: Centrum voor Wetenschap en Levensbeschouwing. (In Dutch).

Binkley, C.S. 1980. Economic analysis of the allowable cut effect. *Forest Science* 26(4): 633-642.

Binkley, C.S. 1987. When is the optimal economic rotation longer than the rotation of maximum sustained yield. *Journal of Environmental Economics and Management* 14: 152-158.

Binkley, C.S. 1997. Preserving nature through intensive plantation forestry: the case for forestland allocation with illustrations from British Columbia. *The Forestry Chronicle* 73(5): 553-559.

Blaug, M. 1983. *Where Are We Now in the Economics of Education?* Special Professorial Lecture, University of London Institute of Education.

Bowes, M.D., and J.V. Krutilla. 1989. *Multiple-Use Management: The Economics of Public Forestlands.* Washington, D.C.: Resources for the Future.

Bracewell-Milnes, B. 1982. *Land and Heritage: the Public Interest in Personal Ownership.* The Institute of Economic Affairs, England.

Braverman, A., and J.E. Stiglitz. 1986. Cost-sharing arrangements under sharecropping: moral hazard, incentive flexibility, and risk. *American Journal of Agricultural Economics* 68(3): 642-652.

Brazier, D. 1991. A review of changes in B.C. forest seedling market during the period 1986 - 1991. In: F.P. Donnelly and H.W. Lussenburg (compilors) *Proceedings of the 1991 Forest Nursery Association of British Columbia Meeting,* pp.37-42.

British Columbia Forest Service. 1974. Annual Report. Victoria, B.C.

British Columbia Ministry of Forests. 1992. Ministry of Forests Fact Sheet on Seed Orchards. Victoria, B.C.

British Columbia Ministry of Forests. 1993. The British Columbia Forest Practices Code Discussion Paper. Victoria, B.C.

British Columbia Ministry of Forests. 1995. *1994 Forest, Range and Recreation Resource Analysis.* Victoria, B.C.

Bromley, D.W. 1989. *Economic Interests and Institutions.* New York: Basil Blackwell.

Bromley, D.W., and I. Hodge. 1990. Private property rights and presumptive policy entitlements: reconsidering the premises of rural policy. *European Review of Agricultural Economics* 17:197-214.

Buchanan, J.M., and G. Tullock. 1962. *The Calculus of Consent, Logical Foundations of Constitutional Democracy.* Ann Arbor, MI: University of Michigan Press.

Buongiorno, J., and J.K. Gilless. 1987. *Forest Management and Economics.* New York: Macmillan.

Calish, S., R.D. Fight, and D.E. Teeguarden. 1978. How do nontimber values affect Douglas-fir rotations? *Journal of Forestry* 76(4): 217-221.

Calvo, G., and S. Wellisz. 1978. Supervision, loss of control and optimum size of the firm. *Journal of Political Economy* 86: 943-952.

Canadian Council of Forest Ministers. 1999. *Compendium of Canadian Forestry Statistics 1998.* Ottawa.

Carmichael, D.M. 1975. Fee simple absolute as a variable research concept. *Natural Resources Journal* 15: 749-764.

Cartier, K. 1994. The transaction costs and benefits of the incomplete contract of employment. *Cambridge Journal of Economics* 18: 181-196.

Cheung, S.N.S. 1969. Transaction costs, risk aversion, and the choice of contractual arrangements. *Journal of Law and Economics* 12(1): 23-42.

Cheung, S.N.S. 1983. The contractual nature of the firm. *Journal of Law and Economics* 26: 1-21.

Cheung, S.N.S. 1989. Economic organization and transaction costs. In: J. Eatwell, M. Milgate and P. Newman (eds.) *Allocation, Information and Markets*. The MacMillan Press Limited, pp.77-82.

Ciriacy-Wantrup, S.V., and R.C. Bishop. 1975. 'Common property' as a concept in natural resources policy. *Natural Resources Journal* 15: 713-727.

Clarke, H.R., and W.J. Reed. 1989. The tree-cutting problem in a stochastic environment. *Journal of Economic Dynamics and Control* 13: 569-596.

Coase, R.H. 1937. The nature of the firm. *Economica*, New Series 16(4): 386-405.

Coase, R.H. 1960. The problem of social cost. *Journal of Law and Economics* 3(October): 1-44.

Coase, R.H. 1972. Industrial organization: a proposal for research. In: V.R. Fuchs (ed.) *Policy Issues and Research Opportunities in Industrial Organization*. New York: National Bureau of Economic Research, pp.59-73.

Coase, R.H. 1988. The nature of the firm: influence. *Journal of Law, Economics, and Organization* 4(1): 33-47.

Coase, R.H. 1992. The institutional structure of production. *American Economic Review* 82(4): 713-719.

Coase, R.H. 1998. The new institutional economics. *American Economic Review* 88(2): 72-74.

Commons, J.R. 1951 [1934]. *Institutional Economics; Its Place in Political Economy*. New York: Macmillan.

Conrad, J.M. 1997. On the option value of old growth forest. *Ecological Economics* 22: 97-102.

Conrad, J.M., and D. Ludwig. 1994. Forest land policy: the optimal stock of old-growth forest. *Natural Resource Modelling* 8: 27-45.

CPB (Netherlands Bureau for Economic Policy Analysis). 1997. *Challenging Neighbours. Rethinking German and Dutch Economic Institutions.* Berlin: Springer.

Crocker, K.J., and K.J. Reynolds. 1993. The efficiency of incomplete contracts: an empirical analysis of air force engine procurement. *RAND Journal of Economics* 24(1): 126-146.

Crocker, K.J., and S.E. Masten. 1988. Mitigating contractual hazards: unilateral options and contract length. *RAND Journal of Economics* 19(3): 327-343.

Crocker, K.J., and S.E. Masten. 1991. Pretia ex machina? Prices and process in long-term contracts. *Journal of Law and Economics* 34(April): 69-99.

Cyr, H. 1998. *Handmade Forests – The Treeplanter's Experience.* New Society Publishers. Gabiola Island, B.C., Canada & Stony Creek, CT, USA.

Dahlman, C.J. 1980. *The Open Field System and Beyond: A Property Rights Analysis of an Economic Institution.* Cambridge: Cambridge University Press.

Datta, S.K., D.J. O'Hara, and J.B. Nugent. 1986. Choice of agricultural tenancy in the presence of transaction costs. *Land Economics* 62(2): 145-158.

Davis-Case, D'Arcy. 1982. *The British Columbia Reforestation Labor Force.* Unpublished bachelor of art thesis. Department of Sociology, University of British Columbia. Vancouver.

Davis-Case, D'Arcy. 1985. *Worker Participation in the Reforestation Labor Force in British Columbia.* Unpublished master of science thesis, Faculty of Forestry, University of British Columbia, Vancouver.

de Alessi, L. 1980. The economics of property rights: a review of the evidence. *Research in Law and Economics* 2: 1-47.

de Palma, A., G.M. Myers, and Y.Y. Papageorgiou. 1994. Rational choice under an imperfect ability to choose. *American Economic Review* 84(3): 419-440.

de Saussay, C. 1987. *Land Tenure Systems and Forest Policy.* FAO Legislative Study No. 41. Rome.

Demsetz, H. 1966. Some aspects of property rights. *Journal of Law and Economics* 9: 61-70.

Demsetz, H. 1967. Toward a Theory of Property Rights. *American Economic Review* 57: 347-359.

Demsetz, H., and K. Lehn. 1985. The structure of corporate ownership: causes and consequences. *Journal of Political Economy* 93: 1155-1177.

Dohan, M.R. 1976. Cost maximization and buyer dependence on seller provided information. *Journal of Economic Issues* 10(2): 430-452.

Drushka, K. 1999. *In the Bight – The BC Forest Industry Today*. Harbour Publishing, Madeira Park, B.C., Canada.

Dugger, W.M. 1976. Ideological and scientific functions of the neoclassical theory of the firm. *Journal of Economic Issues* 10(2): 314-327.

Dugger, W.M. 1977. Institutional and neoclassical economics compared. *Social Science Quarterly* 58: 449-461.

Dugger, W.M. 1979. Methodological differences between institutional and neoclassical economics. *Journal of Economic Issues* 13(4): 899-909.

Dugger, W.M. 1983. The transaction cost analysis of Oliver E. Williamson: a new synthesis? *Journal of Economic Issues* 17(1): 95-114.

Easterbrook, F.H., and D.R. Fischel. 1989. The corporate contract. *Columbia Law Review* 89(7): 1416-1448.

Eggertsson, T. 1990. *Economic Behaviour and Institutions*. Cambridge, UK: Cambridge University Press.

Eswaran, M., and A. Kotwal. 1985. A theory of contractual structure in agriculture. *American Economic Review* 75(3): 352-367.

Faustmann, M. 1849. On the determination of the value which forest land and immature stands possess for forestry. In: M. Gane (ed.) Martin Faustmann and the Evolution of Discounted Cash Flow. Institute paper No. 42, Commonwealth Forestry Institute, Oxford University, 1968. Reprinted in *Journal of Forest Economics*, 1995, 1(1): 7-44.

Feder, G., and D. Feeny. 1991. Land tenure and property rights: theory and implications for development policy. *The World Bank Economic Review* 5(1): 135-153.

Fiddler, G.O., and P.M. McDonald. 1990. Manual release contracting: production rates, costs, and future. *Western Journal of Applied Forestry* 5(3): 83-85.

Fischer, S. 1977. Long-term contracting, sticky prices, and monetary policy: comment. *Journal of Monetary Economics* 3: 317-324.

Food and Agriculture Organization of the United Nations. 1988. *Forestry Policies in Europe*. FAO Forestry Paper No. 86. Rome.

Food and Agriculture Organization of the United Nations. 1999. *1997 Forest Products Yearbook*. Rome.

Frank, S.D., and D.R. Henderson. 1992. Transaction costs as determinants of vertical coordination in the U.S. food industries. *American Journal of Agricultural Economics* 74: 941-950.

Fukuyama, F. 1995. *Trust: The Social Virtues and the Creation of Prosperity.* New York: The Free Press.

Fukuyama, F. 1999. *The Great Disruption: Human Nature and the Reconstruction of Social Order.* New York: The Free Press.

Furubotn, E.G., and R. Richter. 1984. The new institutional economics. *Journal of Institutional and Theoretical Economics* 140(1): 1-6.

Furubotn, E.G., and R. Richter. 1997. *Institutions and Economic Theory. The Contribution of the New Institutional Economics.* Ann Arbor, MI: University of Michigan Press.

Furubotn, E.G., and S. Pejovich. 1972. Property rights and economic theory: a survey of recent literature. *Journal of Economic Literature* 10(4): 1137-1162.

Gallick, E.C. 1984. *Exclusive Dealing and Vertical Integration: the Efficiency of Contracts in the Tuna Industry.* Bureau of Economics Staff Report to the Federal Trade Commission.

Glüeck, P., G. Oesten, H. Schanz, and K.-R.Volz (eds.). 1999. *Formulation and Implementation of National Forest Programmes. Volume II. State of the Art in Europe.* Proceedings No. 30. Joensuu, Finland: European Forest Institute.

Goedecke, E.J., and G.F. Ortmann. 1993. Transaction costs and labour contracting in the South African forestry industry. *South African Journal of Economics* 61(1): 67-83.

Goetz, C.J., and R.E. Scott. 1985. The limits of expanded choice: an analysis of the interactions between express and implied contract terms. *California Law Review* 73(2): 261-322.

Goldberg, V.P. 1976. Regulation and administered contracts. *Bell Journal of Economics* 7: 426-452.

Goldberg, V.P., and J.R. Erickson. 1987. Quantity and price adjustment in long-term contracts: a case study of petroleum coke. *Journal of Law and Economics* 30(October): 369-398.

Gordon, J.C. 1984. Nurseries in the Northwest: a unique opportunity for improving forest yield. In: M.L. Duryea and T.D. Landis (eds.) *Forest Nursery Manual: Production of Bareroot Seedlings.* The Hague/Boston/Lancaster: Martinus Nijhoff/Dr W. Junk Publishers.

Gordon, S. 1954. The economic theory of a common-property resource: the fishery. *Journal of Political Economy* 62: 124-142.

Gordon, W. 1980. *Institutional Economics: the Changing System*. Austin and London: University of Texas Press.

Grant, P. 1979. One hundred million and still growing. *ForesTalk* 3(2): 13-19.

Greene, W.H. 1993. *Econometric Analysis*. Second Edition. New York: Macmillan Publishing Company.

Greene, W.H. 1995. *LIMDEP Version 7.0 User's Manual*. Econometric Software, Inc., Bellport, Australia.

Gregory, R. 1997. More planning documents, less wood – the paper trail that leads to the harvest. *Business Logger* 7(5): 19-22.

Greif, A. 1998. Historical and comparative institutional analysis. *American Economic Review* 88(2): 80-84.

Groenewegen, J. 1996. Transaction cost economics and beyond: why and how? In J. Groenewegen (ed.) *Transaction Cost Economics and Beyond*. Boston-Dordrecht-London: Kluwer Academic Publishers, pp.1-9.

Grossman, S.J., and O.D. Hart. 1983. An analysis of the principal-agent problem. *Econometrica* 51: 7-45.

Grossman, S.J., and O.D. Hart. 1986. The costs and benefits of ownership: a theory of vertical and lateral integration. *Journal of Political Economy* 94(4): 691-719.

Groves, J. 1996. B.C. green and their pockets full of greenbacks: tree planting-- a growth industry. *The Vancouver Courier*, vol. 87, No. 37, May 8.

Gruchy, A.G. 1972. *Contemporary Economic Thought: the Contribution of Neo-Institutional Economics*. Clifton: Augustus M. Kelley Publishers.

Haley, D. 1996. *Paying the Piper: The Cost of British Columbia's Forest Practices Code*. Working Paper. Department of Forest Resources Management, University of British Columbia, Vancouver.

Haley, D., and M.K. Luckert. 1986. *The Impact of Tenure Arrangements on Forest Management and Forestry Investment in Canada*. A report commissioned by the Department of Supply and Services under the endorsement of the Canadian Forestry Service. Faculty of Forestry, University of British Columbia, Vancouver.

Haley, D., and M.K. Luckert. 1990. *Forest Tenures in Canada - A Framework for Policy Analysis*. Forestry Canada, Economic Directorate, Information Report E-X-43.

Haley, D., and M.K. Luckert. 1998. Tenures as economic instruments for achieving objectives of public forest policy in British Columbia. In: C. Tollefson (ed.) *The Wealth of Forests: Markets, Regulation, and Sustainable Forestry.* Vancouver: UBC Press, pp.123-151.

Hamilton, D. 1970. *Evolutionary Economics.* Albuquerque: University of New Mexico Press.

Hanson, P. 1985. *Seed Orchards of British Columbia.* Ministry of Forests. Victoria, B.C.

Hardin, G. 1968. The tragedy of the commons. *Science* 162: 1243-1248.

Harris, M., and A. Raviv. 1979. Optimal incentive contracts with imperfect information. *Journal of Economic Theory* 20: 231-259.

Hart, O.D. 1989. Incomplete contracts. In: J. Eatwell, M. Milgate and P. Newman (eds.) *Allocation, Information and Markets.* The MacMillan Press Limited, pp.163-179.

Hart, O.D., A. Shleifer, and R.W. Vishny. 1997. The proper scope of government: theory and an application to prisons. *Quarterly Journal of Economics* 112(4): 1127-1161.

Hart, O.D., and B. Holmström. 1987. The theory of contracts. In: T. Bewley (ed.) *Advances in Economic Theory.* Cambridge: Cambridge University Press.

Hart, O.D., and J. Moore. 1990. Property rights and the nature of the firm. *Journal of Political Economy* 98(6): 1119-1158.

Hartman, R. 1976. The harvesting decision when a standing forest has value. *Economic Inquiry* 14: 52-58.

Hayek, F.A. 1937. Economics and knowledge. *Economica* 4: 33-54.

Hayek, F.A. 1945. The use of knowledge in society. *American Economic Review* 35(4): 519-530.

Heady, E.O. 1947. Economics of farm leasing systems. *Journal of Farm Economics* 29: 659-678.

Heath, J.R. 1992. Evaluating the impact of Mexico's land reform on agricultural productivity. *World Development* 20(5): 695-711.

Hirshleifer, J., and J.G. Riley. 1992. *The Analytics of Uncertainty and Information.* Cambridge: Cambridge University Press.

Hof, J. 1993. *Coactive Forest Management.* San Diego, CA: Academic Press.

Holmström, B. 1979. Moral hazard and observability. *Bell Journal of Economics* 10: 74-91.

Holmström, B. 1982. Moral hazard and teams. *Bell Journal of Economics* 13: 324-340.

Hubbard, R.G., and R.J. Weiner. 1991. Efficient contracting and market power: evidence from the U.S. natural gas industry. *Journal of Law and Economics* 34(April): 25-67.

Hummel, F.C. 1989. *Forestry Policies in Europe: An Analysis*. FAO Forestry Paper No. 92. Rome.

Hutchison, T.W. 1984. Institutionalist economics old and new. *Journal of Institutional and Theoretical Economics* 140(1): 20-29.

Jeppe, W.J.O. 1980. *Bophuthatswana, Land Tenure and Development*. Cape Town: Maskew Miller.

Johnson, D.G. 1950. Resource allocation under share contracts. *Journal of Political Economy* 58: 111-123.

Joskow, P.L. 1985. Vertical integration and long-term contracts: the case of coal-burning electric generating plants. *Journal of Law, Economics, and Organization* 1(Fall): 33-81.

Joskow, P.L. 1987. Contract duration and relationship-specific investments: empirical evidence from coal markets. *American Economic Review* 77(1): 168-185.

Joskow, P.L. 1988. Asset specificity and the structure of vertical relationships: empircal evidence. *Journal of Law, Economics, and Organization* 4(1): 95-117.

Kennedy, P. 1992. *A Guide to Econometrics*. Third Edition. Cambridge, Massachusetts: The MIT Press.

Klein, B. 1983. Contracting costs and residual claims: the separation of ownership and control. *Journal of Law and Economics* 26(2): 367-374.

Klein, B., R.G. Crawford, and A.A. Alchian. 1978. Vertical integration, appropriable rents, and the competitive contracting process. *Journal of Law and Economics* 21: 297-326.

Kleindorfer, P.R., and M.R. Sertel. 1979. Profit-maximizing design of enterprises through incentives. *Journal of Economic Theory* 20: 318-339.

Kluender, R.A., D. Lortz, W. McCoy, B.J. Stokes, and J. Klepac. 1998. Removal intensity and tree size effects on harvesting cost and profitability. *Forest Products Journal* 48(1): 54-59.

Knight, E. 1990. Reforestation in British Columbia: a brief history. In: D.P. Lavender et al. (eds.) *Regenerating British Columbia's Forests*. Vancouver: UBC Press, pp.2-8.

Knight, F.H. 1965 [1921]. *Risk, Uncertainty and Profit*. New York: Harper & Row.

Kostritsky, J.P. 1993. Bargaining with uncertainty, moral hazard, and sunk costs: a default rule for precontractual negotiations. *Hastings Law Journal* 44(3): 623-705.

Kreps, D.M. 1988. In honour of Sandy Grossman, Winner of the John Bates Clark Medal. *Journal of Economic Perspectives* 2(2): 111-135.

Kwon, Y.K., J.C. Fellingham, and D.P. Newman. 1979. Stochastic dominance and information value. *Journal of Economic Theory* 20: 213-230.

La Porta, R., F. Lpez-de-Silanes, A. Shleifer, and R.W. Vishny. 1999. The quality of government. *Journal of Law, Economics, and Organization* 15(1): 222-279.

Laffont, J-J. 1989. *The Economics of Uncertainty and Information*. Cambridge, Massachusetts: The MIT Press.

Landes, D.S. 1999. *The Wealth and Poverty of Nations*. New York: The Free Press.

Lazear, E.P. 1986. Salaries and piece rates. *Journal of Business* 59: 405-431.

Lazear, E.P. 1989. Incentive contracts. In: J. Eatwell, M. Milgate and P. Newman (eds.) *Allocation, Information and Markets*. The MacMillan Press Limited, pp.152-162.

Leffler, K.B., and R.R. Rucker. 1991. Transactions costs and the efficient organization of production: a study of timber-harvesting contracts. *Journal of Political Economy* 99(5): 1060-1087.

Leibenstein, H. 1984. On the economics of conventions and institutions: an exploratory essay. *Journal of Institutional and Theoretical Economics* 140(1): 74-86.

Leland, H.E. 1979. Quacks, lemons, and licensing: a theory of minimum quality standards. *Journal of Political Economy* 87(6): 1328-1346.

Leland, H.E. 1980. Minimum-quality standards and licensing in markets with asymmetric information. In: S. Rottenberg (ed.) *Occupational Licensure and Regulation*. Washington, D.C., London: American Enterprise Institute for Public Research, pp.265-284.

Lewinsky, J. 1913. *The Origin of Property and the Formation of the Village Community*. London: Constable & Company Ltd.

Llewellyn, K.N. 1931. What price contract?—An essay in perspective. *Yale Law Journal* 40: 704-751.

Lohmann, S. 1994. Information aggregation through costly political action. *American Economic Review* 84(3): 518-530.

Lousier, D., R. Jones, et al. 1989. *Silviculture Employment Issues*. Vancouver: Western Silviculture Contractors Association.

Lucas, R.E.B. 1979. Sharing, monitoring, and incentives: Marshallian misallocation reassessed. *Journal of Political Economy* 87: 501-521.

Luckert, M.K. 1988. *The Effect of Some British Columbia Forest Tenures on the Distribution of Economic Rents, the Allocation of Resources, and Investments in Silviculture.* Unpublished Ph.D. thesis. University of British Columbia, Vancouver.

Luckert, M.K. 1991. The perceived security of institutional investment environments of some British Columbia forest tenures. *Canadian Journal of Forest Research* 21: 318-325.

Luckert, M.K., and D. Haley. 1993. Canadian forest tenures and the silvicultural investment behaviour of rational firms. *Canadian Journal of Forest Research* 23:1060-1064.

Luckert, M.K., and D. Haley. 1995. The allowable cut effect as a policy instrument in Canadian forestry. *Canadian Journal of Forest Research* 25: 1821-1829.

Maddala, G.S. 1983. *Limited-Dependent and Qualitative Variables in Econometrics.* Econometric Society Publication No. 3. Cambridge: Cambridge University Press.

Majumdar, S.K., and V. Ramaswamy. 1994. Explaining downstream integration. *Managerial and Decision Economics* 15: 119-129.

Martin, F. 1994. Sustainability, the discount rate, and intergenerational effects within a regional framework. *The Annals of Regional Science* 28: 107-123.

Masten, S.E. 1984. The organization of production: evidence from the aerospace industry. *Journal of Law and Economics* 27(October): 403-417.

Masten, S.E. 1996. Empirical research in transaction cost economics: challenges, progress, directions. In: J. Groenewegen (ed.) *Transaction Cost Economics and Beyond.* Boston-Dordrecht-London: Kluwer Academic Publishers, pp.43-64.

Masten, S.E., and K.J. Crocker. 1985. Efficient adaptation in long-term contracts: take-or-pay provisions for natural gas. *American Economic Review* 75: 1083-1093.

Masten, S.E., J.W. Meehan, Jr., and E.A. Snyder. 1989. Vertical integration in the U.S. auto industry: a note on the influence of transaction specific assets. *Journal of Economic Behavior and Organization* 12: 265-273.

Masten, S.E., J.W. Meehan, Jr., and E.A. Snyder. 1991. The costs of organization. *Journal of Law, Economics, and Organization* 7(1): 1-25.

Mathews, R.C.O. 1986. The economics of institutions and the sources of growth. *Economic Journal* 96: 903-918.

Mirrlees, J.A. 1976. The optimal structure of incentives with authority within an organization. *Bell Journal of Economics* 7(1): 105-131.

Monteverde, K., and D.J. Teece. 1982a. Supplier switching costs and vertical integration in the automobile industry. *Bell Journal Economics* 13: 206-213.

Monteverde, K., and D.J. Teece. 1982b. Appropriable rents and quasi-vertical integration. *Journal of Law and Economics* 25: 321-328.

Montgomery, C.A., and D.M. Adams. 1995. Optimal timber management policies. In: D.W. Bromley (ed.) *Handbook of Environmental Economics*. Oxford, Blackwell, pp.379-404.

Murphy, E.J., and R.E. Speidel. 1991. *Studies in Contract Law*. Fourth Edition. Mineola, N.Y.: Foundation Press.

Natural Resources Canada. 1997. *Selected Forestry Statistics Canada 1996*. Ottawa: Industry, Economics and Programs Branch, Canadian Forest Service, Natural Resources Canada.

Natural Resources Canada. 1999. *The State of Canada's Forests 1998 – 1999*. Ottawa: Canadian Forest Service, Natural Resources Canada.

Nee, V. 1998. Norms and networks in economic and organizational performance. *American Economic Review* 88(2): 85-89.

North, D.C. 1968. Sources of productivity change in ocean shipping, 1600-1850. *Journal of Political Economy* 76: 953-970.

North, D.C. 1972. *The Creation of Property Rights in Western Europe 900-1700 A.D.* Unpublished manuscript.

North, D.C. 1984. Transaction costs, institutions, and economic history. *Journal of Institutional and Theoretical Economics* 140: 7-17.

North, D.C. 1990. *Institutions, Institutional Change and Economic Performance*. Cambridge, UK: University Press.

North, D.C. 1991. Institutions. *Journal of Economic Perspectives* 5: 97-112.

North, D.C. 1994. Economic performance through time. *American Economic Review* 84(3): 359-368.

O'Hara, K.L., and C.D. Oliver. 1992. Silviculture: achieving new objectives through stand and landscape management. *Western Wildlands* 7(4): 28-33.

Palay, T.M. 1984. Comparative institutional economics: the governance of rail freight contracting. *Journal of Legal Studies* 13: 265-287.

Pearse, P.H. 1970. Conflicting objectives in forest policy: the case of British Columbia. *The Forestry Chronicle* 46: 281-287.

Pearse, P.H. 1976. *Timber Rights and Forest Policy - Report of the Royal Commission on Forest Resources*. Victoria, B.C.

Pearse, P.H. 1988. Property rights and the development of natural resource policies in Canada. *Canadian Public Policy* 14(3): 307-320.

Pearse, P.H. 1990. *Introduction to Forestry Economics*. Vancouver: UBC Press.

Pearse, P.H. 1998. Economic instruments for promoting sustainable forestry: opportunities and constraints. In: C. Tollefson (ed.) *The Wealth of Forests: Markets, Regulation, and Sustainable Forestry*. Vancouver: UBC Press, pp.19-41.

Pearse, P.H., A.V. Backman, and E.L. Young. 1974. *Forest Tenures in British Columbia*. Policy background paper prepared by the Task Force on Crown Timber Disposal. Victoria, B.C.

Pejovich, S. 1972. Towards an economic theory of the creation and specification of property rights. *Review of Social Economy* 30(3): 309-325.

Pejovich, S. 1990. *The Economics of Property Rights: Towards a Theory of Comparative Systems*. Dordrecht, The Netherlands: Kluwer Academic Publishers.

Pejovich, S. 1995. *Economic Analysis of Institutions and Systems*. Dordrecht, The Netherlands: Kluwer Academic Publishers.

Perlin, J. 1989. *A Forest Journey: The Role of Wood in the Development of Civilization*. New York: W.W. Norton.

Phillips, L.T. 1991. Contractual relationships in the deregulated transportation marketplace. *Journal of Law and Economics* 34: 535-564.

Pittman, R. 1991. Specific investments, contracts, and opportunism: the evolution of railroad sidetrack agreements. *Journal of Law and Economics* 34: 565-589.

Powelson, J.P. 1987. Land tenure and land reform: past and present. *Land Use Policy* 4(April): 111-120.

Powelson, J.P. 1988. *The Story of Land: A World History of Land Tenure and Agrarian Reform*. Cambridge, USA: Lincoln Institute of Land Policy.

Pressey, R.L. 2000. The end of conservation on the cheap, revisited. In: G.C. van Kooten, E.H. Bulte and A.E.R. Sinclair (eds.) *Conserving Nature's Diversity: Insights from Biology, Ethics and Economics*. Aldershot, UK: Ashgate, pp.45-67.

Pryor, F.L. 1972. Property institutions and economic development: some empirical tests. *Economic Development and Cultural Change* 20: 406-437.

Randall, A. 1975. Property rights and social microeconomics. *Natural Resources Journal* 15: 729-747.

Reed, F.L.C. 1985. *The Case for Investing in Forestry*. Paper presented to the 12th Commonwealth Forestry Conference, 9-20 September 1985, Victoria, B.C.

Reed, W.J. 1993. The decision to conserve or harvest old-growth forest. *Ecological Economics* 8: 45-69.

Reed, W.J., and J.J. Ye. 1994. The role of stochastic monotonicity in the decision to conserve or harvest old growth forest. *Natural Resource Modeling* 8: 47-80.

Reid, J.D. 1975. Sharecropping in history and theory. *Agricultural History* 49: 426-440.

Reyner, K.M., W.A. Leuschner, and J. Sullivan. 1996. A silviculture investment model for industrial forests. *Forest Products Journal* 46(1): 25-30.

Ross, S. 1973. The economic theory of agency: the principal's problem. *American Economic Review* 63: 134-139.

Roumasset, J., and M. Uy. 1980. Piece rates, time rates, and teams: explaining patterns in the employment relation. *Journal of Economic Behavior and Organization* 1: 343-360.

Sahajananthan, S., D. Haley, and J. Nelson. 1998. Planning for sustainable forests in British Columbia through land use zoning. *Canadian Public Policy* 24(supp2): S73-S81.

Samuelson, P.A. 1976. The economics of forestry in an evolving society. *Economic Inquiry* 14: 466-492.

Sappington, D.E.M. 1991. Incentives in principal-agent relationships. *Journal of Economic Perspectives* 5(2): 45-66.

Scagel, R., R. Bowden, M. Madill, and C. Kooistra. 1993. *Provincial Seedling Stock Type Selection and Ordering Guidelines*. Ministry of Forests, Victoria, B.C.

Schweitzer, D.L., R.W. Sassaman, and C.H. Schallau. 1972. Allowable cut effect. *Journal of Forestry* 70(7): 415-418.

Scott, A. 1955. The fishery: the objectives of sole ownership. *Journal of Political Economy* 63: 116-124.

Scott, A. 1983. Property rights and property wrongs. *Canadian Journal of Economics* 16(4): 555-573.

Scott, K.E. 1984. Corporate governance and the new institutional economics. *Journal of Institutional and Theoretical Economics* 140(1): 136-152.

Sedjo, R.A. 1996. Toward an operational approach in public forest management. *Journal of Forestry* 94(8): 24-27.

Sedjo, R.A. 1997. The Forest Sector: Important Innovations. Discussion Paper 97-42. Washington, D.C.: Resources for the Future.

Sedlack, J.P. 1965. *The Improvement of Forest Nurseries through the Introduction of Better Soil.* Unpublished bachelor of forestry thesis. Faculty of Forestry, University of British Columbia, Vancouver.

Seitz, W.D., and J.C. Headley. 1975. Changing natural resource property rights: an overview. *Natural Resources Journal* 15: 639-642.

Shand, Angus. 1999. Personal communication.

Shapiro, C. 1983. Premiums for high quality products as returns to reputation. *Quarterly Journal of Economics* 98: 659-680.

Shavell, S. 1980. Damage measures for breach of contract. *Bell Journal of Economics* 11: 466-490.

Shleifer, A. 1998. State versus private ownership. *Journal of Economic Perspectives* 12(4): 133-150.

Shleifer, A., and R.W. Vishny. 1998. *The Grabbing Hand.* Cambridge, MA: Harvard University Press.

Simon, H.A. 1957. *Administrative Behavior.* New York: The Free Press.

Simon, H.A. 1962. New developments in the theory of the firm. *American Economic Review* 52(2): 1-15.

Simon, H.A. 1978. On how to decide what to do. *Bell Journal of Economics* 9: 494-507.

Simon, H.A. 1991. Organizations and markets. *Journal of Economic Perspectives* 5(2): 25-44.

Sinclair, A.R.E. 2000. Is conservation achieving its ends? In: G.C. van Kooten, E.H. Bulte and A.E.R. Sinclair (eds.) *Conserving Nature's Diversity: Insights from Biology, Ethics and Economics.* Aldershot, UK: Ashgate, pp.30-44.

Sloan, G.M. 1945. *Report of the Commissioner Relating to the Forest Resources of British Columbia.* King's Printer, Victoria, B.C.

Sloan, G.M. 1956. *The Forest Resources of British Columbia.* 1956. Queen's Printer, Victoria, B.C.

Sowell, T. 1999. *The Quest for Cosmic Justice.* New York: The Free Press.

Spence, A.M. 1975. The economics of internal organization: an introduction. *Bell Journal of Economics* 6(1): 163-172.

Steen, H.K. (ed.). 1992. *The Origins of the National Forests: A Centennial Symposium.* Durham, North Caroline: Forest History Society.

Stigler, G.J. 1961. The economics of information. *Journal of Political Economy* 69(3): 213-225.

Stiglitz, J.E. 1974. Incentives and risk sharing in sharecropping. *Review of Economic Studies* 61: 219-256.

Stiglitz, J.E. 1975. Incentives, risk, and information: notes towards a theory of hierarchy. *Bell Journal of Economics* 6(2): 552-579.

Stolz, C. 2000. The Treeplanting Web Page http://www.canuck.com/~chstolz/index.html.

Stuckey, J. 1983. *Vertical Integration and Joint Ventures in the Aluminum Industry*. Cambridge: Harvard University Press.

Swallow, S.K., and D.N. Wear. 1993. Spatial interactions in multiple-use forestry and substitution and wealth effects for the single stand. *Journal of Environmental Economics and Management* 25: 103-120.

Swallow, S.K., P. Talukdar, and D.N. Wear. 1997. Spatial and temporal specialization in forest ecosystem management under sole ownership. *American Journal of Agricultural Economics* 79: 311-326.

Swallow, S.K., P.J. Parks, and D.N. Wear. 1990. Policy-relevant nonconvexities in the production of multiple forest benefits. *Journal of Environmental Economics and Management* 19: 264-280.

Thompson, W.A., P.H. Pearse, G.C. van Kooten, and I. Vertinsky. 1992. Rehabilitating the backlog of unstocked forest lands in British Columbia: a preliminary simulation analysis of alternative strategies. In: P.N. Nemetz (ed.) *Emerging Issues in Forest Policy*. Vancouver: UBC Press, pp.99-130.

Thomson, D.N., and M.C. Lyne. 1993. Constraints to land rental in KwaZulu: analyzing the transaction costs. *Oxford Agrarian Studies* 21(2): 143-50.

TimberWest. 1996. *TimberWest Information Report No. 2*. Tree Farm License No. 47. Management Plan No. 2 – Density Management: Assumptions in Timber Supply Analyses and Relationships to Future Opportunities.

Umbeck, J. 1981. Might makes rights: a theory of the formation and initial distribution of property rights. *Economic Inquiry* 19(1): 38-59.

United Nations. 2000. Forest Resources of Europe, CIS, North America, Australia, Japan and New Zealand (industrialized temperate/boreal countries). UN-ECE/FAO Contribution to the Global Forest Resources Assessment 2000. Geneva Timber and Forest Study Paper, No. 17. New York and Geneva.

van Kooten, G.C. 1993. *Land Resource Economics and Sustainable Development: Economic Policies and the Common Good*. Vancouver: UBC Press.

van Kooten, G.C. 1999. Preserving species without an Endangered Species Act: British Columbia's Forest Practices Code. In: M.B.R. Brännlund and B. Kristrom (eds.) *Topics in Environmental Economics*. Dordrecht, The Netherlands: Kluwer Academic Publishers, pp.63-82.

van Kooten, G.C., and E.H. Bulte. 1999. How much primary coastal temperate rainforest should society retain? Carbon uptake, recreation and other values. *Canadian Journal of Forest Research* 29(12): 1879-1890.

van Kooten, G.C., and E.H. Bulte. 2000. *The Economics of Nature: Managing Biological Assets*. Oxford, UK: Blackwell.

van Kooten, G.C., and S. Wang. 1998. Estimating economic costs of nature protection: British Columbia's forest regulations. *Canadian Public Policy* 24(supp2): S63-S71.

Vance, J.E. 1990. *Tree Planning: A Guide to Public Involvement in Forest Stewardship*. Public Interest Advocacy Centre, Vancouver, B.C.

Vandeman, A., E. Sadoulet, and A. de Janvry. 1991. Labor contracting and a theory of contract choice in California agriculture. *American Journal of Agricultural Economics* 73: 681-692.

Vaupel, S., and P.L. Martin. 1986. Farm labor contractors. *California Agriculture* 40(3/4): 12-15.

Vaux, H.J. 1973. How much land do we need for timber growing? *Journal of Forestry* 71(7): 399-403.

Vickers, J., and G. Yarrow. 1991. Economic perspectives on privatization. *Journal of Economic Perspectives* 5(2): 111-132.

Vincent, J.R., and C.S. Binkley. 1993. Efficient multiple-use forestry may require land-use specialization. *Land Economics* 69(4): 370-376.

Wang, S. 1997. *Contractual Structure in British Columbia's Silviculture Sector: A Transaction Cost Economic Analysis*. Unpublished Ph.D. thesis. University of British Columbia, Vancouver.

Wang, S. 1999. Small scale forestry in selected jurisdictions of the world: status, characteristics and challenges. *World Forestry Research* 12(4): 38-44. (In Chinese).

Wang, S., and B. Wilson. 1999. Silvicultural investment in British Columbia: economic efficiency and employment. In: B. Slee and I. Hughes (eds.) *New Opportunities for Forest-Related Rural Development*. Proceedings of IUFRO Group 6.11.02 Symposium, August 1999. Aberdeen, Scotland: University of Aberdeen, pp.395-401.

Wang, S., and G.C. van Kooten. 1999. Silvicultural contracting in British Columbia: a transaction cost economics analysis. *Forest Science* 45(2): 272-279.

Wang, S., G.C. van Kooten, and B. Wilson. 1998. Silvicultural contracting in British Columbia. *The Forestry Chronicle* 74(6): 899-910.

Wang, S., G.C. van Kooten, and B. Wilson. 2000. Remuneration for silviculture in British Columbia. *Forest Policy and Economics* 1(1): 71-79.

Wiggins, S.N., and G.D. Libecap. 1985. Oil field unitization: contractual failure in the presence of imperfect information. *American Economic Review* 75(3): 368-385.

Williamson, O.E. 1975. *Markets and Hierarchies: Analysis and Antitrust Implications*. New York: The Free Press.

Williamson, O.E. 1976. Franchise bidding for natural monopolies – in general and with respect to CATV. *Bell Journal of Economics* 7: 73-104.

Williamson, O.E. 1979. Transaction-cost economics: the governance of contractual relations. *Journal of Law and Economics* 22: 233-261.

Williamson, O.E. 1980. The organization of work: a comparative institutional assessment. *Journal of Economic Behavior and Organization* 1: 5-38.

Williamson, O.E. 1981. The modern corporation: origins, evolution, attributes. *Journal of Economic Literature* 19(4): 1537-1568.

Williamson, O.E. 1984. The economics of governance: framework and implications. *Journal of Institutional and Theoretical Economics* 140: 195-223.

Williamson, O.E. 1985. *The Economic Institutions of Capitalism*. New York: The Free Press.

Williamson, O.E. 1988. The logic of economic organization. *Journal of Law, Economics, and Organization* 4(1): 65-93.

Williamson, O.E. 1996. Efficiency, power, authority and economic organization. In: J. Groenewegen (ed.) *Transaction Cost Economics and Beyond*. Boston-Dordrecht-London: Kluwer Academic Publishers, pp.11-42.

Williamson, O.E. 1998a. The institutions of governance. *American Economic Review* 88(2): 75-79.

Williamson, O.E. 1998b. Transaction cost economics: how it works; where it headed. *De Economist* 146(April): 23-58.

Wilson, B., and S. Wang. 1999. Sustainable Forestry: The Policy Prescription in British Columbia. In: Atsushi Yoshimoto and Kiyoshi Yukutake (eds.) *Global Concerns for Forest Resource Utilization – Sustainable Use and Management*. Selected papers from the International Symposium of the FORESEA Miyazaki 1998. Dordrecht, The Netherlands: Kluwer Academic Publishers, Forestry Sciences Vol. 62, pp.35-45.

Wilson, B., G.C. van Kooten, I. Vertinsky, and L. Arthur (eds.). 1998. *Forest Policy: International Case Studies*. Wallingford, UK: CABI Publishing.

Wilson, R. 1975. Informational economies of scale. *Bell Journal of Economics* 6(1): 184-195.

Wright, P.J., and D. Rideout. 1990. Recent experiences with end result contracting on national forestlands in the West. *Western Journal of Applied Forestry* 5(4): 119-123.

Young, B. 1989a. The Green Timbers Plantations: a British Columbia forest heritage. *The Forestry Chronicle* 63(3): 183-184.

Young, B. 1989b. Proceedings of the Forestry Nursery Association of B.C., 9th Annual Meeting, October 16 - 19, 1989, Victoria, B.C.

Zhang, D. 1994. *Implications of Tenure for Forest Land Value and Management in British Columbia*. Unpublished Ph.D. thesis. University of British Columbia, Vancouver.

Zhang, D. 1996. Forest tenures and land value in British Columbia. *Journal of Forest Economics* 2(1): 7-30.

Zhang, D., and C.S. Binkley. 1995. The economic effect of forest policy changes in British Columbia: an event study of stock-market returns. *Canadian Journal of Forest Research* 25(6): 978-986.

Zhang, D., and P.H. Pearse. 1996. Differences in silvicultural investment under various types of forest tenure in British Columbia. *Forest Science* 42(4): 442-449.

Zhang, D., and P.H. Pearse. 1997. The influence of the form of tenure on reforestation in British Columbia. *Forest Ecology and Management* 98: 239-250.

Index

196

For Product Safety Concerns and Information please contact our EU representative GPSR@taylorandfrancis.com Taylor & Francis Verlag GmbH, Kaufingerstraße 24, 80331 München, Germany

Printed and bound by CPI Group (UK) Ltd, Croydon, CR0 4YY
05/05/2025
01860770-0001